EDUCATION TODAY

Development through Drama

EDUCATION TODAY

For a full list of titles in this series, see back cover

Development
through Drama

BRIAN WAY
Director, Theatre Centre, London

LONGMAN

LONGMAN GROUP LIMITED
London

*Associated companies, branches and
representatives throughout the world*

First published 1967
New impression 1972

ISBN 0 582 32075 5

Printed in Singapore
by New Art Printing Co., (Pte.) Ltd.

Foreword

A book of this kind takes a long time to write; by the time it is finished and printed, the author has discovered a great deal more about the subject matter; this is as it should be. I have tried to put down some thoughts and details of practical experience of drama with young people, in an attempt to help teachers in an ever-growing sphere of educational practice; within a decade, the book may read as history, for the subject matter is still so new that there is much yet to be discovered and understood.

It is impossible to attempt to name all those to whom I am indebted – over a period of twenty years – for sharing their own thoughts and ideas and experiences. As a free-lance lecturer I have been privileged to work with drama advisers, training college lecturers, H.M.I.s, education officers, drama school staffs and people involved in every aspect of theatre as well as education; I owe something to them all, and thank them all especially Stanley Evernden, Michael MacOwan, John Morley and Peter Slade. But particular thanks are due to Margaret Faulkes, both for the many years of experiment at Theatre Centre and for much practical help with this book.

BRIAN WAY
Theatre Centre London 1966

Contents

FOREWORD   V

1 THE FUNCTION OF DRAMA   I

2 CONSIDER A HUMAN BEING   10
Facets of personality: points on a circle – concentration
exercises: listening, looking, touch – linking the senses –
age groups – application to the theatre – method of
approach

3 BEGIN FROM WHERE YOU ARE   28
Sound participation – stories made up by class and teacher
together

4 IMAGINATION   42
Using the senses to stimulate imagination – stimulation
through objects

5 MOVEMENT AND THE USE OF SOUND   65
Approaches to beginning movement – activities with a ball
– discovering the body – the use of sound and music – discovery and use of space – early work in groups – music,
emotion and logic

6 SPEAKING   118
Speech and personality – feeling for language – emotional
mastery: the importance of practice – beginnings: topics
of conversation – Developments: dramatic scenes, working
in pairs – developing a crowd scene: boldness and sensitivity, dialects – Making up our own language – movement
and speech

7 SENSITIVITY AND CHARACTERISATION   156
Consciousness of self – sensitivity and personal control –
practical work: exercises in awareness, group sensitivity,
dramatic moments – characterisation

8 IMPROVISATION   183
Subject matter – the teacher's approach to the class – practical work: stimulating ideas – conflict – infants: individual
and group experiences – juniors and secondary: 'stretching': simple, direct experience, conflict, climax and de-
climax, mood and atmosphere, emotion, characterisation,
intellectual consideration, development of form, subject
matter of original improvisations – secondary beginnings:
looking with the eye of a camera

9 FIGHTING AND VIOLENCE   235
Practical suggestions: working out a fight – building improvisations round a fight

10 PLAYMAKING AND PLAY-BUILDING   254
Developing a story about refugees – an episode at an airport – enriching experience

11 A SPACE WHERE ANYTHING CAN HAPPEN   268
Using the classroom – using the hall – rostrum blocks – a
drama room – sharing

12 SOCIAL DRAMA   286
Manners and behaviour – aspects of general living – Broader
social awareness

BOOK LIST   299
RECORD LIST   300
INDEX   303

I

The Function of Drama

The answer to many simple questions might take one of two forms – either that of information or else that of direct experience; the former answer belongs to the category of academic education, the latter to drama. For example, the question might be 'What is a blind person?' The reply could be 'A blind person is a person who cannot see'. Alternatively, the reply could be 'Close your eyes and, keeping them closed all the time, try to find your way out of this room.' The first answer contains concise and accurate information; the mind is possibly satisfied. But the second answer leads the inquirer to moments of direct experience, transcending mere knowledge, enriching the imagination, possibly touching the heart and soul as well as the mind. This, in over-simplified terms, is the precise function of drama.

Naturally, like all over-simplifications, the second answer is unsatisfactory, particularly to those whose rightful concern is academic achievement, in quantity as well as quality. Direct experience is time-consuming, is intangible, and therefore not measureable; it is often successful in least expected quarters and therefore tends to upset the more exact modes of educational assessment; it contains transitory and fleeting moments which, however enjoyable, real or important they may be for those actually having the experience, are difficult to trace in terms of 'progression'. And there are other more precise objections – self-consciousness, lack of space or other facilities, pressures of time and, perhaps most important of all, the feeling among many teachers that they are ill-equipped.

Over the last generation, many strong and valid arguments have been put forward as to the philosophical reasons for using drama as education, and there have been official white papers pointing out its importance and significance. The major part of this book is therefore concerned with practical matters – the 'what' to do rather than the 'why' – on the assumption that many education-ists are already familiar with at least the basic necessities. Never-theless, as with all controversial issues in education, it is both expedient and commonsense to put forward the theoretical basis for practical intentions; accordingly, each chapter will have some concern with the 'why' as well as the 'what'. In particular, this first chapter will review some of the fundamental issues which concern not only drama but education as a whole. Indeed, it is true to say that drama, so far from being new, is closely inter-woven in the practical implementation of both the spirit and substance of every Education Act that has ever been passed, especially the idea of the development of the *whole* person.

But it must be this whole person upon whom our concentration is centred; to make drama another subject in an overcrowded curriculum is to shift the emphasis away from the many 'whole persons' to drama itself. It is comparatively easy to develop drama, but more difficult to develop people; it is equally simple to assess and measure some aspects of the development of drama itself, but to do so can negate the primary intention of developing people through drama. So far as is humanly possible, this book is concerned with the development of people, not with the develop-ment of drama. There is little or no problem in developing good drama – indeed, as is demonstrable, human beings who are little more than puppets in the hands of a highly skilled exponent will quickly master good drama. But, whereas 'good' or 'exciting' or 'brilliant' drama does not necessarily prove that the people doing it are good or exciting or brilliant, nevertheless 'fully developed' people will seldom *make* poor or uninteresting drama, even though it may not be brilliant.

Full understanding of this apparent anomaly is dependent on the realisation that there are two activities, which must not be con-fused – one is theatre, the other is drama. For the purposes of this book – that is, for the development of people – the major difference between the two activities can be stated as follows: 'theatre' is largely concerned with *communication* between actors and an audience; 'drama' is largely concerned with *experience* by the participants, irrespective of any function of communication to an audience. Generally speaking, it is true to say that communication to an audience is beyond the capacities of the majority of children and young people, and attempts to coerce or impose communication too soon often lead to artificiality and therefore destroy the full values of the intended experience. The fact that there are a very few children who, by natural gift, are able to achieve the intentions of both theatre and drama merely highlights the question of who is to be helped by the activity.

Theatre is undoubtedly achievable with a few – a very small minority; but drama, like the rest of education, is concerned with the majority, and, as later chapters will suggest, there is not a child born anywhere in the world, in any physical or intellectual circumstances or conditions, who cannot do drama. The moment the development of people becomes our aim this factor becomes clearly apparent.

Education is concerned with individuals; drama is concerned with the individuality of individuals, with the uniqueness of each human essence. Indeed this is one of the reasons for its intangibility and its immeasurability. 'No two people are alike' may well be an accepted truism of physical appearance, but it is equally true of emotion and imagination, which comprise the root of full individuality, and yet are often the antithesis of academic education, which inevitably (because of tests and examinations) tends to be concerned with the samenesses rather than the differences of people. The differences are often most clearly reflected through the arts, and opportunity for actually 'doing' the arts is sometimes the wisest way of developing individuality. But to do so among young people necessitates an appreciation of the fact that all people are fundamentally creative; the arts are an outlet for this creativity if – and only if – they are viewed from the standpoint of the doer and from that person's personal level of readiness and experience, no matter how primitive this level may be. To view from the standpoint of traditional or conventional professionalism is to adopt a scale of values that are entirely irrelevant, leading to judgments that exclude the majority, particularly in the early stages of discovery.

Individuality is also concerned with originality and deeply personal aspirations; drama encourages originality and helps towards some fulfilment of personal aspiration, and this is important to the full development of personality because even among the best teachers there can develop a tendency to help pupils to fulfil only teachers' ambitions for them. Ultimately, long after a youngster has left school, some part of human happiness and wellbeing is dependent upon the development of individual uniqueness, which in its turn is dependent on the factor of personal aspiration. Are the factors of happiness and wellbeing any less important than physical prowess and intellectual achievement? If not, can they be attained by chance or do they too need some 'teaching'? They are fundamentally dependent on inner resources, but the resources themselves are atrophied if not in constant use. Talking about the arts, learning and studying in order to appreciate the work of professional artists is one important aspect of this process, but not the most important; actual practising of the arts, at one's own level, builds firmer foundations, even for appreciation, and many educationists have made a strong case for protecting young children from too early exposure to professional products because of the danger of undermining confidence in their own simple beginnings. If each person is helped to enjoy and to know what it feels like to use the creative part of themselves when they are young, their eventual appreciation of the arts is richer, without depending on pseudo-intellectualism or the re-echoing of someone else's tastes. In education, the arts are not another academic subject concerned with the development of intellect; to place them in this context often makes them boring for children. They are concerned with the development of intuition, which is no less important than intellect and is part of the essence of full enrichment of life both for those who have intellectual gifts and those who have not; but intuition, like intellect, needs training, though not the same kind or means of training. With intuition, all individual differences are developed to their full; there is no single criteria of what is right or wrong, or good or bad. Perhaps, again, it is this intangible and immeasurable factor which makes it so difficult for the academic mind to accept intuition as part of general education.

4

Intuition might well be considered the most important single factor in the development of inner resourcefulness, and for much of life – certainly for that part called leisure – full enrichment depends on this inner resourcefulness. If this is neglected, then substitutes become a growing necessity both as a means of simple escapism from a reality that cannot be faced and as a general titivation of facets of personality that unconsciously still demand some form of fulfilment. The negative and base aspects of these demands are easily fulfilled because they can be momentarily satisfied by outer circumstances provided by purveyors of mass entertainment: the cheap, the vulgar, the sensational, the shallow and glittering, the exciting vicarious experience, these are the current coinage of a general culture which makes few demands on the inner resourcefulness of the majority. Purveyors of this innocuous and boring entertainment are hardly to be blamed for their products, for the only alternative appears to be a 'higher' culture which is dependent on a genuine or pseudo-intellectualism and has become the plaything of an intellectual élite, many of whom are equally devoid of this inner resourcefulness and find their satisfactory substitute from a different angle, which often includes the necessity to give up the pretence of enjoying the 'higher intellectual' and to seek relief and relaxation in a new pretence of enjoying the 'popular and general'.

The positive and higher aspects of the inner demand for personality fulfilment are less easy to satisfy, but are still common to all people, each at his different level, and are fully dependent on inner resourcefulness. The attempt to equip young people to achieve these aspects fails if the approach is through the intellect rather than through intuition, that is, through a tangible and examinable process of understanding and thinking, rather than through an imaginative and emotional and therefore intangible process of relishing and enjoying, irrespective of whether or not there is full understanding. The appeal of Shakespeare as a playwright is to the intuition; Shakespeare the poet can also appeal to the intuition, until his poetry is dissected and analysed in such a manner and to such an extent that the only possible form of appreciation is intellectual; then the non-intellectual loses a struggle for which he is not equipped. The enjoyment and appreciation of art is within the compass of every human being, each in his different way, each concerned with some fulfilment of this positive and higher aspect of personal fulfilment; but this is a deeply individual factor, dependent on a full development of inner resourcefulness, personal uniqueness and a simple awareness that one's own feelings and imaginings are as important as an acceptance of other people's thoughts. 'I like what I know and know what I like' may well be the motto of the majority when confronted with art; the function and opportunity for education is to develop the farthest horizons of intuitive knowledge so that the motto becomes a broadening rather than a narrowing, a reaching towards the positive rather than an apathetic acceptance of the negative.

For full and rich living art is an important factor, but neither the only nor the most significant factor. Living in this sense means living with the whole of oneself. If education is concerned with preparing young people for living rather than for a job in life, then it must concern itself with the whole person, and even the most complacent of educationists must be prepared to face the fact that whatever else has been or is being achieved in education today there are still some gaps when we consider this wholeness. The factor of intuition discussed above is one such gap and is possibly so all-embracing that there is no need to list others until they arise in more practical contexts, each concerned with some aspect of skill at living. But the achievement of skill in all human activities is dependent, in the final analysis, on practice; skill at living is equally dependent on practice, and the intention of this book is to suggest ways of providing practice at this particular skill. In this sense, a basic definition of drama might be simply 'to practise living'. The same definition might well be both adequate and precise as a definition of education; for this reason it is suggested that opportunities for drama should be provided for every child and should be the concern of every teacher. However, for both child and teacher this becomes possible only if we discard the limitations of theatrical conventions and consider drama as a quite different activity, calling upon different skills, different standards of judgment and entirely different results. The aim is constant: to develop people, not drama. By pursuing the former, the latter may also be achieved; by pursuing the latter, the former can be totally neglected, if not nullified. By pursuing professional theatre conventions – some dating back more than three hundred years – the point may be missed altogether, the activity reduced to one of interest to only a few, achievable by fewer still, and all quite outside any fundamental aspect of general education. Ultimately, theatre may always remain the concern of the few – drama will increasingly become a way of teaching and a way of learning for everyone.

However, the idea of drama being a way of teaching can in itself create another confusion by suggesting that drama is a useful tool for teaching other subjects. This is indeed so, but only after drama exists within its own right. We cannot use number to solve interesting problems until we have experienced and to some extent mastered number itself: no more can we use drama to understand or experience history or bible stories or literature until we have experienced and mastered certain basic aspects of drama itself. Ultimately, drama is a valuable tool, but first the tool itself must be fashioned.

Does this then mean that drama is yet another subject that has to be fitted into an already overcrowded curriculum? No. Drama is not another subject; theatre might be, with its groundwork in history and its study of playwrights and their works, but not drama. Drama is as intangible as personality itself, and is concerned with developing people. Indeed, it is as necessary to discard educational conventions as to disregard theatre conventions. The thirty or forty minute lesson may be considered an important factor in academic study (tragic as it is that interest and absorption should be abruptly ended by a bell), but in drama the five minute lesson can be as important as the longer one, and its place on the timetable governed as much by factors of human need as of academic necessity – a few minutes active drama can do much for tired, strained and possibly bored minds. So drama need never interfere with crowded curricula; it is a way of education in the fullest sense; it is a way of living and, as such, aids rather than interferes with other study and achievement. Children and young people will still continue to pass various tests and examinations even if time is given to drama; indeed there is some evidence (though not as yet scientifically presented) to suggest that where drama is encouraged those who are going to pass such tests or examinations anyway will pass them more easily, and others who are less likely to pass will in fact do so.

The most important single factor in the use of drama as a genuine part of education is the teacher. It would be preposterous to pretend that a teacher needs no preparation for doing drama – but it is equally preposterous to suggest that a teacher who sees the values of using drama needs a course in theatre. A really full, generous and compassionate interest in children, irrespective of academic ability or gifts, is the first requisite; a knowledge of why to use drama is another; the freedom to approach the matter from where he or she feels happiest and most confident is another. For the latter reason, many rules and conventions, both of drama and of teaching, may have to be ignored. (After all, rules are made for mankind, not mankind for rules.) Thus, as already mentioned, it may be wisest to start with the three or five minute lesson; it may be necessary to begin a drama lesson with, say, 'difficult' fifteen-year-old boys by a discussion of the Tottenham Hotspur's XI, or, with similar girls, to discuss hair-styles or dating boy friends. These subject matters are a far cry from the so-called progressive rules of drama – (e.g. start with movement and progress to speech), but are entirely relevant if our basic premise is that of developing people rather than drama. By the same token, a book such as this can be a positive menace! The book itself must contain a certain degree of form, and its form may suggest a factor of progression which is entirely erroneous and unintended. For any teacher who may find some help from the practical suggestions put forward, I would add the thought: 'Start from where you yourself are happiest and most confident; this may be the telling of a story or it may be a simple discussion about appropriate behaviour in certain situations; it may be the problems of the school play or a discussion on Hamlet's attitude to Claudius; it may be a deep concern with teaching Christian charity or simply asking someone to take a telephone message; it may be a simple concern with sharing physical space and material objects or the complex understanding of racial problems. Start from that point – from where you yourself feel interested and confident.

Keep reminding yourself that what you are concerned with is the development of every one of the manifold facets of human beings; a circle can start at any point on the circumference of that circle. Ultimately there may be only one goal, but the means to that goal are manifold and individual, depending on where you, as teacher, are, and growing out of the particular bond you have made with the children or young people you are helping to develop.'
But to develop people we need to start by considering some aspects of the basic nature of human beings; whatever practical manner we find for beginning drama, these basic aspects of humanity are relevant.

2

Consider a Human Being

When considering the uses of drama as part of the development of people it is necessary to reconsider some accepted practices of general education; for instance, there is little if any correlation between I.Q. and ability to do drama. Again, this emphasises the necessity to differentiate between theatre, which usually requires the study of scripts, and drama which may eventually include some use of script but in no way depends upon it. Unfortunately, whilst drama continues mainly within the domain of English, the tendency is for teachers of brighter children to look upon theatre and scripts as the correct starting place, relegating drama to an alternative activity useful only for those who are unable to read fluently. As later chapters will attempt to show, this approach may be entirely valid for English teaching, but leaves out a whole realm of other training, which does not come under the ægis of the English department. Emotional, intuitive and social training are as necessary for the gifted person as they are for the less gifted – indeed some facets of such training are more necessary for those who, because of academic achievements, are going to pursue careers which include responsibility for and authority over less gifted people.

However, the idea that there is no correlation between I.Q. and drama is open to misunderstanding; many teachers of drama will rightly claim that A stream classes make swifter progression in drama and sometimes bring to the early stages a deeper and more consistent concentration; the C stream class may show more initial eagerness and may throw themselves into drama with less caution, but then make less and slower progress.

Facets of personality

Progression is a natural mode of thinking about academic subjects; there is tangibility of content and both the necessity and the opportunity to start at point A and move on to point B and then to point C and so on – the progression might be considered as continuing along a straight line. Once established and mastered (learnt?) there is seldom need to return to any early point on the line, even though subsequent points depend upon the earlier ones. But the analogy of a straight line is incorrect when considering the development of a human being. Instead, we need to consider a circle; however many points there are on the circle – facets of personality – each is permanent and each is a valid point from which to begin; moreover each is concerned with the potential of continuing development and needs to be returned to over and over again; each is subject not only to possible progression but to equally possible regression. But both progression and regression are to an extent intangible, the degree of tangibility being dependent in many cases on the factor of time. Perhaps the analogy of the growth of a tree is pertinent; if we attempt to watch that growth day by day or even week by week we see little if any tangible change; after three months, the change or growth may be very apparent; the growth itself will depend on the consistency of certain conditions, for example sunlight, rain and soil. There would be no growth if the tree were given these factors for a short while and then left without them thereafter. So with drama and the development of people; drama provides opportunity for the development of many points on the circle, but the development depends on consistency; to this extent, in many aspects of drama there is no such factor as progressing from point A to point B, either within the drama itself or within the people doing the drama. There is growth in quality, there is difference in content, but both points A and B – and all the other points – contain their own forms of progression which, intangible as they may be, are ultimately visible as a factor of personality development.

If we make drama another subject, then we make another 'progressive straight line' – in fact many straight lines, one for infants, one for juniors, and so on through the different age groups; and the multiplicity of straight lines grows as we then start further divisions in terms of such factors as I.Q. If drama is not another subject but a way of helping each person develop, then we are concerned with a circle for each individual from infancy to adulthood. There will be a difference in the detail of each point on the circle for each person because of the uniqueness of personality; nevertheless each and every person has the same points on the circle and the same potential to develop each point to its own fulness.

For this reason, the majority of practical suggestions in this book are considered from the viewpoint of all age groups; it is difficult, if not impossible, for instance, simply to look at suggestions for infant schools for these are spread throughout the book. So far as is possible, each point on the circle is considered for all age groups before considering another point on the circle.

If drama is considered in the manner suggested above, one important advantage – perhaps necessity is not too strong a word – is that whatever point on the circle is chosen as a desirable, useful, expedient or simple starting point will be a point that *already exists* for those who are to do the drama. The teacher's function is not that of imposing a whole new set of (possibly) artificial factors, but of starting with facets of human beings that exist from birth in *all* people.

All possible points on the circle exist in each person. The diagram below shows the points on the circle that are considered in this book. At this stage, only the inner circle really concerns us, as at the beginnings of drama we are concerned with helping each individual to discover and explore his or her own resources, irrespective of other people. At a later stage, drama includes the discovery and exploration of one's environment, and within that environment are seen to exist many other people towards whom one begins to feel a growing sensitivity through each of the basic personal resources (i.e. the next circle outwards). Again at a later stage one feels the need for the enrichment of resources quite outside of oneself and one's own immediate and explored environment, as denoted by the outer circle. But for each circle, the points remain valid for every individual, and are concerned

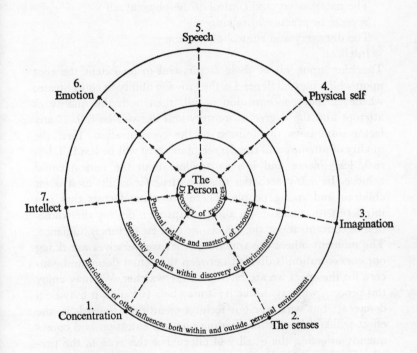

with existing human resources. Each point will be considered in detail in subsequent chapters; at this stage, only a list of factors involved need be considered:

The use of the five major senses: hearing, seeing, touching, smelling and tasting

Imagination

The use, mastery and control of the physical self

Speech, or practice at talking

The discovery and control of emotion

Intellect.

Touching upon all of these factors and to an extent the root upon which they all depend is the growing ability to concentrate; whenever that concentration is full, then both the quality of attempt and the degree of mastery will likewise be full. If any factor diminishes the fullness of the concentration, then the quality of attempt and the degree of mastery will be less full, less real, less sincere and less worthwhile than the person could achieve. In many activities this is as true for adults as it is for children and young people. There are many factors that can interfere with, break down and perhaps even destroy the whole-ness of concentration; the major one of these factors is audience. The moment others are watching what we ourselves are doing our concentration is divided between the actual doing and con-cern for the effect we are having on the watcher. We may enjoy this process, we may dislike it; it may be a stimulus, it may be a deterrent; but whatever our feelings or attitude towards it, the effect will still be that of dividing our concentration and conse-quently affecting the quality of effort. For this reason, the pre-school child and all other age groups need protecting from experi-ences of audience until they are ready within themselves to avoid the emotional reaction to being watched; to gauge this moment of readiness is by no means easy and certainly has nothing to do with the personal wishes of those involved. Children in an infant or junior school are not equipped within themselves to judge the moment of readiness, and an expression of their desire for an audience is symptomatic of all kinds of inner conditions which can guide us to the types of further experience they require – but still leave us with the responsibility of protecting them from the audience experience in order to retain and develop factors of far greater importance.

Here again is the difference between theatre and drama; schools do not exist to develop actors, but to develop people, and one of the major factors in developing people is that of preserving and enriching to its fullest the human capacity to give a full and undivided attention to any matter in hand at any given moment. The beginnings of this capacity to concentrate exists within and is developed unconsciously by the preschool child in its play; nursery and infant schools may develop and enrich it, but are mistaken if they consider that they start it; the function is already there in every child. Some conditions of life at home may have, to a lesser or greater extent, affected it for good or ill; if it has been diminished, perhaps even broken down altogether, the teacher's task is that of rebuilding what already once existed.

This rebuilding of concentration is generally more necessary at later stages of school life, particularly in secondary schools where self-consciousness may affect a very high proportion of young people; of the few ways of overcoming self-consciousness, the re-building of concentration is perhaps the most important and the most advantageous. Part of the function of drama is to develop concentration. Accordingly, this is the first of the many points on the circle which we shall consider in practical terms.

Concentration exercises

Concentration is not an abstraction; one cannot concentrate on concentration. To concentrate is to hold the fulness of attention on a single circumstance or set of circumstances; practice at doing so regularly and consciously results in an ability to do so automatically, and part of this ability is the unconscious shutting out of factors that might detract from the full attention on the particular matter in hand at any given moment.

Early exercises in concentration can start with the use of other factors that already exist within all human beings – the five major senses, hearing, seeing, touching, smelling and tasting. Of these, hearing is the easiest point of starting; listening is a fully personal activity and, in group work, can most easily help each person to exclude the presence of other people; this can be aided still further by closing the eyes.

The exercises that follow are listed in the order: listening, looking, touching, smelling, tasting. Before attempting them in practice with a class several points should be clearly understood.

1. The whole class works at one and the same time; to begin with, the exercises are probably best attempted in the classroom in normal class conditions. Later on, when sessions of drama take place in the hall, the exercises can be done there.

2. The exercises should be set in very simple terms with particular care not to use such instructions as 'Let me *see* you listening'. We are concerned with genuine listening, not with a capacity to *illustrate* an activity called listening.

3. The atmosphere should be calm and uncritical; this factor will be mentioned over and over again, but it is important to stress it even at this stage. We are not concerned with finding out who is 'best' or 'worst' at the activity, and it is important in this, as in all aspects of drama concerned with developing people, to remove all fear of failure. If there is need – and there *will* be need, certainly in the early stages, and particularly with those who are self-conscious – to discipline or control certain people in the class this should be done not for its own sake but as part of social training. To say: 'It isn't easy for people to listen if others are talking', is constructive and starts a process of personal responsibility. To punish or embarrass an individual who has little concentration not only does nothing to help his concentration, but also destroys the atmosphere of the class as a whole, thus probably affecting the concentration of many others. (See chapters 7 and 8 for further comments and suggestions regarding discipline and control.)

4. A few exercises, for a short space of time, *regularly*, brings eventual results. Keep in mind that the progression is within each person, each at his or her own rate; the point on the circle is there for the whole of life. These are not exercises to do once and then pass on to something else.

5. There is no need, with any age group, to associate the exercises with the idea of drama; often it is wisest not to do so. There is no problem in using them with infants and juniors, nor generally

with the first two years in secondary schools. With top secondary groups, there may be need to arrest interest in the first place. This again can be achieved more easily if we avoid talking about 'drama' or 'theatre', but instead discuss factors of particular interest to the group itself, concerned with some general or particular aspect of life. Sport of one kind or another is often a good starting point for discussion. For example:

'What does a famous footballer feel like at the moment of taking a penalty kick at Wembley Stadium, watched by 100,000 people?

'What does a Wimbledon finalist feel at the moment of serving or receiving for match point?

'What does a famous diver or swimmer feel at the moment of diving?

'What does a test match batsman feel as he takes the first ball or perhaps at the moment his score stands at ninety-nine?'

In each case, the question has asked 'What does such and such a person *feel*' in certain circumstances. From a discussion of their possible feelings, we are one short stage from discussing what in fact they have *to do*, where their thoughts must be at that moment. We arrive at consideration of the factor of full concentration.

There are, of course, many starting points other than sport. Many different aspects of transport, from landing a heavy jet aircraft to simply crossing a busy street, are useful. We find for our group the particular from life as a whole that will arrest their interest and attention and start them discussing. In each case we eventually arrive at the point of concentration – which can then be linked to factors in their own lives, for each and every one of us has the same need for concentration, in many activities besides school study; and, most important of all, whoever we are, whatever our walk of life, we can, by practice, increase our capacity to concentrate. And so we introduce the exercises.

LISTENING

(*a*) Listen to sounds outside of the building (in the street or the playground).

(*b*) Listen to sounds outside of the room (in corridors or adjacent rooms).

(*c*) Listen to sounds inside the room.

(*d*) Become aware of – i.e. listen to – your own breathing; do not breathe in any special way; simply become aware of your own normal breathing.

Only 15–30 seconds per exercise.

Further developments

1. Repeat exercises (*a*)–(*c*), adding 'Try to identify each separate sound as you become aware of it'.

Repeat exercises (*a*)–(*c*), holding the whole of your attention on one particular sound to the exclusion of any others.

Repeat exercises (*a*)–(*c*), not only trying to identify each particular sound, but also trying to imagine very clearly a person or persons connected with the sound. (Example: Imagine some details regarding the driver of a passing lorry, or the passengers on a bus, or what people are doing on an aeroplane passing overhead. N.B. Holding the attention on a moving sound until it is out of earshot is always valuable.)

After each group of exercises, it may be useful:

(*a*) To have a class discussion on the various sounds heard. This can be of considerable help to those who, perhaps because of lack of concentration or even hearing that is defective in one way or another, have not been aware of sounds to hear. Do not turn this stage into any form of competition, otherwise tensions will be created that make it impossible for some people to listen at all. Or

(*b*) Let each person in the class discuss *privately* with the person next to him or her all of the various sounds heard. This may or may not lead to a moment or two of general class discussion, depending on the general atmosphere and the stage at which the class has reached.

N.B. Awareness of, or listening to, one's own breathing is entirely personal and individual and should not be part of any form of discussion. This is important as it is essential not to interfere with any person's natural breathing as it is deeply connected with personal rhythm of life. Nevertheless, this is a most important part of the sequence of exercise as it helps each person to become aware of himself as a living entity, different from the many other factors, both near and far, within the immediate and more remote environment of existence.

2. *After* a sequence of some of the above exercises, the teacher can make particular sounds (e.g. tapping different kinds of surface, turning switches on or off, opening or closing cupboards or other doors, moving pieces of furniture a few inches) and ask the class to identify the sounds made, with their eyes closed. These sounds may be many or few according to the intention and stage of development. The class might be asked to (a) speak as soon as the sound is identified; (b) remember each sound and identify later either in class discussion or in discussion with one other person, or in discussion in small groups.

After some practice, a further challenge might be that of remembering the exact sequence in which a number of sounds were made. Later still, if the teacher is moving about the room in order to make different sounds, the class might also be asked to become aware of and remember the number of footsteps made between each sound.

3. Listening can become an important early stage in the development of imagination; see chapter 4 for further details.

4. (*For 9 plus upwards*)

After considerable practice at many variations of the above, and not before there is some certainty that concentration is beginning to become quite strong:

(a) Divide the class into pairs. One of each pair makes a sequence of simple sounds whilst the other listens with eyes closed. After the sequence, the listener either repeats the same sequence or simply identifies the sounds heard and the ways of making them. Then the pairs reverse activities. All pairs work at one and the same time.

(b) Divide the class into pairs. One of each pair talks to the other, who is reading something from a book or paper quietly to themselves. The reader ignores the speaker and concentrates on reading. The reader then tells the disturber some of the detail of what they were reading, checking the content together. Then the pairs reverse activities.

(c) Similar to (b) above, but instead of reading a passage, try to work out on paper or mentally some simple arithmetical problem e.g. how many inches in the length of a cricket pitch. The problem can be set by the teacher according to the age or stage of development of the group.

N.B. For (b) and (c) above, emphasise that the persons speaking must not shout, and must not physically touch their partner.

5. The above and similar exercises can be repeated in groups that gradually grow larger in number: after the pair stage, then groups of three, of four, of five, of six and of seven. Seven is probably the largest number of any value. All groups work at one and the same time.

LOOKING

(a) Look around the room. How many different colours are there, excluding people's clothing? It is wise to exclude clothing in the early stages as this involves people deliberately looking at one another and possibly aggravating self-consciousness.

(b) Look at some surface close to you – e.g. a section of floor, the back of the chair in front of you, the top of the desk – and see clearly the lines or marks or patterns in the surface.

(c) Look at the lines on the palm of your own hand.

As suggested for the exercises in listening, each group of exercises can be followed by either class discussion or private discussion in pairs, but it must be repeated again that there should be no form of competition involved in this or any subsequent exercises.

There is no limit to the number of objects or surfaces the teacher can choose for the class to look at, but it should be noted that, as with the exercises suggested for listening, the activities are suggested from the viewpoint of three different levels of attention:

1. Intimate and personal (e.g. awareness of own breathing, looking at own hand).

2. Close to one's immediate environment, but not part of oneself (e.g. sounds in the same room, a surface close by).

3. In the world outside of the immediate environment (e.g. distant sounds and sights).

Although it is possible to find an infinite variety of different exercises for each one of the senses it is not always possible to arrange them at these three levels. However, it is suggested that there is intrinsic value in having a few seconds in which the different levels of attention are used, even if it means repeating the same example each time. As will have become apparent, these exercises are not only aiding concentration, but are also giving direct practice in the use of the senses, constantly limbering them and keeping them in first-class condition, helping each human being to become a fully sensitive instrument, aware of itself, aware of its immediate and ever changing environment, and sensitive to the large whole containing the smaller. This acute sensitivity and awareness takes time to develop and is, to start with, entirely personal: the instrument is built and taken care of constantly – hence the need for continuity right through school life. An analogy might be made with hair and teeth: without constant and continual attention early efforts are negated. Hair and teeth are tangible so there is no problem in seeing clearly the need for constant attention; the five major senses are intangible – and yet how much more important they are to the business of living a full sensitive and rich life. As will be seen later, once the instrument is working fully, its concerns cease to be merely personal and begin to involve detailed consideration for other instruments – other people.

Further exercises in looking

Look at the overall architecture of the hall or room; look in such a way that you could make a sketch plan of it when no longer in the room; discuss with a partner the different features each have observed.

Look at – examine in detail – one particular feature in the room or hall, e.g. a chair, a radiator, a window. Really examine it so that you know exactly how it was put together. In pairs, show and tell each other the details one has discovered. (N.B. It is advisable to exclude any feature of the room that involves electricity, e.g. switches, plugs etc.)

Repeat similar exercises, in pairs, with one of each pair looking whilst the other talks about anything they like; the person looking ignores the talker, keeping full concentration on the job in hand. Then the pairs reverse activities.

Arrange a number of different objects on a table; invite the class to observe the arrangement for, say, thirty seconds. All close eyes whilst you make some changes in the arrangements – then each person looks and decides what changes have been made. This can be done individually and discussed in pairs or as a class, or pairs can work together from the outset. To start with, the re-arrangements of objects needs to be fairly obvious, but can become subtle at a later stage. The same exercise can, of course, be done by pairs sitting in desks, one of each pair arranging and re-arranging a few simple objects (e.g. books, writing materials, etc.) on top of the desk. A similar exercise can be done with the whole class in which they observe the arrangements of articles such as furniture in the whole classroom or hall and then observe any changes that are made whilst they have closed their eyes. Links with listening can be made, as they follow the sound of teacher's foot-steps around the room, and perhaps even hear some of the rearranging.

Show the class a picture from a newspaper or magazine (adver-tisements are often useful). Allow observation for, say, thirty seconds; then in pairs, small groups or with the class as a whole, discuss the detail of what was seen. The more dramatic the picture, the more interest will be aroused. Link with such ideas as being witness to an incident and describing in court or to the police exactly what one saw.

Further developments

In pairs; one of each pair goes through a simple sequence of movements, using only hands and arms. The other watches care-fully, then repeats the same sequence. Reverse activities. At a later stage, use a similar exercise, moving the whole body instead of just hands and arms. N.B. Emphasise that the object is not to outwit the other person, so movements should not be fast and 'fiddly'. If there is no absorption, or if the outwitting urge is dominant, then they are not yet ready for this type of exercise, so give more practice at the simpler, individual exercises and try again later. Small groups, two groups, the same in number, working together. One group arranges itself as a statue or still photograph – the other group observes the full detail and then makes itself into the same statue or photograph.

As with listening exercises, it will be noted that the exercises can and should be arranged to grow from the individual working on his own, through working in pairs, threes, fours, fives, sixes and sevens, according to the stage that has been reached.

TOUCH

Many of the exercises concerning touch are best attempted, to start with, when the eyes are closed; often the use or sensitivity of one of the senses is increased by removing the use of another. One might start by asking the class to be aware of the exact feeling of whatever their fingers are resting on – it may be the desk lid, or one hand on the other, or the sleeve of a jacket, or the material of skirt or trousers. Whatever it is, become fully aware of it through the tips of the fingers – is it rough or smooth, warm or cold, soft or hard and so on. Then discover one or more (eventually *many* more) surfaces that feel different from the first and different from each other. Discuss in pairs the different textures and in what way they are different.

Further development

Work in pairs. One person keeps their eyes closed and the other guides them to a sequence of different surfaces, which the 'blind' person identifies by touch. Reverse activities.

One of the pair describes to the other the details of the feel of a particular surface or object without naming the surface or object. The other describes a different surface or object. Then both attempt to discover by touch precisely what was described to them.

LINKING THE SENSES

To link sight and sound, or sight and touch, or sound and touch, or a combination of the three, becomes possible after there has been some practice at using each individually. For example, rub or tap a surface (or sequence of different surfaces) at the same time listening to the sound made and/or looking in detail at the surface itself and/or being aware of the feel of the texture. An infinite variety of exercises can be found through the combined use of two or more of the senses.

It is suggested that teachers themselves try some of these exercises at home before inviting their use by a class; at the least, the exercises can afford adults some amusement, at best they are a source of considerable enrichment; further, they will find their own imaginations stimulated to the formulation of other examples; obviously the greater the variety of exercises the better, particularly if, as suggested, there is going to be regular and continual opportunity to do them over a long period of time.

THE SENSES OF TASTE AND SMELL

A natural objection to a great deal of the kind of training suggested in this book is that too much time is necessary in preparation. Perhaps it is now clear that for listening, looking and touching no preparation is necessary, nor is it necessary to leave the classroom. However, it is more difficult to arrange exercises for either taste or smell, and there is really no need to do so. Subsequent chapters suggest ways of using imaginary rather than actual examples concerned both with taste and smell. Meanwhile, once there has been practice at using the ear, the eye and the fingers, we can help the class to become aware of taste and smell and to suggest that they themselves find moments for practising the use of each; for example, becoming fully aware of the many different kinds of smell as they move about the school or go from school to home or home to school; or again, that they might try actually tasting each mouthful of a meal now and again instead of simply shovelling food into themselves at top speed (this is always good for a laugh where school dinners are concerned).

If class exercises are attempted, it is important to remember that the sense of taste and the sense of smell are both delicate and dependent on a very full concentration; it is therefore wise to establish and build concentration through work on the other senses before starting on these.

Age Groups

It will be noted that no particular grading of the foregoing exercises has been made from considerations of age groups or such factors as ability or I.Q. Such grading is both impossible and unnecessary. What is important is that we all know that every human being is equipped with these five major senses and that they need regular practice for full development. Through the practice we also have a natural way of developing personal powers of concentration. Each class will be at its own particular stage of development, and can be helped to develop further. An attempt has been made to suggest early exercises that are valid for any age group that has not done this kind of work before, and further to suggest some natural developments. The point of starting, the manner of development, the type of continuity are all matters that only each individual teacher can decide for his or her own class at any given moment. But every member of the class is involved in equal opportunity, all working at one and the same time, each developing at his or her own rate in a constructive and uncritical atmosphere, entirely free from exposure to audience, from systems of marking or any other device that leads to fear of failure or the labelling of some people as good and others as no good. We cannot all see with the eye of a great painter, hear with the ear of a great poet or musician or touch with the skill and sensitivity of a great sculptor. This is beside the point. We can, in fact, all hear and see and feel, and our sensitivity as people, our awareness of ourselves and the world about us, and therefore our own personal enrichments in life are all partly dependent on developing our sensory instruments to the fullest extent of their powers, different as these powers might be for each individual.

Application to 'Theatre'

For those schools which have drama or theatre clubs, or for particular reasons are concerned with performance, a great deal will be gained by using some of the above exercises for a few minutes before every rehearsal and before every performance. Good performances arise from maximum concentration, maximum awareness and maximum control, and each of these qualities is strengthened by regular practice. Furthermore the detail of the three levels of attention are closely associated with Stanislavsky's circles of attention, growing outwards from the personal self to embrace the environment in which that personal self is performing within a larger environment that includes the audience with whom one is sharing. The many various factors of sharing are touched on in subsequent chapters; perhaps for the present it suffices to point out that only the best is worthy of sharing, and that each person's best arises from the fullest and most absorbed effort. The exercises contained in this chapter will all help that quality of effort, partly by helping the indigenous qualities of the person making the effort and partly by increasing the sensitivity to the responsibilities involved in all facets of sharing with other people. See also chapters 10 and 12.

Method of Approach

One false idea of drama and the approach to developing people through drama is the notion that the activity is free, implying that the participants are left to swim in the limbo of self-experience without assistance. It is important to remember that in the early stages of all creative work the participants experience a kind of fear of freedom, which can be a total uncertainty as to *what* to do; ideas either don't come or are self-rejected as inadequate; there is need for someone to give a start. In the realm of ideas on *what* to do and, later on, *who* to be, each member of the class is fully dependent for all the beginning stages. All the exercises in this chapter, and many in each subsequent chapter arise entirely from the teacher. Do this, do that, do the other thing. But never on any account, in any circumstances, is this accompanied by any indication, instruction or demonstration on *how* to do it. Each person thinks out the 'how' for himself, and makes his own attempt, different as these attempts may turn out to be. It is quite simple, and perfectly meaningless, for a whole class to imitate teacher's way of doing the exercise; what is valuable is for each person to discover for himself his own way of doing it. This is genuine freedom of opportunity.

It may be that we shall be less satisfied with what comes from the class than we would be if we saw a shadow of our own effort – but we must console ourselves that it is *of* them and *from* them and this is ultimately what is important. The imitation of another person's experience is never as deep as our own experience, even if, through lack of practice, our own experiences are on the shallow side in the early stages of the work.

3

Begin from Where You Are

Now we consider a starting point that leads directly out of the kind of work that every teacher of primary age children is familiar with and experienced at: the telling or reading of a story. The story session is the most comfortable way of easing into the beginnings of drama; work can be confined to the classroom or a corner of the hall with the class sitting informally around the teacher – in fact, exactly whatever physical circumstances are the established practice of each individual class. Then, just before starting the story, the teacher invites the class to help bring the story to life by making some of the *sounds* that happen in the story. 'Let us try one sound now; in the story I am going to tell you there is, for instance, the sound of the wind. Everybody make the sound of the wind – now.' And the class will make the sound of the wind. If they have never done this before, the sound will probably be very gentle and tentative; accept this – it is unwise to try to whip it up into a great roar of excited sound, as this eventually leads to an unabsorbed, almost hysterical noise that bears no relation to genuine participation. As confidence grows, tentative sounds will quite naturally become bold and strong without our having to coax or cajole. In fact it is wise before starting such a session to have some simple means of controlling the sound, and to build one's bond with the group by explaining to them and trying out with them, whatever arrangement you have decided on. One control factor that always seems to work is to have a simple arrow which is used in the same manner as the volume control on a radio or television set. When the arrow is pointing downwards, there is no sound at all; as the arrow begins to turn upwards, sound starts and can go on growing in volume until, when it is pointing straight upwards the sound can be at full volume, and as it turns down again, the sound begins to fade away to silence. Explain the arrangements and try them out, using the sound of the wind. And, just before starting the story, remind the class to keep their eyes on the arrow so that they know when *you need their help with the story*. This is a most important point – we, as teachers, need help with the telling of the story. Ultimately, over a longish period of time, we are gradually going to hand over the responsibility for *every* aspect of the story to them; at this starting point, most of the responsibility is ours, but we are inviting early co-operation through simple participation. Incidentally, the arrow can be as simple as a pen or pencil or paint brush, providing all the class can see it clearly; but to have a special arrow is quite useful, as one can then build up sessions of 'Arrow Stories'.

The above approach is utterly simple and therefore suitable for infants and younger juniors. For older juniors, the same basic approach is possible, but the detail needs to be a little more sophisticated. We might discuss the problems of building the atmosphere of a story through sound only – through radio rather than through television. Once interest is arrested through some such discussion, the procedure, including the use of the arrow, is similar. For each age group, we are concerned with the early beginnings of drama through class participation by sound, with the participation fully in our control.

Here is an example of a simple (original) story, with marginal indications of opportunities for sound participation.

STORY	SOUNDS *(controlled by arrow)*
'One hot, sunny day some friends went to the sea-side and hired a boat; they put all their belongings into the boat, helped one another in, and then started up the engine.	*Engines starting up*
Then, off they went out to sea, as fast as	*Fast engines* ....
the boat could go. When they were a long	....*continue*.......
way from the shore, they switched off the	...*engines turned off.*

STORY	SOUNDS
(*continued*)	(*continued*)

engine, and threw the anchor overboard into the sea. Now the boat was very still, with just the gentlest of waves lapping against the side of it. Away in the distance they could see the shore, and when they listened very hard, they could just hear the sounds of traffic in the town.

Anchor plunging into sea.
Lapping waves......

Faint sounds of traffic.

'Then, quite suddenly, they heard a new sound – the sound of a breeze getting up. And the breeze became stronger until it was a wind, and then stronger and stronger until it was a fierce gale.

Breeze............
...growing wind...
..growing wind ....
.....gale force wind

(N.B. *Stop telling story for this strong sound...suddenly drop arrow to end sound, and immediately continue story.*)

'And the gale lashed the sea into waves... bigger and bigger waves... and one enormous wave went right over the boat...and soon the sun was covered by great dark clouds...and there were flashes of lightning...and a great roar of thunder...

....sea sounds.....
....heavy sea.....
....maximum wave sound....
....possibly lightning sounds.....
....thunder ....

'And then the rain started... By now, the friends were so worried, that they quickly pulled up the anchor and started the engine, and went as fast as they possibly could back to the safety of the shore. They turned off the engine, and ran up the shore into shelter until the storm had passed. They were soaking wet and needed some new clothes; they listened very hard, and way off in the distance, very, very faintly, they could hear people in a market-place calling out the things they had to sell....So they set off for market, and as they got nearer the voices in the market

Rain........

Engines......
.....engines continue
.....Engines off...

Distant market voices
....grow-ing gradually in volume
....

STORY	SOUND
(continued)	(continued)

became clearer and clearer and clearer...   *full sound*.......
>   *turn arrow quickly down to cut sound alto-*
gether
And they bought themselves some new,
dry clothes, and went happily home together.'

The above story is concerned with sound participation only.
Several points should be kept in mind:

1. Make sure to have at least one practice with the arrow before
starting.

2. Do not give the arrow to one of the class to use; this is your
medium of control.

3. There may well be moments when, with maximum sound, it
is impossible for them to hear you telling the story – so don't try;
leave them making the sound, then fade it down with the arrow,
and continue the story. (Two such places are indicated above,
but others might arise.)

4. Do not be worried if they do not make some of the sounds you
expect or hope they will make. For example, in the above story,
they may not make such sounds as that of the anchor plunging
into the sea, or perhaps that of lightning. Do not stop the story
to comment on this – though it might be a useful discussion
point after the story is over. Similarly, they may make sounds
other than with their mouths – tapping of hands or some such
for rain, perhaps drumming on desk lids for thunder. This is perfectly valid, and again we can discuss other ways of making
particular sounds when the story is over.

5. Do not, before, during or after the story either tell or demonstrate how to make the sounds. They will discover for themselves.

6. During the first few stories with participation of this kind, it
may be necessary to remind them to keep their eyes on the arrow
and to work carefully with it. This is perfectly natural – all forms
of personal control arise from practice and are unlikely to be
perfect from the outset.

7. If excitement grows to a point where you feel worried about control, despite the arrow, then either cut the story short or bring in the use of very quiet and delicate sounds. N.B. One great advantage of making up our own stories is that we can adapt all of the participation factors to the circumstances of the moment. Stories read from a book are not quite so easily adapted to suit our ends. (See pp. 39 below and chapter 4 for suggestions about making up stories.)

The excitement mentioned here may be the result of lack of absorption from lack of practice, so try not to give up, but to give more practice; or the excitement may simply be a clear sign that we have stimulated the need for more positive activity, going beyond participation only through sound. (See repeat of story below.)

8. Do not expect or hope that for the first few attempts these stories with sound participation will last for more than a few minutes; they may do so. But they will be of more value if we do not attempt to force them to last longer than the experience of the class will allow.

9. It is not suggested or implied that this kind of participation in stories should in any way supplant the activity of simply listening to stories, either read or told by the teacher. This is a different activity for a different purpose. The two activities can exist side by side.

The following list, which is by no means exhaustive, gives some idea of the wealth of sound opportunities that exist for this kind of sound participation. It should be noted that many items on the list are no more than heading indications – e.g. railway stations, fairgrounds, zoos. Class discussion will soon lead to the building up of a very wide range of sound under these headings. Other items have been broken down into more detail – e.g. domestic, fantasy and supernatural. But again these are by no means exhaustive in their detail and are intended only as a stimulus – discussion with the class will reveal many other sounds.

THE ELEMENTS	DOMESTIC	TRANSPORT
Rain	Hoovers	Buses
Lightning	Cookers	Cars

THE ELEMENTS
(*continued*)
Hail
Thunder
Wind
Fire
Water of all kinds
including sea and
waterfalls etc.
Sandstorms
Volcanoes
Earthquakes
Swamps
Jungles

NATURE
Birds
Insects
Animals
Leaves, etc.
Pebbles and stones

ANIMALS
Farms
Circuses
Zoos
Wild-life parks
Pet-shops
Aquariums
Markets

SUPERNATURAL
Magic spells
Witches
Witches' cauldrons
Ghosts
Haunted houses

DOMESTIC
(*continued*)
Cutlery
China
Glass
Washing machines
Scrubbing
Washing
Door and doorbells
Telephones
Clocks
Domestic animals
Babies
Parties

STREET NOISES
Footsteps: walking,
running, limping,
dragging etc.
Walking sticks
News-vendors
Cars etc.
Prams
Ambulances
Fire Engines
Police cars
Tractors

OCCUPATIONS
Offices of all kinds
Farming
Hospitals
Shops of all kinds
Restaurants and

TRANSPORT
(*continued*)
Lorries
Motor-cycles
Scooters
Aeroplanes
Ships and boats
Trains
Horses (and carts)
Railway stations
Airports
Dockyards
Bus stations
Waiting-rooms

INDUSTRY
Machinery of all
kinds, heavy and
light
Sirens
Hooters
Canteens
Bulldozers
Road drills
Tipping lorries
Concrete mixers
Picks and shovels

ENTERTAINMENT
Funfairs and fair-
grounds
Holiday camps
Bowling alleys
Skating rinks

SUPERNATURAL
(*continued*)
Movement of
'spirits'
Fairies and goblins
Caves, caverns and
deep dark places
Toy shops

OCCUPATIONS
(*continued*)
cafes
Schools
Post Offices
Banks
Armed forces
Dentists

ENTERTAINMENT
(*continued*)
Swimming baths
Cinemas and
theatres
Television and
radio studios
Film studios
Greyhound
stadiums
Horse racing
Regattas
Pubs and clubs
and posh hotels

SPACE STORIES
Rockets taking off
Radio communica-
tion
Control room
Bleeps – all kinds
Talk-back etc.
Satellites
Rocket landings
Moon noises

OCCASIONS
Royal and other
processions
Coronations and
other royal
occasions
Weddings
Funerals
Christenings
Launching of
ships etc.
Sports days etc.

WARFARE
Guns of every kind
– including revol-
vers, rifles,
machine-guns,
bombs, shells, anti-
aircraft etc., etc.
Flame-throwers
Tanks etc.
Bows and arrows
Boiling oil pouring

SPORT
All games: cricket, football, rugby, tennis, etc.
Swimming
Various sounds by or among sporting crowds, including whistles,
starting pistols, rattles, programme sellers, hot-dog vendors, ice-
cream sellers, newspaper boys, rosette sellers, ticket touts, etc.

Consideration of the above lists will show that there are very few
stories that one can read to a class that do not give some valid
and simple opportunities for participation through sound. Perhaps
they also indicate the limitless possibilities when making up

simple, original stories in order deliberately to provide particular opportunities. Naturally one chooses story material according to the degree of or type of sounds that one feels ready to control and to accept. If, in the early stages, one is worried about strong and loud sounds such as those under the heading 'warfare', then one simply avoids that type of subject matter.

Top Juniors and Secondary Schools

As already indicated, a similar approach to the use of sound and full class participation will work satisfactorily with older age groups if the method of approach and the content suit the age group. This is one way of making vital use of the school tape-recorder; the background sounds necessary for a story can be built up and recorded by the whole class. For example, consider the sounds that might be built for a story on a desert island – the sounds of the sea and surf, of the birds and insects, perhaps of small animals, and the sounds of the wind and the movement of palm trees. If the class is divided into sections, each section being concerned with one particular sound, then a whole sound picture can be built up of the desert island, either as an introduction of, as a background to, or for particular moments within the story of the desert island.

Building and recording background sounds can be an exciting and important way of starting with older secondary children, with the use of the tape-recorder for final recordings. Assist the class to think in terms of sounds that are very close, sounds that are in mid-distance and sounds that are far away; (link with the exercises in listening contained in chapter 2); point out the non-selectivity of a microphone – it picks up every sound about it. The full use of the tape-recorder is beyond the scope and intention of this book, but reference will be made to it every now and again, and the above can be an excellent way of slowly introducing some factors of drama.

Participation with Action

From the simple and natural way of beginning drama through sound participation in a story, it is a comparatively easy matter to go on to the use of participation with action. Conditions remain the same: the class is still either in the classroom or in a corner of the hall, grouped around the teacher; there is no need for any member of the class to get up and away from these positions until we as teachers feel ready in ourselves for that to happen.

The story about the friends at the seaside can serve as a useful example of the approach. We now invite the class not just to participate with sounds, but 'to do all the various things that happen in the story, *sitting where they are*'. The sounds might well be added, fully controlled by the use of the arrow; or we may feel that it would be better to have action without any sound, in which case we need simply add the words: 'Don't make any sounds this time; simply do all of the actions that happen in the story'.

And we tell the story again:

STORY	POSSIBLE ACTION
'One hot, sunny day some friends went to the seaside and hired a boat; they put all their belongings into the boat and then started the engine; they left the engine warming up, and pulled up the sail; it was a heavy sail and they had to pull really hard to get it up. They tied off the rope to keep the sail up; then they returned to the engine and accelerated until it was going as fast as it could...and they steered the boat right out to sea....When they were a long long way from the shore, they turned off the engine, and lowered the sail...and folded it tidily so that they would have no difficulty in raising it again. Then they threw the anchor overboard, so that the boat was quite still. Etc., etc.	*Starting the engine* *Pulling up the sail* *Tying off rope* *Accelerating engine* *Steering the boat* *Turning off the engine* *Lowering the sail, and making tidy* *Throwing the anchor overboard*

The story is now mainly concerned with action. However, again several points should be kept in mind.

1. The class may well introduce some sounds, particularly if they

have experienced the same story with the use of sound. They may, for example, make the sounds of the engine even though we may have mentioned that we want them to do only action; do not be worried by this, and have the arrow standing by in case it should happen. Action often stimulates sound, which then enriches action.

2. Do not be worried if they do not do all of the actions; some are very difficult to start with. Do not stop the story to comment on this; keep it in mind as a possibly useful point of discussion after the story is over.

3. Never – before, during or after the story – either tell or demonstrate how to make the actions. They will discover for themselves. If less confident children copy others, do not worry about this – they will gain in confidence if the atmosphere is uncritical, and there is far less harm in one child copying another than arises from copying the more exact communicative actions of an adult.

4. Do not worry them about exactness of detail or accuracy of mime. Such detail and accuracy are concerned with communication and belong to a very much later stage. They are not actors – they are simply experiencing at the very simplest of levels.

5. Do not expect stories with action to last for very long to start with.

6. In this version of the story, not only have many of the incidents involving sound been left out, but the ending has been deliberately changed, with the visit to the market place left out. Just as the sounds could have been left in, or else could occur in another reading or telling of the story incorporating both sound and action, so too could the visit to the market-place be used as *the first step towards* permitting or encouraging part or all of the class to leave their seats and begin to use a little more of the space around them. For example, a section of the class could have become people in the market place who are going around buying from the other half who are selling various articles from their seats. Then activities could be reversed, and buyers and sellers change functions. Or perhaps the whole class can come away from their seats. 'Who', we ask, 'wants to sell things in the market?' Of the many volunteers, we appoint (or cast) perhaps twelve, fourteen or sixteen people, working in pairs to help each

other, to set up their stalls (quite imaginary) in different parts of the room, each pair calling out what it is they have to sell. The remainder of the class, again perhaps working in pairs, go shopping round the market. (See pp. 125 for further developments of 'A Market place', including ways of ending.) The whole incident in the market has lasted no more than perhaps one minute to a minute and a half; nevertheless we have taken the first bold step in allowing an even more active form of drama to arise quite logically and naturally from what has gone before. This is quite enough for a first time. If this is a new experience there will be more excitement than absorption, but we must not judge too severely; only further opportunity will provide the practice that will bring improvements in concentration and sincerity. (See also chapters 6 and 7 regarding factors of discipline and noise.)

N.B. A note regarding selection of individuals or 'casting'. Try always to make it appear quite arbitrary, no matter how much careful thought you may have given to the kind of opportunity that you are concerned with providing at any given moment for any given youngster. Do not comment on your selection and reveal your reasons for it; you may have decided that John is ready for a little responsibility – but do not say such things as: 'I think we'll have John do so and so; he's been trying very hard lately and I think he deserves a little encouragement.' John may well have been trying hard and he may well need the encouragement, but his gain lies in the fact that you have observed both his need and his opportunity and are making suitable provision; nothing will be added for him if you make the procedure conscious for him and for the rest of the class. Nothing will be gained – some things might well be lost. Also, don't ask John if he would 'like' to be so and so; he may not like, or he may be quite indifferent until you set up the idea of choice by your question. Say, quite simply: 'John is so and so.' John will accept this, so will the rest of the class, and the matter is settled without any fuss. Similarly, keep words of praise or encouragement general to the whole class, not particular to a few children. It does not necessarily encourage John to say to the whole class: 'I'm sure you'll all agree that John did jolly well today, don't you?' They may or may not. It is irrelevant. John doesn't need this kind of praise and the rest of the class probably resent it or else become ambitious to collect the laurels for themselves next time. We keep the atmosphere wholly uncritical, with occasional words to the entire class such as: 'Good – we've worked hard today', or perhaps 'I don't think we've all worked quite as hard today as we did last time – never mind, perhaps we can make up for it next time'. These generalisations are quite sufficient; they are not concerned with the attitude to 'good, better and best' which is basically highly competitive, which leads to fear of failure, the undermining of the less gifted and a potential arrogance in the more gifted. Slowly we become interested in work for its own sake, not for the laurels it might win us. This is a healthy attitude to work of any kind, and an absolute necessity for work concerned with individuality and personal creativity, no matter how simple the level of that work. The idea that 'this is a highly competitive world and the sooner children get used to it the better' may or may not hold true for academic work or for physical factors on the playing field or in the gymnasium, but is quite erroneous where the creative arts are concerned. We are not training people to be competitive artists, we are using the creative arts to help make fully developed people; a backward or retarded person's one hundred per cent is of as much value to that person as the potential university graduate's hundred per cent is valuable to him; each is valuable in its own right.

Stories made up by Class and Teacher Together

We have considered the method by which sound and/or action participation can start from the teacher reading or telling a story; the procedure follows through the suggestion that in all the early stages of drama it is necessary to give ideas on what to do or who to be, but to avoid any suggestion of how to do it. One extension that soon becomes possible from such beginnings is for the teacher to allow the help given by the class to include the actual making up of the story itself. (This is not necessarily *the* next step; there are many points on the circle which can be equally valuable for the next step, but this is a clear step that arises from what has gone before.)

Many people have written variations on the theme of the 'Ideas Game', which is particularly useful for any teacher who feels unskilled or inadequate at making up stories.

The ideas game will work with all age groups from infants to old age pensioners. The procedure is as follows.

Ask the class to suggest three ideas, quite simple ideas of any kind, e.g. a telephone, a stick, a rocket; ask them to help you remember the ideas – this at once makes the bond of cooperation: they are not going to sit and listen to you, they are going to help you. Perhaps they have already helped you to build the atmosphere of a story by making the necessary sounds; now they are going to help again. Start your story with any one of the objects and, at any moment in the story, according either to your needs (i.e. you are 'stuck') or to the deliberate opportunity you wish to provide, stop and ask such questions as:

'And what do you think they saw...?'

'What do you think the man did...?'

'What do you think so and so said...?'

'What do you think they heard...?' etc.

Each time you stop and ask such a question, you will undoubtedly receive one or more replies. *Accept* the suggestions made; if there are several, then you need to make a quick decision (not a great issue) as to which one will fit best with the story you are telling; select that and go straight on with the story until you feel the necessity to ask another question, and so on. Do not be alarmed if some of the suggestions seem a little unlikely; you will quickly sense what is genuine interest and help, and what is clearly playing you up; it is usually possible to ignore the latter suggestions and select others, but if it is done tactfully then general cooperation will soon grow.

Do not try to make the stories too long to start with; they will grow quite naturally as you and the class gain confidence from practice. If possible, try to arrange for the answers to be given to you without the necessity for putting up hands and waiting until selection; this holds up the flow and places you in some difficulty if you do not happen to like the suggestion made by the person you select; if several suggestions come at once, you have a wider range from which to select. There is no need for disorder because hands are not raised, and, if you feel the need, you can make quite clear that it is only for this particular activity that they need not put up their hands. Try also to use suggestions from many different people rather than only from the one or two who seem to be on your wavelength or already have acknowledged status as being clever or bright. At the same time, do not be surprised or bothered if, particularly in the early stages, there are some who have no suggestions to make. Do not suddenly point at such people, demanding suggestions from them; they probably have little enough confidence as it is, and to be picked on suddenly will only exacerbate the difficulty. One of our objectives is slowly to build confidence in each individual; for some this will take a very long time indeed; as has been mentioned before, we must remove the fear of failure and the notion of being no good. Infinite patience is necessary.

When first making up stories through the ideas game, the teacher may well need to take the major responsibility, but little by little, as the confidence of the class grows, the teacher hands over more and more responsibility to the class. Sometimes it is interesting to let different endings to the story be made up by the class itself, divided into small groups (anything from two to five in number); or perhaps the end could be written individually by each member of the class. There are many ways of setting about it, according to the particular goal we have at any given moment. But our primary objective is that of handing over some of the responsibility for the 'what' and 'who' as well as for the 'how'.

At present only the making up of the story is important. Later, in chapter 5, ways are considered of an approach to the actual doing of the stories as well. The story is a vital factor in drama, and is deeply concerned with imagination.

4

Imagination

Every human being is born with imagination. Unfortunately, however, in education, imagination is usually equated with 'art'; art is equated with professional practice; those children who show some degree of achievement in one or other of the arts are labelled imaginative, and the closer their work is to the accepted criteria of 'good' professional art then the more imaginative they are. The remainder are 'no good' at art, and, because imagination and art are equated, are therefore 'unimaginative'. Human dignity being the bastion that it is, the majority effortlessly accept this quality of unimaginativeness.

In fact, imagination is closely interwoven with the fabric of life as a whole; home and environment, clothes and cooking, activity and relaxation, the capacity for full enjoyment of all kinds and, possibly most important of all, every aspect of personal friendship and sensitivity to others, all these and many other factors of life are closely bound up with imagination. Appreciation and practice of the arts as leisure pursuits will also undoubtedly arise from a fully developed imagination, but they are not the criteria of the quality of that imagination and the imagination itself will exist to a greater or lesser extent both before and after any factors concerning appreciation and practice of the arts. In terms of education, it is vital that each human being is helped both to develop his or her own imagination and to feel confidence in it. Neither the development nor the confidence will happen if educationists confine acknowledgement of imagination to the comparatively narrow field of the arts and then judge quality of imagination according to interest in, appreciation of and skill at either one or all of the arts, comparisons often being made with professional activity.

To develop imagination there is need for constant opportunity to practice the use of *one's own* imaginative faculties. This is different from learning to appreciate the products of other people's imaginations; the latter will follow more easily from the former, but there is little evidence to suggest that the former will ever arise from the latter. Indeed it might be true to suggest that personal imaginative development can be undermined by too early exposure to the products of others. Further, to build confidence in personal imagination it is necessary for the practice in using imaginative faculties to take place in a constructive atmosphere, free from fear of failure, from competition and comparison, free from sarcastic or caustic comment, free from criticism (either praise or blame), free from audience reaction and free from judgments based on ability at other activities.

How to Start

The problem of starting, with any age group, is again reduced to the minimum if we keep in mind the fact that we are not attempting to add something new and strange – we are simply taking what already exists and working outwards from there. We have already considered the problem of concentration and linked this with the existence of the five major senses; by exercising these senses we are helping to develop them more fully and at the same time providing simple practice in concentration. We can start our work on imaginative development from the same source – the use of the five senses – and, perhaps, make our first goal that of creating *stories*, one facet of which was considered in the previous chapter.

On page 18 an indication of one early approach was given in the suggestion that the class be invited to listen to sounds outside of the building, and, if these sounds should include traffic, for instance, to try to imagine the actual source of the sound and people connected with it – e.g. drivers of vehicles, passengers etc. In such cases we are using the senses to *stimulate* imagination.

Using the Senses to Stimulate Imagination

LISTENING

Actual sounds

Listen to sounds 1. outside, or 2. inside the building we are in, or 3. inside the room we are in.

Try to identify the cause of each sound – to see clearly and precisely what or who is making the sound and how it is being made. If the sound is made by a person, think of everything you can about that person; what he or she looks like; what they do; where they are going; where they have come from; why they are associated with the sound; what sort of place they live in and all the details of that place. What they might do for a living, what their friends are like, and so on.

N.B. This kind of exercise and those that follow – as indeed with many that have already been suggested – can be done entirely on one's own or in pairs, threes, fours, fives, sixes or even groups of seven, depending on *the stage of development that has been reached*. There is really no hard and fast rule about this, but generally speaking it is wisest to allow opportunity for early practice and mastery to be entirely personal, individual and isolated; following this, little by little one learns how to share with other people, developing from the few to the many, often working with one's own friends in natural social grouping.

Further developments from listening to actual sounds

Even to imagine the circumstances and causes concerning a particular sound is a step towards the creating of a story, and there are many ways in which this can be developed to an intended story form.

1. Link one or more sounds together, e.g. the sound of a clock inside the room we are in with the sound of footsteps outside, or perhaps the sound of a moving vehicle.

2. Link one or more sounds to imaginary circumstances concerning yourself, e.g. footsteps or traffic sounds concerning someone you are waiting for, or are hoping will not be coming, or perhaps fear the arrival of.

3. Imagine the sounds you are listening to are part of the sound

track of a film or television story – it could be the opening or the ending or any point during the film. You can hear the sound track; imagine for yourself what is happening on the screen.

4. Make very personal to yourself the circumstance of the sound and add to it any particular wish you yourself would like fulfilled, e.g. an aeroplane goes overhead; you are in it. Where do you wish you were going and for what reason?

5. As in 4, make the sound personal to yourself, but be somebody else listening to them, e.g. a pop singer, a spy, a politician etc. Follow on the circumstances in terms of this other person.

6. Add a particular 'if' circumstance to those concerning the sound, e.g. What would happen *if* the aeroplane engine suddenly cut out? What would happen *if* the clock suddenly stopped and time stood still? What would happen if...? Wouldn't it be nice if...? Wouldn't it be exciting if...? Wouldn't it be terrible if...? Wouldn't it be funny if...?

This is the 'if' that is often at the root of much creative use of imaginative circumstances, leading to the making of stories.

All of the foregoing exercises are based on sounds that exist inside or outside of the immediate environment. To these the teacher can add other sounds, each of them actual and real, but deliberately made by the teacher in particular imaginative circumstances. For example, the teacher might suggest that each person in the class is a blind person sitting at home in the evening; or someone in a lonely and deserted house, late at night; or a prisoner waiting to hear news of his future. Having established the circumstances, the teacher then carries out a sequence of sounds, e.g. turning door-handles, letting a door swing slowly open, footsteps, sounds against the window or concerned with the opening and closing of a window, the sounds of switches etc. Such an exercise is best carried out by each person having his or her eyes closed, so that they do not see precisely how the sounds are being made.

Other sounds and music

Children hear sound emotionally, not intellectually. Sounds of all kinds will therefore evoke pictures and ideas for stories, and a ong sequence of sounds will perhaps suggest an entire story. At this stage we are concerned with the use of sound only for making up stories; in chapter 5 sound is considered again in relation to movement and dance. The division is partly artificial as one activity can so easily be linked with another. But there are many occasions when for one reason or another teachers feel unable to pursue factors of movement and dance (e.g. lack of space; uncertainty; working with an older group that has done little movement work before) and yet would find story-making easily stimulated and enriched by the use of sound.

In the early stages, with any age group, the sounds need to be simple, not too many in number and of not too long duration. Some can be made simply by using the fingers or the hands on the top of the desk or a chair.

Examples:

1. With one finger, lightly tap a continuous time-beat on the desk or chair, keeping the pace constant at any speed from fast to slow.
2. With the hand, strongly beat the same kind of sounds as in 1.
3. Using all of the fingers, make short running sounds on the desk.
4. Using both hands, make a climax of sound, 'rolling' from very quiet to very loud and then suddenly cutting out.
5. As with 4, only instead of cutting out at the climax, let the sound slowly return to very soft, finally fading away.
6. Reverse 4, going from a sudden very loud sound, rolling away to silence.

(N.B. Teachers are advised that with only a little practice at home they will become very adept at making such sounds – but practice may well be necessary.)

When using such tapping sounds – and the above are only a few of the many possibilities – the approach to the class will naturally differ according to the age group. With infants and young juniors, the teacher might say something like: 'Close your eyes and listen; what does this sound make you think of?' or 'What does this sound remind you of?' For older juniors or secondaries, the approach will need to be more sophisticated, as for example: 'I am going to make the sound track of the opening of a film (or television story). With your eyes closed, see for yourself what is happening on the screen to this soundtrack.'

The sound is then made. What follows after the sound will depend on the stage of development the class has reached, but it should always be borne in mind that the exercise is being used to develop and stimulate *their* ideas, not for them to read into our minds what *our* idea might be; by the same token, there may well be *many* different ideas – possibly every person in the class might have a different one – and each one is equally valid. There should be no selection of the *best* and rejection of those that simply do not appeal to our adult mind or our particular tastes. If our procedure necessitates the using of only one idea from the many, then the choice should be made simply, without reference to quality. Little by little we shall develop each person's confidence in the fact that his imagination matters; to do so, the framework of the class must be uncritical. With teenagers the atmosphere may also need to be *private* to avoid all sense of ridicule and fear of failure. By 'private' is meant the opportunity to talk quietly to their neighbour about what ideas they had, rather than having to tell the whole class. Perhaps they didn't have an idea on this first occasion; or perhaps they did have one, but do not feel it is the kind of idea that will be acceptable to us as teachers; or perhaps, whatever their idea was, they have had insufficient experience at putting personal ideas into their own words and so are partly or wholly inarticulate; all of these factors are important and through other stages of drama we must hope to be able to stimulate further, to build confidence, to develop the capacity to put ideas into words – but if our immediate aim is simply that of stimulating imagination, then we must not risk defeating that aim by suddenly introducing others. Even when we feel we have reached the stage of sharing ideas together, the circumstances of doing so should be fully concerned with sharing, not with other new factors such as communicating to an audience of listeners. If the class is seated informally for such exchange of ideas, confidence is sustained. To ask one member of the class to come out to the front, to stand up straight and not fidget, to speak up, to speak 'properly' and so on, will soon undermine the confidence of many. There may well be some in the class who are very clever at this latter kind of exposed situation; such people will do no less well in the informal situation, and others will be greatly helped. Factors of communication will arise in good time – to force such factors too soon will simply undermine all the early stages of the work, which are concerned with developing confidence etc. for every member of the class.

Here are examples of the use of some of the above sounds, and the results from their use, with different age groups.

Infants

ME: Listen. What does this make you think of?
THE SOUND: *With flat of hand on desk, a strong continuous time beat.*
ANSWERS FROM CLASS: Giant. Soldier. Big animal.
ME: Listen again. This is what the giant or the soldier or the big animal saw.
THE SOUND: *Short bursts of scraping sounds with the fingers on the desk.*
ANSWERS FROM CLASS: A mouse. An insect. A bush moving.
ME: Listen again. This is what the giant or the soldier or the big animal did when he saw the mouse or the insect or the bush moving.
THE SOUND: *Using both hands, climax roll of sound on desk, cutting out at climax.*
ANSWERS FROM CLASS: Ran away and hid. Jumped in a hole. Chased it away. Ran after it and caught it.

The sounds have stimulated various ideas. In the next chapter (see p. 89) details are given of a similar sequence involving movement.

Some of the ideas given above could also be used for the 'Ideas Game' building of a story, teacher and class sharing ideas together.

Secondary:

ME: Here is the soundtrack of the opening of a film. With your eyes closed, each of you see for yourselves what is happening on the screen. Close your eyes now and listen.
SOUND: *Quiet tapping of one finger on desk in regular time beat.*

ME: Now, with the person sitting next to you, talk about what you were seeing on the screen.

A minute or so was given for this discussion. At this stage it was entirely private to them; what they had seen was none of my business. Some had probably seen nothing. For me, the important thing was for each member of the class to realise that there was nothing to worry about – they need feel no sense of failure, and they were not going to be publicly exposed or criticised.

ME: Now the next part of the sound track. You may find this fits exactly where you left off, or it may seem to introduce some quite different events. In films this often happens, doesn't it? We see one scene, and then suddenly cut away to another scene, perhaps even introducing a different set of people. Either something new or continuing from where you left off will be fine. And if you didn't see anything last time, then perhaps you will this. Close your eyes now and listen.

SOUND: *A slow roll of sound to climax and then fading away again to silence.* (The sounds were made using both hands on the desk. The fade in was very slow, so as to give time for new thoughts to be stimulated.)

Again there was the private discussion, after which there was general discussion, many different people telling all or part of their story. Some were fairly fluent, others contributed only a sentence or two; in each case I was helped to see what stage each individual had reached and therefore what kind of opportunity each was to need in the future; similarly, some spoke up, others were at various stages of mumbling. There was no comment on either. This class was concerned with stimulating and quietly sharing imagination; factors of communication were quite irrelevant. Because all the ideas were accepted as being of equal value, simply by taking an interest in them and not suggesting one was better than another, and because the whole atmosphere was kept informal, it was possible actually to feel the growth of confidence and interest.

There were many different stories for each of the two sounds; some had found an easy way of connecting the sounds into a single story; others had two quite distinct stories, one for each sound.

No comment was made on those who could not connect the sounds. Here are some of the ideas stimulated by the sounds separately:

The continuous tapping sound

Water dripping (in a cellar; down a castle wall; a tap in a basin etc.), also Chinese torture – water on man's forehead, boring hole.

'Signals' (warning to robbers in a bank; start of a revolution – echoes of '*Viva Zapata*'; two prisoners planning an escape and communicating by tapping)

Blind man walking with stick

Various kinds of clock (railway station; condemned man listening to seconds going by; time-bomb; count down of rocket; spy given limited time to confess 'or else')

Footsteps (along embankment in dark; various tense situations, to do with robbery, escaping prisoners of war, guards on duty etc.)

Various forms of chipping at rock, coal face, etc.

The roll to climax and fade to silence

Earthquake

Mining disaster

Approach and passing of avalanche

Approach and passing of horses, running people, stampeding cattle, train, aeroplane, various kinds of rescuers.

Many of these were linked, particularly those which started with 'prisoners' and formed a natural continuation into attempted or actual rescue or escape.

Small groups followed up some of these initial ideas, taking the story a stage further, without the need for additional stimulation by sound. Such a lesson could easily lead into art or story writing, if not into actual practical drama. (See chapters 8 and 10 for follow up.)

Similar sounds, and entirely different kinds of sound, but with the same possibilities of time-beat, rhythm and climax, can be made with such instruments as a tambour or a cymbal – in fact, any of the percussion instruments. Again, the use of these for movement as well as for stimulating story-making is considered in chapter 5, and in chapter 6 in relation to speech.

These simple sounds, whilst being basically in themselves 'music', have one major advantage over the use of recorded music in that they are under the full control of the teacher, who can make the sounds as long or as short and as contrasting in detail as is necessary or appropriate for the particular intention of each class. Even a fully sensitive feeling for mood and atmosphere can be achieved with such sounds after only a little practice. (Another practical advantage, of course, is that the teacher does not have to depend on always having a record-player available for this story-making activity which, certainly in early stages, is often best done in the classroom rather than the hall.)

Recorded music

However, the time comes when recorded music has immense value, not only for movement and dance (see chapter 5) or for music dramas (see chapter 8) but also for fuller stimulation and enrichment of the imagination in sessions of story-making. A full list of music that has been found useful for different age groups will be found on page 300.

The story-making procedure when using recorded music is similar to the suggestions given above for the use of simple sounds. It is wise to keep the passages of music short to start with. Play approximately one minute from the opening of the passage and allow group discussion of the first part of the story to follow this; continue with a second section of music, followed again by discussion, and so on until the full passage has been heard. The full passage itself should not be too long in the early stages – say, three to four minutes all told.

Stimulation through Objects

SIGHT

In the same way that the sense of hearing can be used to stimulate the imagination so, too, can the senses of sight and touch. Objects of all kinds, both real and imaginary (in the sense that the object is named without necessarily being to hand) can be used for this, and group stories be made up.

If the teacher possesses the object, then it can be held up or passed round for all groups to see or handle; for example: a key, a ring, a lighter, a rare coin, a charm, etc. Alternatively, the word denoting the object can be written on the board. Another interesting alternative is for the teacher simply to say the word, denoting, perhaps, several different possible objects or ideas. For example, to say the word 'Key' may lead to a story that is concerned with 'Quay', or perhaps the key to a secret code, and not to the kind of key associated only with locks. The word 'ring' was used by one secondary group in several different senses within one story – an actual finger ring, the ring of people around the body of the person wearing the ring, the ring of the telephone and the wringing of wet clothes. The story was amusing and inventive, and there was great enjoyment at this deliberate play on words.

If a group appears to be stuck when working from the point of view of only one object, then often they will be helped by being allowed to use two or maybe even three objects.

Further development

1. Increase the range of type of object to include those that could not possibly be seen or handled in the class, e.g. the time-fuse, a tree, the rudder of a ship, a hair-drier, etc., in fact almost any object.

2. On some occasions, deliberately add a descriptive adjective before the name of the object, e.g. the mysterious box, the weird tree, or even more extravagantly – the bouncing aeroplane, the trembling ship, etc. The addition of the adjective will often lead to attempts at making up a particular kind of story because we, as teachers, feel that such an attempt might have some particular value, as for instance, if we want them to move away from comic stories, or crook stories, and so on.

3. On some occasions, add a time or place factor to the object, with perhaps a different time/place suggestion for each group:

Example: the object – a ring. All groups have this in common.

Add:

1st Group – Time: 2000 years ago
2nd Group – Time: the year A.D. 2000
3rd Group – Place: an old farm house
4th Group – Place: top of a mountain
5th Group – Time: Xmas Eve
                    Place: under the floorboards

and so on with different time and/or place factors for each group.

4. On some occasions, give the first sentence of the story.

5. On some occasions, give the final line of the story.

With either 4 or 5, the 'line' can be either something somebody says or simply a narrative line.

6. On some occasions, give both the opening and the final line. The suggestions of an opening or ending line, or both, help gradually with the factor of form in a story, working towards a fuller feeling for beginning, middle and end, factors which will not exist in the early stages. It is wise not to criticise this lack of form when the class begins story-making; we are concerned with building confidence in personal imagination – finding and using ideas is what is important. Form grows out of regular practice.

7. With older infants, juniors and young secondaries, it is often useful (particularly in the early stages of story-making) to give groups an actual physical object, which they can imagine is anything they choose: e.g. a blank sheet of paper, a pebble, a stick. One or all of these objects might be given to each group to have in their midst. Make quite clear to them that they can use the objects as they wish including, for instance, writing on the paper. The paper might turn into maps of various kinds, or secret messages, or commands from the king; the stick might become a magic wand, the periscope of a submarine, a rifle, teachers' cane, a crutch; the pebble might be a jewel, a pill for making you invisible, a nugget of gold; the examples quoted are from the large number that have been experienced, but no doubt there are many more possibilities.

Pictures

Picture material of all kinds will be found a most useful way of stimulating stories. Generally speaking, it is wise to remove all captions or other written material, including titles, that may be attached to the picture. Sources of material for pictures are:

1. Newspapers and magazines: news pictures, feature story pictures, cartoons, advertisements. In the early stages, the more action in the picture, the more the stimulation, but after a lot of practice even very simple and subtle pictures will serve.

2. The sleeves of gramophone records often have exciting and stimulating picture material on them; if the sleeve cannot be cut up, then fold away the part that shows the title of the music.

3. Medici and other reproductions of paintings etc. from various art galleries. It is interesting to use abstract pictures of every kind.

4. Groups can of course paint and use for story purposes their own pictures. Useful as part of this is the ink-blot or paint-blot type of abstraction. Fold a piece of paper and drop blobs of ink or paint into the fold; squeeze the fold tightly, running the fingers up and down the fold.

TOUCH

The sense of touch of objects of various kinds can also be used as stimulation – but it is important for everyone to keep their eyes closed until the object has been passed round. For example, stones or driftwood of exciting shape, peeled fruit (a peeled grape electrified one group, many members of which decided it was a human eyeball!) pieces of cloth of different kinds, etc. In schools where craft activities exist, many links can be made; all kinds of objects made in pottery or with salt, soap or wood carving can be useful for this particular manner of stimulating.

SMELL

Generally speaking, it is not easy to set up circumstances for using real smells for stimulating stories, but the sense itself can still be used within a framework of imaginary smells. If it is possible to set up any circumstances for real smells, this is useful; for example, a piece of leather, a piece of wood, an empty scent bottle (or other empty bottles?), driftwood or pebbles from the beach, plants, flowers, shrubs etc. But with imaginary smells, the scope is broadened. The teacher can suggest a smell – for example gas, fire of different kinds, smells associated with town or country or seaside, with industry or transport, with any kind of occupational activity, with food, medicine, hairdressing etc. Alternatively, the teacher can simply say 'Make up a story that is concerned with some kind of smell', and can always exclude certain smells if necessary for particular reasons. For instance, the smells of gas and fire are so obvious that the teacher may want the groups to attempt a story from a different basis of smell. In this case the words 'excluding gas or fire' could be added. (We must not be surprised at what may come – the smell may turn out to be a cat, or even Granny, rotting under the floorboards.) Equally, of course, by the use of an adjective, we can guide the story in a particular way for particular reasons – a pleasant smell, a mysterious smell, a terrifying smell, an intriguing smell, and so on.

TASTE

The circumstances are even more difficult to set up for using the sense of taste for stimulating the imagination, so that use of imaginary tastes is often the only manner in which this sense can be incorporated. The procedure is very much the same as that above for using the sense of smell.

It is important to bear in mind that if we are using imaginary tastes or smells we are, in the very moment of doing so, asking for a process of using imagination that depends on there already being a degree of confidence in imagination and some practice at using it. For this reason, it is often wise to start the whole process of developing imagination through story-making by using the other senses in connection with a factor that really exists instead of one that has to be imagined. Once there has been some practice we are able to move on to more subtle uses of the senses. It is also necessary to be ready for – and to accept – story themes that are not always pleasing to us as teachers; stories may include various forms of blood and thunder, violence and other aspects of strong adventure. These things are strongly dramatic, broad rather than subtle, and are an almost inevitable stage of growth. (In terms of practical drama, the tendency to use this kind of story is considered thoroughly in chapter 9.) Teachers generally accept this aspect of growth in the field of child art; we do not ask children to paint a rose or 'mother' too early on, because these subjects are 'too beautiful' and many youngsters would at once be intimidated by their own fear of failure; ask them to paint a picture of a nightmare – something ugly rather than beautiful – and the hesitancy disappears and confidence is bolstered. Much the same happens with early story-making and with practical drama. If we are using the sense of smell to stimulate ideas for a story, we must not be surprised or worried if their choice of smell is from stark or unpleasant odours; if we are using taste, then early choices are likely to be concerned with poison or witches' brews or some other unpleasant factor. More 'civilised' or 'cultured' choices will come eventually, but much depends on our acceptance of the early primitive selections; it is our acceptance, in an uncritical framework, that helps to build confidence and therefore lay the foundations for future work. There will also be, particularly with top juniors and secondary youngsters, many extremely funny stories, with a breadth of humour much akin to farce, which again we should learn to accept in the early stages of story-making. Many teachers are put off by the apparent and actual triteness of the early themes in stories, but there is, in fact, nothing to worry about providing we are recognising the triteness as a stage of development concerned with early practice and building confidence; once confidence is established, there is a great deal we can and should do to help the development of richer, more complex and more interesting themes (see chapter 8).

In chapter 2, we began our consideration of a human being in terms of how we can help each one to develop a capacity for devoting undivided attention to any matter in hand through concentration exercises linked to the five major senses. Now we have considered ways of using these five major senses to develop another facet of each human being's resources: imagination. Practice at each factor will not only develop that particular factor, but will enrich another. By practising the use of imagination in story-making we have been further enriching the major senses. It is important *not* to make these processes conscious to the class at the beginning, except in very special circumstances with more mature youngsters who may need to be given some aspect of the whys and wherefores in order to obtain their full cooperation. But it is interesting and important to sense the moment when we can make at least part of our intention quite clear, together with the suggestion that many other exercises of the senses can be undertaken personally by each one of us during the ordinary course of life each day. The exercises can make each day more interesting by helping us to be more alive and more aware, and they can help us to know and understand other people. Certainly older teenagers can become fascinated by what is, after all, simply a way of living, partly concerned with using the whole of oneself, partly concerned with sympathy for others. The processes involved can often include a full identification with other people and thus fully seeing both their point of view and the way they feel about things. This aspect of the development of people is more fully considered in chapter 7. Meanwhile it has its logical relevance in connection with the development and full use of the senses.

The types of suggestion we can make to teenagers, when we have aroused their interest and given them some initial practice, are manifold and depend very much on our particular bond with them, and how much we, as teachers, are able to see things from their point of view. (Incidentally, this is sometimes worth reflecting on. How much do we stop to consider our teaching from the point of view of the recipients – this is part of the factor, already mentioned, of the difference between helping children to fulfil our ambitions for them and giving reasonable opportunities for the fulfilment of their own aspirations? It is part of being human to aspire to being fully human, and there is great satisfaction to be gained from the feeling that one is able to live with the fullness of one's own humanity. It is often because we have not been helped to develop this full humanity – the maximum of which we are capable from what nature has given us – that leads to the type of despair that is connected with being subhuman, or else to the type of frustrating ambition to be super human; either leads us into being, as it were, displaced persons, unable to be fully ourselves because we are unacquainted with that self or else lack any reasonable belief that that particular self is of any importance to anyone, including ourselves. To be and to live fully one's own potential involves living 'skilfully'; and skill at living is as much dependent on practice as skill at any other human activity – only it is applicable to every single one of us.)

Here are some extra-curricular exercises that I have suggested to teenagers. It would be presumptuous to suggest that all of them were interested or that many of them tried out the exercises at all, let alone for any length of time. But there may have been more doing so than I know about; it is none of my business to ask – they have their own lives to live and it is no part of my function to attempt to live that life for them or to demand that they share their inner experiences with me. The few who felt enough confidence in me to share a small part of that experience have certainly given sufficient indication both of interest and of 'results' for me to include some of the suggestions within this context.

LISTENING

Listen — as often as possible to sounds at varying distance from oneself: very near, moderately near, far away, very far away. Dwell with each of the sounds; try to identify what is making the sound; try to envisage any person or persons connected with the sound; wonder about such people.

— to silence, particularly the silence within oneself;

— to sounds as other people might hear them; for example, with mechanical sounds the person involved is concerned with the tune of the sound, which tells him whether the machine is working well or not; the sounds of farm animals mean more to the farmer than to us; a dog's bark means more to its owner than to anyone else;

— to moving sounds, until they have disappeared from hearing, but stretch the hearing so that the point of disappearance is constantly extended;

— to hard and ugly sounds with intended tolerance, by fully understanding the significance of the sound and its effect on someone else – a road drill is a good case in point;

— to the sounds of footsteps; try to feel what they signify in terms of the person walking, for how a person is feeling at a given moment is often reflected in this sound;

— to sounds with which you are very familiar in your own neighbourhood; listen as though you were going to leave the neighbourhood and wanted to store up sound memories;

— to various sounds and, irrespective of whether or not you know precisely how they are being made, consider how you could reproduce a similar sound for, say, a radio play;

consider different circumstances for situations or scenes for a radio play, and consider what kinds of sound would be appropriate;

— and let various sounds evoke memories associated with each.

LOOKING

Look — with the selectivity of the lens of a sensitive camera, able to select particular images that are a long way off, in the middle distance, quite near, in close-up, or even in over-enlarged detail;

use the above in terms both of a movie camera from a static position or when able to pan horizontally or vertically;

use the above in terms of an ordinary stills camera, selecting a precise moment and position for a particular shot (eventually, from closer observation of various forms of photograph, concerning oneself with the composition of each shot);

— with the eyes of, and from the point of view of, many different people:

— an artist working in black and white; an artist working in colour; an artist with a fascination for shadow; a short-sighted person; a long-sighted person; someone who is going blind; a person leaving the neighbourhood, storing up visual memories; a stranger (many strangers in different circumstances, some happy, some unhappy etc.); a person much taller than yourself; a person much shorter; a small child's view-point (and don't forget the open wonder of the newness of experiences);

— a cat or dog very close to the ground; a bird, or the view one might have from an aeroplane; people in different states of feeling: happy, unhappy, anxious, afraid, supercilious, contented and calm, etc. etc.;

Look at the many very different moods of the sky;
— when the weather is exactly as you like it, look at the sky from the viewpoint of other people (perhaps the farmer is hating the heatwave that is making your holiday just perfect);
— when the weather is *not* to your liking, look at the sky from the point of view of other people (the theatre manager is probably liking the rain that might bring you and others into the theatre that summer evening);
— with compassion at the face of every person you pass in the street, and wonder about them; bear in mind that behind every face there is as much worry about something in life as behind yours; wonder what it might be behind each face you observe;
— at objects from the point of view of the people concerned: the person who made it; the person who sells it; the various people concerned with the original raw material;
— look at the 'taken for granted' features of civilisation with a renewed sense of wonder: all electrical gadgets, from telephones to television; water coming out of a tap; means of transportation, from a bicycle to an aeroplane; gas facilities; even pen, paper and pencil, etc.

imagine what life was like before the factors mentioned above were invented; imagine the 'moment' of discovery – particularly in the personal terms of the person or persons concerned with the invention;

at a single object; think back to all the stages of its development to its origin, or from its origin to its present state, for example, a matchstick.

With an example like the one above, the matchstick, we are confronted with an excellent opportunity for controlling and disciplining imagination, permitting ourselves to dwell (at least for the present) only on those factors that are fully relevant to the final objective; consider the match: we might start from the viewpoint of the forest in some far country where the match started as a minute fragment of a giant tree; somebody selects and cuts down that tree – at once we could be over-concerned about this somebody, instead of keeping our imaginative thought with the origins of the match. And so on. Of course, we can well return to that somebody at another time, but for the moment we are concerned only with the progression of the match itself, from original tree to our fingers.

TOUCHING

Touch all kinds of surfaces with full awareness of all the properties of the surface: is it hard or soft, smooth or rough, cold or warm, dry or damp, pleasant or unpleasant, etc.
— be aware of the point of contact, the touching of other parts of the body than only the fingers; sitting in a chair, the feet are touching both the inside of the shoe and through that the floor; the backs of the legs are perhaps against the chair; one leg may be crossing another; the elbows or fore-arms are resting on the arms of the chair; the back is against the back of the chair, the buttocks on the seat of the chair; be aware of the touch of all of these;
— be aware of different kinds of surface, and in different conditions, that one might be walking on: the stone of pavement, asphalt of roads, grass, earth etc.; sometimes when they are dry, at others when they are wet; sometimes when cold, sometimes when hot;
— when walking on one surface in a particular condition, imagine what it would feel like in different conditions;
— look at a surface that one is not touching; imagine what the surface feels like – imagine it within the tips of the fingers, not just in the mind; then move to and actually touch the surface;
— repeat the same kind of exercise with objects that are so out of reach that they cannot be touched; recall what similar surfaces did feel like;
— touch various objects from the point of view of people or the person concerned with making them;
— as with the suggestion under 'looking', touch 'taken for granted' objects with a renewed sense of wonder, e.g. light switches, radio station selection knobs, telephones etc.

SMELLING

Both indoors and outdoors, close the eyes and, turning the head

61

in various directions, become fully aware of all the different smells in the air and try to identify them;

when walking, be aware of the changes in smell; sometimes they can be almost as profuse as the changes of sight and sound;

be aware of the circumstances concerning other people with various smells, both pleasant and unpleasant; for example, the smell of a gasworks may be horrible for some of us as we are passing, but what about the people who live close by and so are constantly exposed to it, and what of the people who are concerned with making the product that is causing the smell?

smell various odours from the viewpoint of other people; this is again interesting with smells we do not ourselves like, for example, we may not like the smell of some forms of foreign cooking, but what about the person who is looking forward very much to that particular meal? Similarly, consider smells that we enjoy from the viewpoint of others;

be always aware of and enjoy smells that you yourself find particularly pleasant, whether they be the scent of flowers or scent from a bottle; let these smells evoke imaginative circumstances;

let different smells evoke memories from the past; remember clearly;

observe the approach of animals to smell; consider what is happening in their own experience (it is not dissimilar from the approach of many humans to such unknown factors as medicines);

by the use of imaginary circumstances, discover an entirely different viewpoint regarding certain smells, for example, the smell of smoke may mean little or nothing to us in our normal lives, but what if we smelt smoke whilst on an aeroplane? The smell of curry may mean little to us (we might not even like it) but what if we were living in a community where it is the staple diet? The smell of ether may be repugnant to us, but what if we were about to have an operation?

Of all the sense organs, the nose is possibly the most delicate, and the most neglected.

TASTING

The pressure of busy and interesting lives leads the majority of
people to approach food rather in the sense of adding fuel to
an engine; try, now and again, to really taste every mouthful
of a meal, particularly if it involves a dish that is a favourite;
— become aware, in detail, of the taste of various foods, with and
without various aids such as condiments and sauces and so
on;
— consider tastes from the point of view of other people – particularly of the person who has cooked the dish and is probably
hoping we are enjoying it;
— let different tastes evoke memories from the past; remember
clearly;
— imagine the taste of things we have, in fact, not tasted for one
reason or another; link this process with smell;
— imagine circumstances of all kinds where something we reject
because of its taste may be extremely tasty to someone else;
the taste of mere bread to someone who is without it is a good
case in point.

Some of the above situations may also be suitable for drama
work in schools in addition to those already mentioned earlier in
the book; they are given here separately, partly in the hope that in
those secondary schools where little or no drama work is done,
for whatever reason, that some teachers may feel the exercises
and the thought behind them are worth passing on to senior
pupils for the enrichment of their own private lives. This kind of
enrichment – and the humanising factors arising from them – are
important as a balancing factor for young people whose intellectual gifts are being fully developed, often to the exclusion of
other human factors. It can only be hoped that grammar schools
are coming, or will gradually come, to the realisation that the
finer the brains are that they have to train, the greater the responsibility they have to make sure that these brains are part of a
personality that has been developed in every way, not least of all
in compassion for others who are less gifted intellectually. Ugly
and unhealthy distortion more often than not arises when one

63

factor is developed beyond others. This is as true of intellect as of any other aspect of a human being. Even the finest intellect is part of a being who has also five major senses and imagination; the intellect will not be harmed by fully developing the senses and the imagination, and the uses to which that intellect are eventually put may well depend, in human terms, on precisely imagination and an acute sensitivity.

But now, for all age groups, we move on to another point on the circle: the human body.

5

Movement and the Use of Sound

When considering movement we are once more concerned with a factor that already exists; it is a fundamental point on the circle, not something entirely new that education must add.

Every human being has a physical self, a body; some people are very fortunate and have either a beautiful or handsome physical self, others an agile or strong physical self; some, at the other extreme, have a body that is neither goodlooking nor particularly strong and agile; and perhaps the majority fall somewhere between these two extremes. Much is done, through education and health services, to help the physical wellbeing and growth of the body, but not so much is done about the emotional wellbeing of the body as part of that growth. This is one of the functions of movement within drama – to help every child and young person to achieve complete mastery of his or her physical self, thus enabling an emotional harmony to develop regarding their own bodies, on a basis of full personal confidence and sensitivity. This process, as with so many aspects of drama, is an intangible one, particularly in the early stages of the work, and its very intangibility leads to a quite understandable feeling by teachers that it is necessary to teach 'steps' or other particular manners of moving the body. In fact it is not necessary to teach steps – and to do so can destroy the intuitive factor of movement and replace it with cerebration. The root of the problem lies in confusing a process of growth with an adult art form. All formal *dance* is adult in basic conception, requiring the learning of and the remembering of sequences and patterns of steps, both individually and in relation to one or more other people; further, these requirements are juxtaposed to sequences of music, often dependent on exact

65

synchronisations of particular steps to particular sounds; together with these, there is often the additional need of mood, which may be quite contrary to the actual emotion stimulated either by circumstance or by the music and therefore has to be created; and finally there is often the need for communication of character or story or ideas or feelings, or some combinations of any or all of these. *Some* children and young people are capable of mastering all of these factors of dance, often quite quickly and without too much difficulty; many never will achieve such mastery. Both the capable and the less capable still require opportunities for movement which are based on intuition and personal mastery, each at his or her own level; to provide such opportunities will enrich more formalised types of dancing, and will eventually bring the formal to within the capacities of many more children and young people. Meanwhile the essential spirit of dance is fostered and developed in each person, alongside an intuitive feeling for and response to time-beat, rhythm, climax, atmosphere and characterisation, the full sensitive use of space and the whole of the body in a controlled use of that space, including sensitivity to others. All of these factors can be achieved by every person without being taught a single step, and irrespective of physical type or any forms of natural talent. Furthermore, teachers can approach this type of movement experience with their classes without themselves having to learn steps to teach.

This chapter is therefore concerned with improvised movement or dance.

Approaches to Beginning Movement

For many teachers a basic problem regarding movement is that they do not have the facilities that seem necessary, particularly that of space. It is always important to bear in mind that although lack of space will clearly hamper some of the richer developments of movement (and of other aspects of drama as well), there is still a great deal that can be done within the limitations of a classroom, even with the class confined to their desks or chairs. Moreover, it can be quite natural for a teacher to be somewhat alarmed by the idea of too much space, and the same feeling may well be experienced by many members of a class who have had no such experience before. In such cases it is often wise to start movement work in the classroom and when first using the hall to confine the class to use of only part of the space, perhaps even dividing the hall with a simple barrier of chairs or balance benches.

These early suggestions are therefore applicable to working either in hall or classroom; the whole class is working at one and the same time, each person working on his or her own to start with, perhaps developing to work with a chosen partner, then in groups of three, then four or five per group.

Activities with a Ball

(a) Each person in the class has a ball – an entirely *imaginary* ball – about the size of a tennis ball. Discover everything that can be done with the ball, from the place where one is sitting or standing: bouncing the ball, fast and slow etc., throwing it up to different heights and catching it; throwing it against different walls and catching it on its return. Spinning it with the fingers. With the feet, kicking it in different directions. Alternately kicking, catching and throwing. Heading the ball, or heading in conjunction with kicking, throwing and catching.

(b) Repeat all of the above with a large, rather heavy ball, e.g. a football.

(c) Repeat all of the above with a large, very light ball, e.g. a beach ball or even a balloon.

(d) Repeating all of the above with a 'googly' ball – i.e. a ball, the size of a tennis ball with a weight or bias inside of it which makes the ball behave falsely, shooting off at all kinds of unexpected angles, necessitating a great deal of leaping and jumping to get at the ball after each throw or kick against another surface.

(e) *Where there is space* (even a confined space), repeat (a), (b), (c) and/or (d) using all the space.

(f) Repeat any of the above at a *tremendous speed*, like an old-fashioned film.

(g) Repeat all of the above in very *slow motion*, again as in a film when we see a horse race, or some such, slowed down.

(h) Repeat any of the above exercises with constant changes of speed from very fast to very slow.

All of the above have concerned each person working on his or her own.

(i) Now, *in pairs*, repeat some of the exercises, both fast and slow.

(j) Also in pairs: let each pair decide on different sport activities they would like to use, in both slow and fast movement: e.g. tennis, table-tennis, football, handball (rugby, only if you are not bothered about possible 'scrums' and 'scrimmages'). Ask what different pairs have been doing, and let the class, still working in pairs, experience the different suggestions.

After every exercise or few exercises in pairs, say: 'Change pairs – find a new partner.' In this way, each member of the class has the experience of working with different people rather than with one chosen companion. It is important not to make an 'issue' of the changing partners, and if the majority of the class are clearly unhappy about it, then leave them with chosen partners until further confidence is established.

CLASS CONTROL

It is important to establish some simple arrangement with the class concerning you, as teacher, having full control at all times. All that is necessary is to be able to make a sound loud enough for the whole class to hear at the same moment. Build the teacher-class bond by explaining that the moment they hear the particular sound they are to be absolutely still and quiet, even if they are in mid-sentence or almost in mid-air. Try it out with them several times, insisting on an absolutely immediate response from everybody. If approached in the nature of an interesting challenge rather than a disciplinary threat, there will usually be a constructive response to the bond; but we must not be surprised if sometimes, when absorption is very deep and interest full and strong, they do not immediately hear the sound (not hearing might even be an indication of the need for some more exercises in listening).

The sound the teacher makes for these moments of control can be as simple as a single, strong clap of the hands; but better still would be a single sound on either a cymbal or a small drum (a tambour); neither of these is very expensive, and as one or the other or both will be very useful for many aspects of drama work – and will always be valuable for class control – teachers are recommended to purchase them. A whistle is not recommended for this kind of control because of its other associations – but, of course, it could be used if nothing else is available.

It is most important for each teacher to make with each class this bond of control. When we provide opportunities for drama of any kind, we are deeply concerned with the emotional development of children and young people; we have a superb, *natural* opportunity of making a reality of the idea of self-discipline and personal responsibility for behaviour, but the process can take quite a long time, depending on the kind of previous opportunity for exercising such personal control the class may have experienced. If full responsibility is given too soon, this can be as unfortunate in its results as not giving enough; in the early stages, the *teacher has full control*, and then gradually hands over more and more of the control according to the class's readiness to handle it. Important, too, is the fact that children will quite understandably test the reactions of their teachers within such a field of activity; we respond to this test with fairness and justice if we know the minimum of our patience and do not allow anyone to exceed those bounds under any circumstances. To allow some forms of behaviour on one day, because we feel on top of our form, and then refuse the same behaviour another day, because we feel a little under the weather, simply creates muddle and confusion in the youngsters and breaks our bond with them. Consistency, with great firmness in the early stages, will help develop a process of liberty which is entirely different from licence.

We need to handle particularly carefully the kind of youngster who seems to remain unabsorbed and tends to play about. Sometimes, merely moving to a position close to such a person or a group of such people will be enough to curb them.

If there is need for even firmer handling of any individual, then as far as possible this should be done from a basis of social training: drama is closely interwoven with opportunities for learning to share many different aspects of life with other people, on a

69

sensitive basis of give and take and consideration for others; sharing space, sharing ideas, problems etc., together with actually sharing in the creating of different kinds of experience, are all an important part of the socialising influence. There may be little or no positive contribution to this by some in the early stages; there may be aggressive refusals to cooperate. If the teacher keeps the potential for social training in mind, strongly protecting the absorbed effort of some from the negative interference of others, then discipline is integrated with processes of growth rather than existing as a separate entity. A general statement to the whole class will often be more effective than dealing with a single individual or small groups, for example: 'The majority of the class are working hard. If any of you don't want to work, then that is up to you, but just make absolutely certain that you do nothing that will interfere with anybody else's effort.' This is a challenge to each individual's personal responsibility, without victimising any particular person. Individual personal responsibility cannot be achieved overnight if it is to grow from within the individual; it requires constant practice – as much practice as reading, writing and arithmetic. Nothing would be achieved within the framework of these activities if the teacher personally did the reading, the writing and the arithmetic for each individual within the class; no more can the emotional factor of responsibility for behaviour be achieved if the teacher persistently dominates within the field of discipline, particularly if, in a kind of abstract manner, discipline is considered for its own sake, unrelated to factors of growth and personal development. Because drama involves personal emotional factors, some traditional forms of exact control are shown up as a shabby, unrealistic expedient which exist for the greater comfort of teachers. Unfortunately the humanising intentions of drama have caused some people to speak of the activity as 'free'; the notion of freedom has so many connotations with licence instead of liberty, that it is necessary constantly to remind oneself of the difference and of the length of time it can take to become fully aware of other people and to consider their needs. Much time is spent on preaching the words 'Love thy neighbour as thyself'. Drama gives a full, personal inner opportunity for discovering the precise philosophy of life embodied in these words as a process of two-way exchange, the give and take of life. This is another point on the circle, applicable to every human being for the whole of life.

NOTES ON 'ACTIVITIES WITH A BALL'

1. The suggestions are concerned with one particular way of starting movement if none has been done before. It is *a* way, not the only way; it has the advantage that all human beings will, at some stage or another of their lives, have had experience of various activities with a ball and so will be working outwards from the familiar and the known.

2. It is important not to worry anyone about accuracy of mime when holding, throwing or catching the ball; accuracy is concerned with detail, often for communication, and comes at a much later stage.

3. The different speeds are very important. They involve personal physical control, which is the basis of many aspects of movement and dance. The slow motion attempt is excellent training for this type of controlled use of the body.

EXTENSION FROM MOVING IN SLOW MOTION

On some occasions one exercise, with its own particular purpose, will give rise to another, possibly with a different purpose. So from the slow motion exercise, the imagination might lead to the use of such movement in a simple story or brief episode. With infants and young juniors, episodes might evolve where, for example, statues or life size paintings come slowly to life. With older juniors and secondaries, an episode or story might evolve from the notion that in outer space, beyond the full power of gravity, people float in the air. One secondary group, which had never done drama before, extended this to assembling and building a space station from materials that had been sent up to them by rocket. The actual assembling and building led quite naturally to cooperation in small and large groups, with the slow motion movement sustained throughout. Subsequently, the space platform was used for a war against the Martians (not only subsequently, but inevitably – at this stage), but as all of the fighting was accomplished through the same slow motion, there was full

71

control throughout. Indeed, moving in slow motion is one excellent approach to the factor of 'fighting', which is considered more fully in chapter 9.

Discovering the Body

When either sitting or standing, it is interesting to discover all the different parts of the body that we can move, either separately or in various combinations. In the early stages of attempting this it is wise not to be too detailed or to ask for any section of the exercise to be sustained for more than a few seconds. Once absorption and interest have grown, then both the detail and the time factor can be extended.

Let us consider this from the point of view of a teacher actually taking the class, with some marginal comments on the types of reaction that have been known to take place.

TEACHER (*to class as a whole*): Let us discover how many parts of our bodies we can actually move. As I call out any particular part, then each of you move it, working in the place you are standing (sitting) on now. Ready. Fingers – move every joint on both hands. (*Only a few seconds – say, five seconds.*) Now – wrists. (*Some may merely shake their wrists, which is excellent for relaxation – but muscular intention is important as well, so we might add:*) Yes, both shaking them and making them work by our own effort.* (*After a few seconds of moving wrists:*) Elbows – bending the elbows and

---

* 'By *our* own effort.' It is always difficult to advise teachers as to when and if it is advisable to join in an activity with the class. Generally speaking it is wisest not to, as if one is genuinely participating (and that is the only kind of participation we should allow ourselves – it is pointless hoping for absorption and sincerity if we ourselves demonstrate external and half-hearted examples) then it is impossible fully to observe how each member of the class is managing. Because we are basically concerned with individuality and the development of intuition and the differences in people, drama makes more demands on our capacities to observe than any other activity. Furthermore, if we are actively participating and happen to be either experienced or gifted in our own use of the activity, it is easy for the class to become fascinated as audience, and therefore to work less fully themselves, or alternatively, they may copy – often rather exactly – our way of doing the exercise, which entirely defeats the object of personal development. However, in a case like this, it is sometimes helpful to certain age groups, particularly top groups in secondary schools, to observe that we are not above feeling value from the exercise. Even in such cases, it might well be wise to take part only in the first few sections of the exercise and then quietly to drop out.

turning the whole forearm in different ways – yes, and see if you can possibly manage it without banging your neighbour. Very difficult, but try. Now – shoulders, including swinging your arms above your head. Now quite still. Now let your neck stretch upwards, as if you were going to dust the ceiling with your hair. Right up. Now let your head fall slowly forward, till your chin is resting on your chest. Don't force it. Now, roll your head slowly to one side, round the back to the other side and then to the front again. Go on doing that...but don't force it. Now still again. Now – faces. Move every muscle in your faces – chew gum, flap your eye-lashes, screw your face up and let it go again. (*If there has not been laughter up to this point there is almost certain to be some now. Try not to worry about it – laughter is a healthy release of tension, and you can, by tone of voice, bring back more serious endeavour as soon as you continue.*) Now – spines, from your neck all the way down to and past your waist, and beyond. Imagine you have a long tail, and swish it about. Now let the weight of your head 'float away', like a great balloon. If you get it really floating off, then you can stand on one leg without falling over. Now – stand on one leg. Keep your head floating away. Now throw the other leg about, really move your leg at the groin and at the knee. Now – that ankle. Now – the toes on that foot. Now change legs. Groins and knees. Toes. Now both legs on the ground. Use them both – groins, knees, ankles and toes.

Now – let's make this very difficult for ourselves (*it is good to offer the challenge*). We are going to add concentration, so that once any one section of ourselves starts to move, we are not going to let it stop. Eventually we shall have every bit of ourselves moving. I'll call out all the sections again. Once each starts moving, try to make sure it doesn't stop. Ready. Fingers. Add wrists. Keep fingers going. Add elbows – but still fingers and wrists. Add shoulders. Add necks. Add faces. But still fingers, wrists, elbows, shoulders and necks. Add spines. Add waists. Add groins. Add ankles. Add knees. Add toes. And when I clap my hands, stop absolutely still in whatever position you are in. (*Then clap hands, or use the cymbal or the drum. On the sound everybody freezes exactly where they are.*) When I flick my fingers move everything, starting them all at one and the same time. Now – (*flick of fingers, and all start moving. On a repeat of the handclap or the drum or cymbal sound, all freeze again.*)

The above is a simple way of discovering a little about the body and of making a first attempt at moving it, linking with concentration. At this moment, we have left the class frozen in whatever positions they were in when they heard the freezing sound. There are many possible developments from this point.

ADD IMAGINATION

TEACHER (*continuing from above*): And again when I flick you are going to move everything – and this time when I clap (or hit the drum or the cymbal), you are going to freeze in the ugliest position you can think of. Ready.

With the flick, everybody moves, and after a few seconds, the louder sound leads to everybody freezing in an ugly position.

Right – absolutely still. Hold it there, and keep your concentration. Now – each of you decide what kind of ugly person or thing or creature you are. Decide entirely for yourself – don't say anything to anyone else about it.

A few seconds pause for each person to decide.

Now – I'm coming round. If I stop close to any one of you, then whisper to me privately what kind of ugly person or thing or creature you have become. Whisper very quietly, so that no one else can hear.

The teacher walks round among the group, stopping now and again very close to different individuals for them to whisper what their decision is.

(The whispering is important as it avoids fear of failure and preserves confidence, even to the point of being fully honest with such replies as 'I haven't thought of anything yet,' or 'I don't know'; it also takes away the audience potential from those who are feeling shy and uncertain about the appropriateness of their decision, or from the 'smart Alec' who wants to show off some 'clever' idea. Ideas will probably differ enormously.) *After hearing several different ideas*, the teacher repeats these to the class as a whole, *without comment* and without identifying who has had which ideas. (*And thus preserves further confidence by showing that all ideas are acceptable.*)

Repeat the exercise; this time everyone freezes as the funniest person or thing or creature they can think of.

ADD MOVEMENT IN CHARACTER

TEACHER (*continuing*): When I flick move everything – and this time you are going to freeze again as the ugliest person or thing or creature you can think of – and it can be quite different from last time if you wish.

With the flick, everybody moves – the teacher encouraging full and vigorous movement of every part. The louder sound freezes them.

Now – absolutely still. You are all statues. Decide for yourself what kind of ugly person or thing or creature you are a statue of. Now – with the sound I am going to make, let the statue *slowly* come to life and start moving about – and when the sound stops, become a solid statue again.

A continuous sound is made, either with the hands, or, more easily, on the drum or cymbal (for one thing it is easier to go from soft to loud and back again to very soft – right through to a full fade out – on one of these instruments) and the statues come slowly to life, moving about, according to space, with attempts to sustain the ugly person, thing or creature that has been decided on. Watch carefully for sustaining of absorption – as soon as it seems that a few are losing their absorption, fade out the sound so that all become once more still as statues.

Repeat exercise leading to 'Funny' statues, which again are brought to life with sound. This time the sound can be a lively rhythm, which the majority of 'funny' statues will respond to with fairly fast and vigorous movement, possibly using the mood of gaiety associated with being funny statues. (They will be all kinds of statues ranging from clowns and monkeys to Gonks and fat old ladies.) Again, watch for decrease in absorption, and the moment a few are losing this, let the sound fade out or stop so that they become statues again. By stopping at this point we again avoid fear of failure. They are unable to sustain anything for very long in the early stages, so we, as teachers, provide for them the legal opportunity for stopping; confidence will soon grow from these opportunities and with confidence a greater capacity for sustaining.

DEVELOPMENT OF IMAGINATIVE OPPORTUNITY

TEACHER (*continuing*): Again when I flick, move everything. I'm not going to say anything about what kind of person or creature or thing you are going to be – but when you are moving everything, do so with great urgency. Ready.

With the flick, movement starts.

More urgent still. And when I make the loud sound, stop absolutely still in whatever position you are in.

A few seconds more of movement – then the loud sound, and everybody freezes in exactly that moment, whatever their position.

Now – each of you decide for yourself as follows: if you were caught by a high-speed camera in exactly this position, who might you be and what might be happening? You are part of a still photograph from a film. Who or what are you in the film, and what is happening? Each of you decide for yourself – and when I come round, whisper privately to me.

A moment is given for the decision to be made, and then the teacher again walks among the class, hearing from some people who they are and what is happening. Some of these can be repeated to the whole class.

And again – when I flick, move everything. Only this time it is almost impossible to move – but you have to. You simply must, no matter how difficult it is. Ready.

Again the flick. Again the freeze after a few seconds.

Now – decide again. Another still photograph from a film. Who might you be and in what situation if a high speed camera caught you in exactly this position.

Again some of the ideas are heard quite privately and repeated to the class as a whole.

TEACHER (*continuing*): Again when I flick, move everything – and this time, the whole of your body feels incredibly light – every part of it, really as light as it can be. Ready.

Again the flick. Again the freeze after a few seconds.

Now – decide again. If you were caught by a high-speed camera in exactly this position, who might you be and what might be happening to you? Another still photograph from a film. And this time when I come round, I shall touch you on the shoulder. If I touch you, then just say what you have decided.

(There is a slight change here, in that the 'private whisper' has been dropped. It should not, of course, be dropped until we are quite certain that confidence is firmly established, which might in fact not come for a very long time, at least for many of the class. For this reason it is important to make no form of comment on the 'volume' of sound when people say what they have decided. If they speak very quietly, accept it, repeat what they have said, and then pass on to the next. In this way, we see how each person is getting on in terms of confidence. Much can be undone by forcing the issue at this stage.)

TEACHER (*continuing*): This time, when I flick, move in any manner you like – fast or slow, light or heavy – or any other way. Each of you decide for yourself, and freeze when I make the loud sound.

Again the flick – again each person moves.

(The greater liberty of personal choice may worry some of the class, possibly resulting in their looking around to see what others are doing and then doing the same kind of movement themselves. This will indicate that we have given full choice a little too soon; at such moments we need to be at our most encouraging, even suggesting that they do something they have done before. Whatever we do or say must be calculated to bring back a return of full confidence and to remove any sudden new fear of failure.)

The loud sound again makes everybody freeze.

TEACHER: Now again, decide entirely for yourselves. If you were caught by a high-speed camera in exactly this position, who might you be and what is happening. You are again part of a still photograph from a film. Not a film you have seen, but an entirely new one. Each of you decide for yourself.

This might be followed up in one of many ways:

(a) The teacher might again hear privately the decisions made.

(b) Various people might be asked to say aloud what they have decided.

(c) Following on these, or instead of either of them, the class might be invited to 'bring the still photograph to life' for a few seconds, the action being both started and ended by a definite sound.

(d) The class might divide into pairs; each person in each pair shows his partner the position he or she was in and tells what they have decided is happening and who they are being; then the other partner shows his or her position and gives their explanation.

OR—

RELAXATION

TEACHER (*continuing – from the moment where all are still, in whatever position they were in at the moment of the last sound. N.B. This exercise can follow any one of the moments of stillness that have already been experienced*):

Now – each one of you is a block of ice, solid ice. The sun is right overhead, and is beating down on you with a really fierce heat, melting you from above – melting you, until you are just a pool of water on the floor. Go ahead in your own time.

In the early stages of such work they will 'melt' very quickly, but once absorption is established, together with some physical control, they will take a very long time, as little by little they relax from the upper extremities until the whole of themselves is fully relaxed on the floor. The exercise is as much concerned with physical control as it is with relaxation.

An alternative to the above is made quite simply by changing the suggested direction from which the heat is coming – instead of it coming from the hot sun above, we can suggest that they are standing on hot metal and are being slowly melted from below, again until they are a pool of water on the floor. Either exercise will help the factor of concentration, leading towards full physical control, and the fuller the physical control the greater the step we have made towards achieving personal responsibility for behaviour. This, of course, is also being helped constantly by the use of the 'finger flick' for starting activity and the loud sound, by whatever means we are making it, for stopping it, freezing on the spot.

Further Exercises in Relaxation

It is perfectly true that the majority of young children relax quite naturally and therefore do not need exercises in relaxation to get rid of immediate tensions; as they get older, many factors in life create tensions – the factors, which in themselves do not really concern us here, vary considerably, ranging from self-consciousness to various fears; fear of failure in the scholastic fields of activity, fear of punishment, fear of freedom, fear of ridicule, and other deeply personal fears to do with one's own personal development and other people's comments on that development, and also deep concern for the future and what it holds. Most roots of tension are emotional, and because drama is concerned with the emotions it can often help to remove some of these emotional causes of tension, which is the best way of removing the tensions altogether. But this can be a long and slow process, and in the meanwhile the body can be helped to lose the actual tension through relaxation; because the body and emotion are always functioning together, the loss of tension can have some considerable effect on the emotion causing the tension, and will at the very least help the body to throw off some of the ills that might arise from long periods of unreleased tension.

Moments of consciously intended relaxation, regularly practised, eventually bring about the ability, at an unconscious and almost reflex level, of being able to recognise the existence of tension and the different feeling within the self when this has been removed, together with an awareness of how to set about actual relaxation. This process becomes more difficult the older we get and the more that tension has set in. For this reason, moments of relaxation exercises with even naturally relaxed young children help to build up, at an unconscious level, habit forming abilities to be able to remove tension, together with an inner awareness of what it feels like when one is relaxed.

If relaxation is the opposite of tension, we can often fully achieve relaxation in any particular part of the body by deliberately creating tension in that part and then letting go of the tension. So, fully to relax one arm, we can deliberately stiffen the whole arm – and then let the stiffness go. Often, we might think the arm is relaxed when it is not necessarily so, and we can gradually discover the difference between partial and full relaxation by deliberately creating and then losing tension. Similarly with other parts of the body, each in turn being tensed and released. The whole body can be relaxed in the following manner, by tensing – really fully tensing – four particular areas in turn, each area creating tension and then relaxation throughout adjacent areas. The exercise should be done lying on one's back on the floor. The four areas are:

1. *The hands.* Clench the fists really tight, so tight that the finger nails are almost biting into the hand, the knuckles almost bursting through the skin. Then – let it all go.

2. *The face*, particularly the eyes. Screw up the eyes really tightly, until it almost hurts – in fact, probably does hurt a great deal. Then – let it all go.

3. *The buttocks.* Contract the buttocks really tightly. Then let go.

4. *The toes.* Clench the toes really tightly – as tight as possible. Then let it all go.

To get a full tension within each of these four areas takes practice, and the fuller the tension, the greater the relaxation when one lets go.

Once full relaxation has been achieved in this manner, remain lying down, feeling the whole body sinking away through the floor – almost as if one was going to leave an imprint of one's body on the floor in the same way as would happen in sand or soft earth.

'GROWING FROM NOTHING'

Now that we have reached the point of relaxing on the floor we can approach the matter in a different way – by *growing* from, as it were, nothing, into whatever person, thing or creature is suggested.

Invite the class to 'make themselves as small as they can'; with younger ones, we can say simply: 'Curl up very small where you are.' Then we say words to this effect: 'You are all going to grow from where you are into...' adding what it is we want them to grow into. It is both advisable and helpful if we use sound to accompany or to lead this growth, giving simple experience of climax at the same time. (We considered this climax sound when concerned with different ways of stimulating stories – see p. 46.) The sound can be made either with the hands, or with one or both hands on a surface like a chair or a desk, or, better still, either on the drum or the cymbal. The sound helps by both stimulation and control, and we can vary the actual pace of the growth of the climax according to the absorption of the class. In the early stages the process of the growing might be a matter of only a few seconds, as there is little detailed thought within it. With practice and confidence, the detail becomes greater and the time-span of growing can be stretched considerably to help deeper experience.

What they will grow into will vary according to age and experience, as must the actual phrasing we use–for example, we might say to infants 'You are all going to grow into giants', but to give the same experience to secondary pupils we might well need to change the word 'giants' to something like 'enormously strong people, twenty times our own size'. The experience of growing into large people, thinking and feeling the quality of largeness, is an interesting experience for all age groups.

The following list may give some guidance on the kind of persons or things or creatures we can suggest for them to grow into:

(a) Variations in size or kind – large, small, strong, weak, heavy, or light people, animals, birds, underwater creatures, or creatures from outer space; trees, plants, and so on.

Either separate from or added to these:

(b) Simple emotional qualities – angry birds, frightened monsters, gay people, determined creatures, etc. etc.

(c) Such creatures as puppets (for stiff movements), rag dolls (for very relaxed movement).

Once the creature, thing or person has grown, we need to make a simple decision whether the group is ready for further experiences as these characters. If not, then they can either 'melt' again, as blocks of ice, or, with another climax sound find their way to the ground. If we want to provide the further experiences (and the quality of absorption is our guide, though it is always worth taking the risk, even if only for a few seconds), then there are many developments we can consider:

1. Simply beginning to move about – in the sea, on the land or in the air, according to what they have grown into.

2. Beginning to move about for a particular purpose – e.g. searching for food; trying to find their way out of one area to another, e.g. from the sea onto dry land, out of a hole, etc. etc.

3. Beginning to move about on one surface and then going into or onto different surfaces – e.g. moving about dry earth, into mud, onto hot rock, through thick undergrowth etc., and to these might also be added the differences between moving in light or darkness.

4. Beginning to move and gradually changing the condition – e.g. strong people or creatures becoming weak, or vice versa; starting determined and gradually giving up; starting sadly and becoming happy, or vice versa, and so on. This kind of change is an interesting way of ending this type of experience; e.g. strong people or creatures gradually lose their strength, losing more and more of it until they can hardly move at all, and finally are unable to move, so come to rest on one spot. And from here, it is simple to say again 'Make yourself as small as possible' and then give a new experience of growing from nothing.

With this 'growing from nothing' we can give experience of the whole evolution of man – from a mere substance into which comes life, to underwater life, to that underwater life crawling on to land and becoming mammals, to getting up on to both feet as apes etc., including such experiences as climbing, to growing wings and becoming birds, and so on.

All of the foregoing suggestions embrace certain factors:

1. The whole class is working at one and the same time, but each individual is working entirely on his or her own.

2. Some simple suggestions have been made regarding the use of sound for control, stimulation and enrichment, but there has

been no need for recorded music, or for any kind of musical instrument; a cymbal or drum has been suggested, but all of the exercises could in fact be done with use only of the hands.

3. Many of the exercises can be attempted as adequately in the classroom as in the hall, even with the desks in the traditional arrangement. Learning to share a small amount of space is useful social training, and youngsters become very adept at using what is available, no matter how inadequate.

However, it is worth considering what can be done to make as much space as possible available in the classroom. The major necessity is that of moving furniture to the sides of the room. This need not be a burden if we make the actual physical moving of each desk and chair part of drama, by suggesting different situations or characters for the class as a whole, both situation and character depending on the age group and the amount of experience they have had.

The following are a few of the many different manners in which we can suggest the furniture is moved:

(a) We (the class) are all members of a secret society; our task is to blow up the enemy headquarters; the classroom is the basement of those headquarters and we are going to pile up great crates of high explosive near the walls of the basement; we have to work with complete silence and secrecy as there are many guards about; we also have to work quickly, as the high explosive is time-fused; the chairs and desks are the crates of high explosive. We can work either on our own, or help each other as a team.

(b) We are all simple shepherds carrying gifts (in the story of the Nativity).

(c) As in (b), but we are all Wise Men.

(d) As above, but we are all kings.

(e) Slaves building the pyramids (or anything else we may decide slaves should build).

(f) Astronauts assembling a space platform in outer space (slow motion).

(g) Builders of some kind, during a go-slow strike.

(h) Miners working against time to reinforce a pit that is in danger of caving in.

83

(i) Clumsy removal men getting a grand piano down a narrow staircase.

(j) A scene from a film: removal men clearing a house; something has gone wrong with the camera, so everything is happening at half-speed.

(k) As in (j) – only the fault in the camera makes everything go at twice normal speed.

(l) Moving very precious and delicate ornaments.

(m) Craftsmen putting their own work on display.

(n) Defence force preparing defences.

(o) Attackers preparing positions for an ambush.

(p) Refugees piling up possessions prior to leaving their country.

(q) Divers clearing a wreck under the sea.

(r) Explorers loading their ship.

(s) Explorers setting up camp.

(t) Witches putting ingredients into a cauldron.

(u) Automatons carrying out the demands of their masters.

(v) Servants preparing a feast or a banquet.

(w) Fairies spring-cleaning.

(x) The toys in a toy-shop at the magic hour of midnight.

(y) Medical supplies arriving for jungle troops in great heat.

(z) Smugglers in a cave or on a ship; or thieves in the night; or pirates.

There are, of course, many other ways, both for clearing the furniture and for reassembling it. In this context it is possible to introduce consideration for other people's property, for co-operating with other people and for not, through noise, disturbing other people when they are working (e.g. the class next door).

The Use of Sound and Music

Children discover and use sound during their preschool years; adults tend to call their use of sound 'noise' because it is basic and primitive and involved with early discovery. If we like the sounds – and liking is usually associated with whether or not the sounds disturb our own lives – then we often encourage them; if we dislike them, then we often discourage them without consideration of the immediate reason for them or for their potential growth to something that may be valuable in the future. From a teaching point of view, it is necessary for us to be very objective about the early use of sound, eliminating judgments that arise merely from expedient likes and dislikes. Observation of children's discovery of and pleasure in sound, of their way of making sounds themselves, gives us a basis from which to start when considering the use of sound and or music as part of drama – including movement and dance.

Considerations of this kind inevitably find connections with work being attempted as part of children's or young people's musical education – or, perhaps more accurately, musical appreciation, certainly with older age groups. There need be no conflict, but there often is, through lack of understanding of the fact that children and young people hear sound emotionally and not intellectually. Perhaps this can be made most clear by considering the effect of words and the sound of them on a young child. If an adult shouts or screams at a small child 'I can't stand you, get out of my sight', quite obviously the child will be frightened or alarmed and probably burst into tears; but the same reaction would happen if again with a shout or a scream the adult used the words: 'You're the nicest child in the world and I love you very much.' Before the intellectual meaning of the words are understood the emotional sound makes its impact. Furthermore, young people do not, where actual music is concerned, make or enjoy the conscious or unconscious intellectual analysis of musical form in any detail. They respond to, discover and enjoy simple straightforward time-beat; the preschool child enjoys thumping a stick on another surface, or a spoon on its plate; the enjoyment may be musical and associated with intense listening, or it may be dramatic and associated with physical action; it is also deeply associated with the personal rhythm of life and with the heart beat. Where actual music listening is concerned, there is often, indeed usually, greatest pleasure in music with a pronounced and regular time-beat, as for instance in martial music.

At a later stage there is discovery and enjoyment of the use of rhythm. This might be quite simply time-beat with regular changes in stress, or it might be a pattern of sound that is constantly repeated. Again, we hear examples of this in their own banging at the preschool stage. Where music listening is concerned, the enjoyment of rhythm is dependent on its lack of subtlety – the clear and obvious time-beat must still be there; again martial music is a good example.

The emotional hearing of sound connects also with listening 'pictorially' and to 'stories in music'; and, included in such experience is a growing feeling for mood and atmosphere – simple, obvious and 'one' in the early stages, subtle and variable later. So music may be jolly and gay or it may be sad. Later, there may be subtler feelings for change from one to the other mood, even within the same piece of music, but this feeling for change is still within the emotional sphere and not the intellectual.

Another early discovery and pleasure in sound is that of climax, and again we can observe examples in simple preschool bangings, again sometimes a largely musical experience associated with listening and at others a mainly dramatic experience associated with action. (Incidentally, a young child's enjoyment and excitement at an express train rushing through a station, or a very fast car racing past down the road, is very much connected with pleasure in climax.) This type of enjoyment is again reflected in listening to music, particularly in terms of stirring endings.

So the young child discovers and enjoys three basic ingredients of sound or music from very early in life: time-beat, rhythm and climax. It also feels qualities of mood and atmosphere and is stimulated to 'seeing' (thinking?) stories. If, as teachers, we approach the use of sound and music with these factors in mind, we have a basis from which to work that is already familiar to children, even though that familiarity is entirely unconscious. This is vitally important because the tendency for adults, arising from the intellectual appreciation of music, is to consider music for movement 'balletically', envisaging precise steps or appropriate actions to specific bars or notes in a passage of music. This may well arise quite simply for older children after a lot of experience, but is far too complex a cerebral activity in the early stages. Further, intellectual appreciation of music tends to make us ignore (even dislike) obvious time-beat, even rhythm; this is particularly obvious in the average adult distaste of pop music which, whether we like it or not, contains very clear time-beat and rhythm and has consequently great appeal to young people. The difficulty for many teachers arises from the fear that if we do not introduce children at an early age to 'good music', then they may never discover it and so will lack a potential source of enrichment and pleasure for the rest of their lives. There is also a feeling that much music with pronounced time-beat and rhythm is vulgar and therefore not to be allowed in school. Consequently we tend to introduce them to – and even to use for movement and drama – music that is 'good' or pure. The results are often, particularly in the early stages of drama or movement, dispiritingly poor, simply because the emotional sound message is too difficult. Consider it this way, again in terms of language. If we require a young child to carry out a simple task, say, for example, handing a book to Johnnie, we would use simple straightforward words: 'Please give this book to Johnnie.' The child understands our request and is able to carry it out. What would happen if instead of saying 'Please give this book to Johnnie', we said something like, 'Would you kindly organise the physical attributes of your own person in order to convey this encyclopædia of cerebral exactness to your fellow pupil whose parental indulgence has resulted in his being bestowed with the sobriquet Johnnie'! The child would stare at us, lost and bewildered, completely unable to understand the simple nature of our request. So is it with music. If the language of music is too complicated, then the child is unable to do anything in response to it; if it is clear, and its clarity lies in its time-beat and rhythm, then its message is easily understood and acted upon.

For this reason, there is need to use the simplest of sounds, giving the clearest of messages, in the early stages, not only for the younger age groups, but for older groups as well, if such groups have never before had any experience of using sound to move to. The simplest sounds are of the kind already suggested – the use of a tambour (or a drum) and of a cymbal or gong. Are both necessary? Yes, they are. The tambour or drum provides experience of short, sharp sounds; the cymbal or gong provides experience of longer, ringing sounds. (This fact is considered in more detail in the chapter on speech, but needs to be pointed out now; for the purposes of a book it may be necessary to consider different

DEVELOPMENT THROUGH DRAMA

aspects of an activity separately, but in practice there is no real separation, and this is a good example. The use of sound is connected not only with movement, not only with the stimulation of ideas for stories and character, not only with mood and atmosphere, not only with teacher control leading to individual personal control by each pupil, it is also concerned with, indeed deeply interwoven with speech. Speech roughly divides into the long sounds of vowels and the short sounds of consonants, and by the use of the long sounds of a cymbal or gong and the short sounds of the drum or tambour, we are providing, at an intuitive level, physical experience of factors deeply concerned with speech experience. In one sense, some aspects of movement might indeed be considered as 'speaking with the body' rather than speaking with words. This is not altogether an exact definition, because speech is often concerned with the expression of experience and movement is concerned with the immediacy of the experience.) After experience of these simplest of sounds, the next obvious kind of sound to use, moving into the realm of music, is that with a clearly pronounced time-beat, as for instance is to be found in Sandy Nelson's drum recordings or Winifred Atwell's honkie-tonk piano. These all have clear time-beat and rhythm, and yet have many different experiences of mood and atmosphere, particularly for young people. Adults tend to think of such music collectively as having only one mood and atmosphere, but again this arises from intellectual thinking rather than emotional and pictorial listening. (Perhaps, as adults, we have to re-learn some of our ways of listening!) Acker Bilk provides another good example of the type of early music to use. It is important for us to differentiate between the kinds of music already mentioned and the type that is essentially 'sentimental goo' or the type of intellectual modern jazz which contains neither time-beat nor rhythm.

Beyond these experiences, we can gradually move towards types of classical music that are less offensive to the adult ear; the music and arrangements of Leroy Anderson are excellent as a first step in this direction, as time-beat and rhythm are still catered for quite definitely and clearly. At the end of the book will be found a list of recorded music that teachers might find useful, some of them concerned with movement and dance, others more concerned with dramatic experience – many concerned with both, in the activity known as dance drama. Meanwhile, before suggesting some actual uses of sound and music for movement, it is important to point out the need not to rush children into experience of gramophone music too soon. When the teacher is supplying sounds, it is possible not only to stimulate, but to *follow* what the class is doing, to provide new or different or contrasting or similar experiences, according to the needs of the moment out of our assessment of the immediate situation. This is not possible with recorded music – or certainly not so without a great deal of prior organisation together with many mechanical changes from record to record. With recorded music, the class tends inevitably to have to follow the music; eventually this has a very particular value as a discipline, and it helps to develop an intuitive awareness of form and structure, both in story-making and in dance. But this takes some while to develop; early attempts need to include the use of only short sections of records – a whole record can be too great a challenge to the capacity for sustaining concentration, interest, characterisation and story content; inability to sustain these factors can lead to disappointment, undermining of confidence and fear of failure, and to the need for the teacher to impose too much in an effort to keep things going. Far better to aim at simpler experiences which avoid these issues.

EXAMPLES OF THE USE OF TIME-BEAT, RHYTHM AND CLIMAX. In the following examples, it should be noted that two distinct types of *teaching approach* are involved – that in which the teacher directly states what to do and/or who to be, and that in which ideas are stimulated by the sound that is made; we have considered both approaches before when establishing the necessity in the early stages of other aspects of drama not to leave the class 'cold' but to make the kind of suggestion which results in immediate activity, and then, as confidence is established, handing over greater responsibility to them to find their own ideas. Perhaps it should also be mentioned again that whichever approach is used, the teacher does not, under any conditions, show or tell 'how' to do things – nor is any one youngster picked out as 'best' and asked to 'demonstrate' to the others; the framework continues to be entirely uncritical.

Let us consider some examples, again through the eyes of the teacher actually taking the class in the hall:

TEACHER: You are all soldiers marching – now.

Sound: straightforward, marching time-beat (tambour). Bring the sound to a simple climax and then sharply stop; the class will stop too, though perhaps not absolutely on the final beat yet.

Now – soldiers with a wooden leg.

Rhythm made by use of same time-beat with alternate loud and soft beats, again to simple climax for stopping movement.

Very, very tired soldiers.

Very slow, measured time-beat; can be done on either tambour or cymbal, preferably latter. Let the sound go slower and slower to a final slightly louder sound for end.

Suddenly the soldiers see the enemy.

Sound: Swiftly growing climax.

The swift climax of sound will bring immediately swift movement to the majority of the class, even though the teacher has not said what the soldiers did when they sighted the enemy; this is an example of stimulating their own ideas; after the movement has stopped, the teacher asks what they did when they sighted the enemy; some may have charged the enemy; some may have run away to hide; some may have stood still and shot up the enemy with machine guns – there may even be many other ideas, and the teacher may decide that everybody should have all of the different experiences and therefore go back on that moment with the same sound, only this time stating exactly what everyone is going to do. After these experiences:

TEACHER. Now be different people and animals in a circus. First – horses.

Sound: The straightforward trotting rhythm of the sound of horses; now and again a short climax of sound, followed by the slightest pause, then continue with the rhythm. Either slow down the rhythm to a stop or else build to a small climax and stop.

Here is an example of mixed directed and stimulated approaches. The teacher has directly stated 'be horses' and has helped the movement with a straightforward galloping or trotting rhythm – but the occasional short climaxes followed by the slight pause are a stimulus to them to find their own ideas. The teacher watches to see who at once has an idea, and, by doing that kind of sound several times, gives others the chance to think of something, too. Some may not think of anything and so copy what other people are doing rather than being left out; teacher does not comment on this in order to avoid undermining confidence and creating fear of failure. What they do at these particular moments will vary from, perhaps, taking jumps to rising up on hind legs – much may depend on what experience they have had of seeing horses in a circus. With the slowing down of the sound, they will also slow down, and stop when the sound does – such is the emotional control of sound!

TEACHER. Tightrope-walkers.

Either a very slow and measured time-beat (which will connect to actual use of feet), or else a continuous drum roll, which will create the mood and atmosphere that surrounds tight-rope walking.

The idea of tightrope-walking has followed that of horses or ponies, because the last activity was fast and boisterous, and being tightrope walkers is slow and quiet and concentrated – a quite different, contrasting experience.

TEACHER. Clowns, jugglers or tumblers. You decide for yourself – and change if you want to.

A variable concoction of gay rhythms, perhaps with moments of short climax – definitely finishing with a moment of climax.

The choice of several different people is given as a general stimulus – and the invitation to change if desired is added in case of inability to sustain first choice. This kind of choice often helps because what first appeals is not necessarily easy to sustain and, by having alternatives to go on to, there is again avoidance of disappointment and undermining of confidence. This point is constantly reiterated on behalf of less gifted children, who can so easily give up if they see the more gifted pressing happily on when they themselves are feeling 'stuck'. The fundamental basis of both education and living is personal confidence – but, for some, it can take a long time to achieve.

Other aspects of a circus might also be added: lion-tamers; the lions; performing seals; trapeze artists; bears; elephants; walking on balls; riding single wheel cycles, etc. and perhaps finish up again with ponies or horses.

Then, a different stimulated experience.

TEACHER

Listen to the sound, and do whatever it tells you to.

A very quiet, slow time-beat on the tambour. The class begins to move about – and after awhile the sound stops and they stop.

Well – what were you doing or being to that sound?
ANSWER: Burglars.
ANOTHER: Stalking an animal in the jungle.
ANOTHER: A prisoner escaping.
TEACHER: All right. Each of you go on doing and being what you were before – and keep listening to the sound.

The same sound is repeated, but this time a sudden really loud bang is added, bringing some kind of immediate reaction from everybody.

Well – what happened then? What happened with the burglar?
ANSWER: A door suddenly slammed shut and scared him.
ANOTHER: I knocked over a chair in the room.
TEACHER: What about those of you stalking animals?
ANSWER: A lion suddenly roared.
ANOTHER: A tiger jumped out of the trees on to me.
TEACHER: And the escaping prisoner? What happened to him?
ANSWER: He got shot.

At this stage, depending on how strong is the general absorption of the class, the teacher might continue to help each person to develop his or her own individual story to other sounds, or might go back to the beginning, now suggesting that all the class are burglars, or stalking animals or prisoners escaping – perhaps do all three stories following each other.

This is a clear example of stimulation by sound; also of how we can control bodies to work vigorously and broadly from loud and strong sounds, and more gently and delicately by quieter, sensitive sounds.

The above examples, or some adaptation of them, are clearly material for younger children, say up to and including the first two years in the junior school. Many of the examples would work equally well with older groups, possibly up to the second year of secondary schools, but not necessarily to start with. This is an interesting fact that often emerges from a long period of work in drama – pseudo-sophistication falls away and a renewed interest is found in quite simple material, when that material involves actual doing and being; so, for example, the concept of circuses may seem very young in the realm of intellectual ideas for young teenagers; they may tend to scoff at it in the early stages; but full mastery of many of the aspects of a circus in the physical-emotional sphere is in fact very advanced, bringing with it superb possibilities of personal satisfaction in achievement; because of this, the circus material may be very useful at a later stage, bringing full absorption and interest. This again is important when concerned about progression; if we feel the necessity for progressing along a straight line, then we tend to search for advances mainly in the intellectual content of drama; if we are concerned with the vertical progression of the many different points on the circle representing all aspects of the whole person, then we can often progress in aspects such as emotion or the body or personal control by returning to simpler, already fully understood intellectual material, which, because of that fuller understanding at one level enables fuller development at other levels to be achieved.

The above examples are concerned with many short and varied kinds of experience, some of them directed (i.e. teacher states what to do or who to be, but not how to do it), others stimulated (i.e. the sounds made by the teacher suggest ideas of who to be or what to do); in both cases, sound controls the experience. It is wise to keep the experiences short until absorption has grown through practice, and until there is the beginnings of basic confidence. Then, however, we can begin to put many different experiences together into a longer, continuous story:

EXAMPLE OF LONGER STORY WITH USE OF SOUND*

TEACHER: All find a space to lie down. I am going to tell a story
and you can all do everything that happens in the story. To start
with you are all fast asleep. (There may be snoring, according to
how much drama experience they have had; very often, in the
early stages, youngsters, when trying to read into our minds as
to what we are expecting them to do, think that we are asking
them to 'show us' their experiences; we are not – we are asking
them simply to experience, not to illustrate the experience for
our benefit or anyone else's benefit; we are not concerned with
communication to an audience, but with sincerity that, at this
stage, will come only when there is regular work without an
audience. Of course, the snoring may be simple fun or intended
'playing about'. Whatever its cause, we deal with it simply,
without making an issue of it.) Very fast asleep, so there is no
snoring. (Now we give the story itself a full start.)

One day, we are very fast asleep, when suddenly the alarm clock
bell rings. (*Very young children will at once become the alarm clock bell
and make the sound of ringing; older ones will simply either stir in their
sleep or suddenly shoot upright in response to an imaginary bell sound.*)
But you are very sleepy this morning, so you turn over and go to
sleep again. (*The use of* you *now begins to make the story personal for
each youngster. Teacher waits until there is full quiet again, noting the
different degrees of absorption.*) But the alarm clock bell rings again –
so you have a great big stretch – and then you sit up in bed.
Suddenly, you remember today is a holiday, so you jump out of
bed and you go to the window to see what sort of day it is. You
decide its going to be a beautiful day, so you go to the bathroom
and have a quick wash and clean your teeth, and when you have
done those things you go and get dressed; and when you have
finished dressing you go and have breakfast.
(Note that the last two statements have slightly changed in
approach from the earlier ones; this is to allow for those who are

* The links between sound as such and the sounds contained in speech have
already been mentioned, albeit briefly. We have also considered the emotional
effect of the use of sound – and it is important now to realise that all the
stimulating and controlling factors that exist when using a tambour or a cymbal
equally exist in the use of words and in the atmosphere created by tone of voice.

more fully absorbed to take longer over the detail of their washing or dressing; it is always necessary to watch the different pace at which a class will work; for much of the time, our story can flow with the majority; but if there are a few who quickly do each action, without, at this stage, much detailed thinking about the experience, then try to hold their absorption by giving them the next thing to go on to, at the same time leaving the possibility for more detailed activity by those whose absorption will carry it.)

TEACHER: Then you tidy up your breakfast things and carry them carefully to the kitchen – because its a holiday you may leave the washing-up until later in the day. Then you go to the front door, open the door and close it carefully after you. Then off you go, walking happily down the street in the warm sunshine. (*Now the teacher adds sound for the first time – a gay time-beat on the tambour. A final slightly louder beat stops them.*)

Now you are by a gate into a large field – climb over the gate – and run across the field through the long grass. (*Again sound – a slightly faster time-beat for running over the field – the sound slows down to bring them to a stop.*) At the other side of the field, you climb carefully through a very prickly hedge – mind the thorns on your clothes (*a more detailed and quieter experience after the running – no need for sound with this*). On the other side of the hedge is another big field with lots of ditches to jump over (*sound again for the running – and now the sound is fast time-beat together with short running climaxes for the leaps over the ditches; the two sounds together, at regular intervals, make a rhythm*) – and over the last ditch there is a wide river, with stepping stones across it (*sound again helps the crossing from one stepping stone to another – again the quieter experience after the running and jumping*) – and across the other side of the river is a huge pool with stones all round the edge of it – and you try to see if you can throw a stone right across the wide pool (*pause to allow several goes at this, according to absorption, in their own time*). Then you pick up a very large heavy rock and throw it right into the middle of the pool – watch the splash – and watch all the rings of water from the middle of the pool right to the very edges (*simple imaginative experience, with the body quite still*).

Then, at your feet you see a very strange stone – it is a blue stone – you pick it up – and start rubbing the mud off of it. As you rub the stone you find yourself beginning to turn around and around and around – and as you go round you feel yourself becoming larger and larger as you grow into a great giant. (*Add sound – a slow growing climax on the tambour or the cymbal – the sounds helps both the turning round and the growing into giants – a clear end to the climax of sound, helps completion of the growth.*) And the giant goes striding across the country-side (*long measured time-beat sounds, perhaps on the tambour*) and there is a tree in the way of the giant. Using all his strength, the giant uproots the tree and throws it away (*climax of sound again to help the full use of 'strength' for uprooting the tree and throwing it away*) and off he goes, striding across the fields again (*repeat of time-beat sound for giant walking – note also that teacher is now saying 'the giant', not 'you'; this helps fullness of concentration on being the character – sound abruptly stops, and the class stops as well*). And the giant looks down from his great height and sees he is by the pool again, and at his feet is a red stone. He bends down and picks up the stone – and starts to rub the mud off of it – and finds himself turning and turning and turning – and as he turns he is getting smaller and smaller and smaller – until he becomes a very small bird (*again the slowly growing climax of sound for the spinning and the changing from one character to another – a final loud sound completes the change*). This bird has never flown before, so he hops around for a bit – then he discovers he has wings and stands very still and begins to try to use them – to practice flying – and gradually the bird gets better and better at flying until at last he is able to go soaring off into the sky. (*Again, a very, very slow, rolling climax of sound for the practice at using the wings, and finally for taking off – then with up and down rolling rhythms, the bird is helped to fly – and a slow de-climax brings it finally back to earth.*) The bird finds itself by the pool and sees a yellow stone – and picks it up and starts to rub off the mud – and finds itself turning and turning and turning and growing very tall and thin and stiff – growing into a puppet (*again the slow climax of sound for the turning and growing into a puppet – the repetition of the formula has many values of its own, including the class's growing readiness for what is coming, and beginning to spin almost the moment that they pick up the new stone*) – and the puppet enjoys dancing by the pool (*and gay rhythms on the tambour or the drum help both the dancing and the 'stiffness' of the puppet – after a while we drop the volume of sound, without losing the gaiety of the rhythm, so that we* *can be heard over the sound, with the dancing still in progress.*) But the puppet is so sharp and stiff that as it dances it begins to get more and more stuck in the mud until it simply cannot move any more (*and we bring the volume of sound up again, still sustaining the rhythm – and then gradually slow down the rhythm to help the experience of dancing in the mud and getting more and more stuck – till finally the puppet cannot move any more – which happens with one final loud sound on the tambour*). And the puppet looks down at the mud and sees a green stone – he bends down stiffly to it, and begins to rub off the mud – and starts to turn and turn and turn – all the time changing back to being *you* again – (*Again the slow climax of sound for the turning and changing character; of course, if absorption is strong, they needn't yet turn back into themselves, but could have other experiences as other characters of contrasting kinds instead.*)

And now you suddenly realise that it is getting very late and you ought to be going home – so you wash the mud off your hands in the pool, and shake them to get them dry – then you turn homewards – and go back across the stepping stones over the river (*sound as on the outward journey*) – across the field with the many ditches (*sound again as on the outward journey – we need now only mention 'where' they are, not what they have to do*) – back through the prickly hedge with the thorns (*no sound – keep level with the general absorption*) – across the field with the long grass (*sound again as on the outward journey*) – over the gate and back home along the road, not quite so gay this time, because you are feeling a bit tired (*slower time-beat of sound will help the tiredness*) – through the front door and into the house – and then you lie down and have a lovely long rest. (*Final opportunity for stillness and quietness after all the many different experiences; it is always wise to end a class of this kind on a quiet note, so that there is no over-excitement before beginning other lessons.*)

Examples of Early Use of Music for Time-Beat, Rhythm and Climax

Earlier in this chapter the necessity for establishing a bond with the class – for full teacher control – was emphasised; some similar arrangement should be made in the early stages when using music, for example 'Whenever the music stops, "freeze" in whatever position you happen to be in'.

The following sequence could take place either in classroom or hall, depending on our readiness and the class's experience.

TEACHER: I am going to suggest various things for you to do with some music; the moment the music stops, freeze absolutely still in whatever position you are in – see if you can stop with the music. Ready. Type a letter to a friend, telling them what you were doing yesterday evening. (*Music in.*)

(We are starting with the simplest and smallest movements of all, simply using the fingers, achieving this through the simple imaginative idea of typing a letter; and in order not to have anyone in the class unable to do anything through not being quite sure what to put in the letter, we add a simple suggestion for that as well. After a few seconds – quickly fade out the music to silence.)

TEACHER: Now – larger typewriters. (*Fade back music again for another few seconds, then fade out again. There may be need for a reminder about 'freezing' the moment the music stops – but the reminder needs to be in the form of a challenge.*) Now – really enormous typewriters.

(*Music in again for a few seconds.*)

Now – you have a big sheet of paper in front of you and a paint brush in your hand – made dots all over the paper with the paint-brush. (*Music in.*)

(Depending on what music we are using for this – and there are suggestions at the conclusion of the examples – we will see a change now from a use of full notation with the fingers to an attempt to use the straightforward time-beat of the music; some may use double-time, some single; few will achieve mastery of either to start with. (Again we fade out the music.)

TEACHER: Now – dashes instead of dots. (*Music again for a few seconds.*) Now – a brush in each hand, making dots and dashes. (*Music again;*) Now – instead of paper, you have a huge wall in front of you and a large paint brush. Paint the wall with the brush. (*Music in – we are now, still with the same time-beat, getting a fuller use of the arms.*) A brush in each hand. (*Music again for a few seconds.*) Now – walls either side of you as well as in front. (*Music again.*) Now – the wall behind you. (*Music again.*) Now – the ceiling, still with a brush in each hand. (*Music again; if they have been sitting in their desks, some may stand for this.*) Now – back to typing your letter; tell your friend about your decorating. (*Music again.*)

At this moment, as is often necessary and wise in drama work, we bring the class back to an activity which they have already experienced. The familiarity of this sometimes helps confidence to grow more quickly, and on second and subsequent attempts there may be fuller mastery. In this case, a return is made to typing in order to sit down those who have stood up, and to give a more controlled, smaller experience if some of the class have been getting a little too excited with the larger opportunities provided by full use of the arms all round the body when painting the walls.

TEACHER (*Fade out music again*). Finish the letter and get it ready for posting. (*Music in.*) Now – you are on your bicycle, pedalling to the post office; (*Music in.*)

(From the use of fingers and arms and the upper part of the body, we are giving experience of using the legs; if the class is in desks in the class room here is an example of a perfectly logical way of developing some aspects of movement even within the limitations of space; in the sequence that follows, all of it on the bicycle, we might try a slightly different use of the music – instead of fading it out completely so that the class 'freezes' we might drop the volume just a little, enough for us to be heard over the music, but leaving the music loud enough for movement to continue uninterrupted. *So – we fade down a little.*)

TEACHER: You're going up a steep hill. (*Music right up again for a few seconds, then fade down a little again.*) You're reaching the top – then fast down the other side of the hill. (*Music right up again.*)

(When going up the hill, we find, perhaps, some of the class discovering and using the slower time-beat, and when going down the other side perhaps changing to a use of the fast time-beat. *Again we fade down a little.*)

TEACHER: Now – free-wheeling round lots of bends in the road. (*Music up again*) – and soon you are going to arrive at the post office and post your letter; (*Music up again; for the arrival, we might do a slow – very slow – fade down and out of the music*).

Many pieces of music by Winifred Atwell, Sandy Nelson and Leroy Anderson are suitable for sequences such as the above.

Many other short and simple sequences can be devised in the same way, with similar music, providing *imaginative* stimulus for using different parts of the body in different ways, together with the use of time-beat, rhythm and climax; always the imaginative stimulus will help movement experience; here are some other simple examples:

1. Making smoke patterns in the sky with flaming torches in either or both hands; this will help a full use of the arms.

2. Making patterns in the sand with one's feet; this will help a fuller use of the legs and feet.

Both of the above experiences can be attempted in many different ways, according to the kind of music being used; brittle, fast, staccato music will lend itself to angular movement, with a predominance of straight lines; slower, more flowing music, will lend itself to movement that contains greater flow in curves, etc.

In the early stages experiences need to be short and varied; but once there is a growth of confidence, longer passages of music can be used, without any interruption by teacher for additional suggestions. With people in secondary schools who have never done any improvised movement before, the early suggestions in this chapter regarding different experiences with a ball are an excellent way of beginning, and can be used with the first introduction of music, and occasionally returned to, both for reasons of confidence, and for more consciously intended use of time-beat, rhythm and climax. There is great skill and control in dribbling an imaginary ball to the time-beat and rhythm, and kicking goals to moments of climax – or in similar activities using the hands; and the experiences can be fast or slow motion, with appropriate speed of music.

It is often wise to consider the early stages of such work with older pupils in secondary schools arising from the use of their own records. They will often willingly bring these, and because of their familiarity and because they like them we are able more easily to foster interest and early attempt. It is then comparatively easy to extend experience once there is a basis of confidence and the beginnings of absorption. The fact that the music may not particularly appeal to us as music is unimportant if, by using such music, we are able to get things started. The type of dances or movement that teenagers do to such music again may not appeal to us – but this is unimportant if by allowing it we have a basis from which to start further developments. The fact that they move at all, limited as the type of movement may be for all kinds of reasons, at least shows us the basic inner need for an activity which gives relief from enforced cerebration and which uses the physical self rhythmically.

All kinds of inhibitions and self-conscious factors account for the paucity of movement within most such dances, but we do not overcome this by attempting to teach broader vocabularies of movement in the early stages; the emotional factors associated with confidence and overcoming self-consciousness must be dealt with first, and these can more readily be overcome through intuitive experience than through intellectual; it can take a great deal of time, enormous patience from the teacher and regular opportunities in an absolutely uncritical framework.

One excellent way of beginning with such groups is to use a Sandy Nelson drum record (e.g. *Let there be drums*) and to say to the class: 'You have just been given a set of drums as a present; go ahead and play them.' We fade in the music – movement is possibly confined to a small area just in front of each person; after a while we fade down the music and say: 'Now you have twice the number of drums'; again after a few seconds we say: 'Some of the drums can be played with the feet'; again a few seconds of full activity – by now more of the body is being used, and the area of space is being increased – and we fade down again to say: 'Now you have drums all round you – in front, to either side, behind you.' Later: 'Now there are drums hanging all round you as well.' Later: 'You play drums so much during the day that you even dream of playing drums, and in your dream there are drums of all kinds and sizes everywhere and you want to play them all.' Now more space is being used, perhaps the whole room. We might then put the speed of the record up from 45 r.p.m. to 78 r.p.m. stating: 'Now you have a nightmare of drum playing.' And then change the speed from 78 r.p.m. to 33 r.p.m., saying something like: 'And the nightmare suddenly changes so that you are playing in slow motion.' This takes the activity from the very fast and excitable to the slower and calmer, and may even bring with it a more deeply considered use of the drums with a corresponding growth of precision. Meanwhile, we have helped them to use more of their own physical selves more fully, and also to begin to use space a bit more fully.*

And it is the question of space that we need now to consider.

Discovery and Use of Space

So far, this chapter has been concerned with each person working mainly on his or her own, discovering a little about their own physical selves, using the body to stimulate the imagination or the imagination to stimulate movement; feeling for time-beat and rhythm and climax, together with attendant factors of personal physical control; evolving, through intuitive processes, a feeling for improvised dance and for physical characterisation, and the involvement of character in story form.

One has only to master a little of the potential of the body's movement before one discovers that body's dependence on space and the need for it; and within that space one is more than likely to come across other bodies also seeking space to use. This section is concerned with space as such, and the next section is concerned

---

* Those attempting improvised movement with teenagers owe a great debt to the film *West Side Story*; the nature of the film, its subject matter and the kind of characters portrayed, has done more, perhaps, than any other single factor, to assure tough and masculine teenage boys that there is nothing sissy about dance and movement work. Any potential teacher of drama and dance with such age groups is recommended to see the film for this reason, and, providing we are using 'similar' types of music in the early work in schools, it is often helpful even to suggest that the intention of the work is similar to that in *West Side Story*. Further mention of the relationship is made later in this chapter and also in chapter 9 on 'Fighting'.

with the factor of other people in that space. We have already met, almost unwittingly and unconsciously, both factors. Now let us consider space in more conscious detail. In the suggestions already made there has been necessity to move from the place where one is standing, and this in itself involves the use of space and therefore the unconscious and intuitive discovery of space. Every time we use such exercises as 'painting the ceiling' or 'making patterns of smoke and flames in the sky' we involve each person in the unconscious use of their body within the full space around their body; and if we use an experience which includes 'journey', as for example in the story which took everyone across various kinds of field from home to the edge of a pond and back again, we once more help the unconscious use of full space; in fact, it is wise that the first uses of space should be thus fully un-conscious, for the conscious use of space is often subject to factors of self-consciousness; it is for this reason that when we first use the hall rather than the classroom, some members of the class will retire to the farthermost corners, unable to come fully into the openness of the hall, let alone across its full width or length. What happens naturally on the floor space is thus always important for the teacher, as it gives indications of indivi-dual confidence, both from within and in relation to the work being done – possibly also in relation to their attitude to the teacher.

The moment comes when we can help the conscious discovery of space and a more conscious use of it; the process is a slow and gradual one – and in the early stages is worth doing for that reason alone, even though it leads very close to the next step, which is a full and conscious awareness of other people within the space.

EXERCISES TO HELP DISCOVERY OF SPACE

1. Suggest to the class that each person is standing in an upturned glass jar, enclosing them on all sides and above, so near to them that the slightest swaying of their bodies or standing on their toes and some part of them will touch the glass sides; close their eyes, and become aware of the jar by slight movement. Now, with a little stronger pressure at any point on the jar, they can

push the sides farther and farther away, until their hands are free to continue the pressing, above and all around them. Gradually they can push them so far away that they have to take several steps in any direction to meet the sides and push them still farther, and have to leap up to push the top farther away.

2. Starting as above, but this time with a sudden strong effort they are able to break the jar around them – only to find that they are in yet another; again they can break the sides of this one, only to find again they are in another, and so on, each jar a little larger than the last one.

3. A similar process to the above, only instead of something as solid as glass surrounding them, they are encircled by light curtains, which they can sweep easily aside with their hands – but there are layers of curtains to sweep aside, each layer a little farther away from them than the last.

4. A similar process to 3 above, only instead of light curtains, they are enclosed by the most delicate spider's webs, which they are anxious not to break, but are able very gently to move aside, layer after layer.

5. They are enclosed in some thick muddy substance, which they can push away from all round them with a great effort, but they have to keep pushing it away on all sides or else it will fill up again around them.

The above can be added to with many other examples; and most of the experiences can be enriched by a very, very slow climax on the cymbal; the pace of the climax can, to start with, follow their absorption, and then, gradually be extended in duration to stretch the fullness of the experience.

GROWING FROM NOTHING TO DISCOVERING SPACE

If we look back at the exercises on 'Growing from nothing' (see pp. 81–82), we can soon find ways of extending these to the discovery and use of more space, still within the imaginative sphere. Here are some examples:

1. Ask the class to curl up small; starting with one finger, they are going to become fire – growing from one finger until the whole of themselves, fingers and arms, whole body, legs, toes, everything is fire. And all round them in every direction is a mass

of combustible material which the fire is going to consume, e.g. they are in the middle of a forest, and they are going to burn up the whole forest. (Again sound will help stimulate and enrich this experience – a slow climax of sound for the full growth of the whole self as fire, and then great rolls of sound with moments of climax for devouring the forest–perhaps ending with a gradual fade to silence for the fire eventually dying out.)

2. Again start from curling up small; this time growing into a gigantic and enormously powerful weed that, once fully grown, begins to strangle and destroy all plant life around it. (Sound use similar to above.)

3. Again start from curling up small; this time growing into a gigantic monster that, once fully grown, begins to uproot trees and bushes and weeds and all other substances or buildings all around. (Sound use again similar to 1 above.)

4. Again start from curling up small; this time growing into some form of underwater life, large or small, beginning to move about over the ocean bed; the large or small are two different experiences and can both be useful – the large creature meandering slowly and the small type of fish darting about in all directions as it discovers more and more space under the sea. (Sound use again similar to 1 above; the cymbal would be most useful for the large creature and perhaps the drum or tambour for the small.)

5. Again start from curling up small; this time as a minute bird inside an egg; gradually the bird grows and grows until the egg can no longer contain it and it bursts out; then it discovers its wings and is very gradually able to fly, finally being able to fly everywhere. (Sound use again similar to 1 above, again with the fade down to silence at the end.)

Again, the above can be added to with many other examples. Suggestions have been made regarding the use of simple sound, but it is equally possible to use music as an accompaniment to each activity. Simple sounds on the drum or tambour are, as in previous exercises, the most useful and clearest forms of sound accompaniment, because with them the teacher can follow the rate of development of the class; sometimes stretching the length of any aspect of the experience, and at others following the average level of absorption. From this, the kind of music already suggested, with clear time-beat and rhythm, and with subtle control of the volume for different moments of experience, is the most useful.

But more difficult music can also be gradually introduced; this is considered in detail in the section 'Music, Emotion and Logic', on pp. 112.

Meanwhile, there is another approach to the discovery and use of space which is more direct and less dependent on imagination. For this, we simply invite the class to discover the space around them with their hands and fingers, even, perhaps, suggesting that they 'feel' the air all around them, above them and low down towards the ground – and then discover more and more space all round as they begin to move their feet a little in any direction from the space on which they are standing. We can invite them to explore outwards, to all points of the compass, to all corners of the room or to each wall of the room they are in. We might suggest that they trace, with their hands and fingers, the full shape of every aspect of the room, as though they were 'drawing in the air' that particular shape, in large or small dimensions according to whether they are remaining on one spot or moving about the room over a small or large area.

Here we are concerned with the direct conscious discovery and awareness of space – often, the imaginative experience, which leads to an unconscious full use of space, is the simpler way to begin; but as confidence grows, the direct approach is both valid and a necessary experience.

Early Work in Groups

There is no rule governing the moment at which a teacher decides the class can and should work in groups; personal discovery, personal effort, personal mastery with each member of the class working at one and the same time has been emphasised throughout. But even in the earliest stages there can be a kind of comfort in numbers, particularly with self-conscious people, and if this comfort is likely to help general confidence and wellbeing, then it is worth starting group work sooner than might appear logical.

At the same time it is wise to bear in mind that there will be no true group entity about such work – rather will there be a collection of individual efforts stimulated and sustained by the existence of the group, often with exchange of ideas or prompted suggestions during the actual doing of any particular activity. This is healthy; it is part of the process of learning to share ideas and to help each other – indeed, of learning to live and work together. It is also a basic root of the growth of sensitivity (see chapter 7.)

The following are suggestions for early group work in movement, with the use of music, for upper primary and secondary schools. The size of each group should be three, four or five; it is very difficult to work in a group larger than five until there has been a lot of experience in smaller groups. There are many important factors involved in this matter of making groups, but they need not concern us now, except to mention that we may often see quite 'natural social groupings' at this stage; people whom we are accustomed to seeing together 'out of school' will tend to work together, and it is wise for us to leave such grouping alone as it often leads to the fullest cooperation. (See chapter 7 for further details.)

EXAMPLE I

TEACHER: Get into small groups – three, four or five in each group.

In a moment I am going to put on some music for you to do a very short story with movement only; there won't be any speaking in the story, but you can have a short while to discuss what you want to do beforehand. This is what the story is about and who you all are in the story. You are all rather stupid and idiotic people – real fools, like the Goons or the Three Stooges. You all mean very well, but it doesn't matter what you try to do you usually make a mess of it or go about it in the wrong way. In this story, you have just robbed a bank, but you are so half-witted that the car you are using to escape in is a really ancient one – the kind used in the old crocks' race from London to Brighton. Now, have a moment or two in your groups to discuss for yourselves the kind of people you are and what they are going to do.

Your story starts at the moment you are leaving the bank with the swag and running from the bank to the car.

(We give them about a minute to discuss; at this stage they won't need more as there will be no detailed planning; they are not actors, they are not producers; they are not script-writers, they are youngsters who are being given, through a simple imaginative idea, an opportunity of using their bodies. If they are feeling self-conscious and 'silly' about movement, then we are helping them to overcome this by giving them a perfectly logical reason for being silly – the sillier the better. By these means we remove fear of failure and so build confidence. And because there are three, four or five in each group, there is no feeling of isolation; they are all in the same boat as it were, and able to help one another. After about a minute, the teacher continues):

TEACHER: Right, stand by. Each group make a still photograph of the robbers leaving the bank. (*By making a 'still photograph' we help the beginning; instead of having to work out the details of how to start – which will come at a later stage – they are able to start right in the middle of the main action of the story.*) As soon as you are all still, I will put on the music.

(A simple moment of training in personal control and coopera- tion – but the teacher, having said it, must stick to it, and not put the music on until all are still; the lack of stillness, if any, may not be anything at all to do with 'bad behaviour'; it may be a factor of self-consciousness; it may be the sudden sharing of a new idea; it may be that the teacher didn't allow quite enough time for discussion.)

TEACHER (*continuing*): As soon as the music starts, bring the still photograph to life. Remember, there is no speaking – only move- ment. And the moment the music stops, freeze the action into another still photograph.

Once they are all still, the music is brought in with full volume. Strong, loud music will help fulness of physical action. A fast section from an L.P. by Winifred Atwell is suggested; the time- beat and rhythm are very stimulating. Now, the class as a whole needs to be watched carefully to see how long they are able to sustain the episode; there will be a great deal more fun than absorption, but for the majority there will be a very free use of their physical selves, and the fun will help to win interest. As soon as it seems that many groups have finished – and at this stage, this may be very soon – the music is faded out and the action ends with another still photograph. Just as the still photograph helped over the problem of 'how to begin' so now it helps with the ending. At a later stage, they will evolve an actual and intended ending, which they will eventually be able to make coincide with the last bars of the music. But the music will be too long at this stage. It is worth allowing a few moments of generally cheerful and excited chatter before continuing, and certainly wise to make no comment nor criticism about any individual or group.

Some developments from Example 1

(a) Repeat the above – or any of the following – allowing speech as well as movement; or perhaps suggesting that when they hear the cymbal crash through the music they can add speech.

(b) Let each group make up its own episode to concern the same characters – nothing to do with bank robberies and cars. After they have done the new episodes, let each group state briefly what their story was. (Entirely informal conditions for this exchange of stories.)

(c) Repeat any one of the episodes after allowing a little time for discussion and 'polishing'; encourage consideration of 'what went well' before they discuss 'what needs improving'.

Here are some different episodes, using the same foolish characters, which have been useful with classes, many of them actually being suggested by the youngsters themselves.

— Decorating a room
— Serving at a banquet
— Sailing a boat
— Artists working in a studio
— Fitting up a suit of armour in a museum
— Erecting a 'do-it-yourself' shed
— Erecting a 'do-it-yourself' space-platform; either on land, fast action, or in space, slow-motion
— Erecting a tent, with or without a gale blowing
— Various aspects of cooking

— Laying a carpet
— Spring-cleaning
— Decorating a village hall for Christmas or a fete
— Dressing a shop window
— The out-patients or casualty department of a hospital.

But each class will have many other suggestions to make as we guide them from the directed stage, when the teacher is suggesting most of the ideas, to the creative stage, when, stimulated by one example, they are able to make up their own ideas. This process of direction, stimulation and creation arises in all aspects of work in drama.

EXAMPLE 2

The above examples are concerned with the physical boldness that arises from 'being foolish' or silly. A later stage, using the already discussed idea of the value of 'ugly' movement, but now incorporating mood and atmosphere as well as early attempts at characterisation, can develop around nightmares; indeed, a nightmare dance might follow immediately after the first 'goon' episode, using the same groups, but allowing them to listen to the record first (e.g. one of Sandy Nelson's drumming records) and then discussing what they are going to do to it. The fantasy elements of nightmares, and later of different (including pleasant) dream sequences – again help a full use of the body in circumstances entirely different from everyday movement, and logically utilise any such worries as self-consciousness or fears of failure in the realms of (so-called) good movement; the movement often is good in itself, particularly if we are not concerned in our own minds about its ability for communicating; the roots are intuitive and imaginative, not cerebral and technical.

EXAMPLE 3

An adventure story, incorporating a fight – but a fight in which there is no actual touching of any kind.

The reader may find it advisable at this stage to turn to the chapter devoted to fighting in order to clear up any worries about this factor. It suffices it to say here, that *fights will arise;* they probably will have done so in the examples already stated above; they invariably do arise, and are one major cause of many teachers giving up attempts to do drama work in schools. Sometimes, we win confidence and interest by ourselves actually suggesting a fight – which, with similar music to that already suggested for examples 1 and 2, may well range from the West Side Story kind of gang fight to a simple episode of savages doing a war dance around captives.

EXAMPLE 4

One excellent way of moving on to other and different themes is to introduce the idea of 'abstract opposites' as subject matters for dance dramas. Examples of these are: hot and cold; war and peace; hard and soft; water and fire; air and earth; past and present; fat and thin; short and tall; darkness and light; black and white; strength and weakness; rich and poor; health and sickness, and so on.

Within all of these, the very factor of opposites introduces a dramatic element of conflict, which stimulates ideas, and the factor of the ideas being carried out in movement or action only (as will be seen in a later chapter they can also form the basis of ideas for spoken improvisations – see chapter 8) impinges fully on the intuitive and emotional facets of personality, through the unconscious or conscious implementation of symbolism whereby 'great thoughts' can be given microcosmic unity. So can the perennial themes of mankind's highest endeavours be experienced by children and young people at the simplest and yet often the most meaningful of levels, through movement.

It is through such subject matter, no matter how primitive and unformed and uncommunicated the movement may be, that some of the full values of movement and dance can be found. In the early stages of such attempts, the type of music that is most useful may well be of the kind already mentioned; but gradually there can be progression to more difficult forms of music – indeed there might be so in all of the above examples. The adventure suggestion in Example 3 and the above concerning abstract opposites may provide the opportunity to move on to music such as Gustav Holst's *The Planets*; or even beyond this to music such as the conclusion of the fourth movement of Sibelius' Second Symphony. Other suggestions will be found in the Appendix. Once there is confidence to use the fullness of the movement of one's own body and confidence to use one's own ideas, then all kinds of music become valid for dance dramas; and often the wisest way of arriving at themes or subject matter is to let each group listen to the music and decide for themselves. As will be seen in the next chapter, it is important not to let movement and dance dominate drama – as they can so easily do – but nevertheless to see the full educational value of such an approach.

Music, Emotion and Logic

One of the objects of this book is to suggest that drama can help with the full, harmonious development of each individual through coordination of body, mind, heart and soul. One of the finest expressions of this coordination and harmony is music. With both drama and dance, the use of music is an important part of the process.

The essence of music is rhythm; the essence of all aspects of the earth, including human life, is rhythm. The use of the one develops an intuitive appreciation of the other, an awareness of the rhythm of life, partly conscious, partly unconscious. Intuitive sensibility depends on unconscious coordination of body, mind, emotion and spirit, the full expression of which is found in individual experience through dance and movement with music.

It has already been pointed out that music can and will stimulate the imagination; it will do more, for being stimulated by music coordinates the rest of the senses and the mind and the spirit without harnessing them, and without the necessity for technical mastery in order to harness them. Music also contains both emotional and intellectual logic (Webster definition: 'a chain of reasoning'), which is unconsciously absorbed during individual and intuitive physical movement to music.

Many educationists today sense a danger in the use of music and the resulting stimulation of emotions. Undoubtedly there are dangers, though these are perhaps only different in kind and possible degree from the dangers of emotional stimulation from highly competitive forms of sport, and even of competitive over-intellectualised training; the latter we are accustomed to, and the effects are subtle and insidious. But all too often there is nothing subtle about emotion when stimulated by music, and it is this breadth of emotion, often in apparent or actual negative forms, that creates concern for the educationist. The problem is exacerbated by some of the resulting influences of medical work in the realms of dance and drama therapy, part of which often includes the most exacting uses of highly evocative music. Medical research in this field is of the greatest importance, but it is equally important that we do not apply what amounts to 'treatment for the abnormal' as a general diet for the 'normal', not even in the best intended sense of prevention. There is a clear and funda-mental difference between *channelling emotional energy* and *indulging in emotional orgies*. For the abnormal, undergoing therapeutic treatment, an emotional orgy may well be the proper manner, at any rate for a time, of channelling both emotional and physical energy, but it needs to be handled very skilfully by a fully trained therapist. It is very unwise for teachers (drama specialists or otherwise) to apply the same fundamental approach, particularly if they lack basic therapeutic knowledge, to a normal class as part of general development through drama. Nevertheless, it is equally important not to become so cautious about potential in-herent dangers in the use of music that one does not use it at all. It is not a question of therapy, nor even of prevention, but a matter of actual and constructive growth. Therapy tends to be concerned with what is 'wrong' with people, thus creating the danger that one may miss the factor or factors that are 'right' within the same people. The drama teacher is or should be con-cerned only with what is right, no matter how infinitesimal this quality may be; thoughts of prevention, though much more positive and constructive, tend again to a presupposition that there must perforce be potential for 'going wrong', and so can again miss the necessary concentration on seeking out what is right.

Constructive growth includes the release of and the exploration of one's emotional self. An educationist's fear of emotion is nearly always embedded in fear of negative emotion and the resulting action or effect of that emotion; hate, greed, sensuousness and so on are all emotions that create this fear. We are prepared to accept love and compassion and kindness and tenderness – all the positive emotions – but tend to assume that these will automatically exist if we succeed in avoiding all manifestation of the negative emotions. This is not so. The positive emotions need equal opportunity to be discovered and practised – without opportunity and practice they will not exist either in depth or in confidence. But the negative emotions will, seemingly, break through, or manifest themselves in one way or another (often subtly and insidiously) no matter how much we ignore them. It is not giving practice to negative emotions to allow them to come to light within the legal and constructive framework of dramatic opportunity – it is doing the opposite, casting light on what in fact needs to be controlled (by practice) and throwing into high relief the opposite kind of experience resulting from positive emotion. We cannot, therefore, give practice in the use of positive emotions without taking the risk of fully using negative emotions. What is important in drama, however, is that these emotions, either negative or positive, can be guided and channelled constructively, so that the negative are seen as negative and, even if only at an unconscious level, mastered, whilst the positive emotions become familiar and, again at a personal level of control, readily available. But we cannot gain the positive without accepting the many risks involved in discovering and mastering the negative. One is not possible without the other, and the positive will often develop simply in contrast to the negative and because of the 'legal' opportunities to 'behave illegally', which only drama can provide without any harm either to individuals or to society as a whole. Occasional and constructively intended permissive opportunity to behave illegally does not teach and consolidate illegal behaviour – indeed, it will do exactly the opposite by creating simple emotional relief and release and therefore dissipate temptation to actual illegal behaviour in real life.

Music will release and heighten emotional experience, both positive and negative. By channelling that emotional and physical energy, children are provided with a constructive opportunity for mastering emotion instead of gradually and insidiously becoming mastered by it. Part of this opportunity arises from use of the mind – or, more correctly, the intuition – under the guidance of the teacher, who must be concerned with stimulating positive and creative activity at however simple a level, never trying to impose 'desirable results', yet always helping to increase horizons of thought and experience rather than allowing wallowing in the immediate and the shallow.

But the experiences and mastery of emotion through the use of music is only part of the overall value of this kind of dramatic experience. It was suggested at the beginning of this section that music is, in its very nature, the finest expression of the coordination of body, mind, heart and soul; furthermore, this coordination is indivisible and its corresponding intuitive experience, both for the individual and the group, is also indivisible, and includes within it a natural development of an awareness of processes of logic that are as much of importance to mental growth as to physical and emotional. Many of the blockages in some aspects of mental growth are physical, emotional and spiritual, and music provides an opportunity for releasing in part or whole both the immediate blockage and some of the root causes, allowing, even if only momentarily, the full, harmonious use of the whole of oneself. Within such moments, the basic structure of musical form, with its inherent logic, impinges on the mind at unconscious levels; the process is again intuitive, but by the process the intuition is enriched and the logical and deductive steps that occur instantly through the intuitive process are helped a little to become more conscious, so that in time intellectual reasoning processes become more defined. In drama this process is often seen quite clearly because music, more than any other source, will help the discovery of form in drama – of, at its simplest, the early awareness of beginning, middle and end. But one of the basic needs within human beings who, by their very nature, are caught in an immediacy of the moment, with an awareness of the past but no knowledge of the future, is to have experiences of wholeness of life, a perspective or God-like view of a whole pattern of existence. This basic need is behind the desire to be audience at a theatre, and, microcosmically, part of the basic need is satisfied.

The basic need in children and young people is equally inherent, but different in kind, because of the child's capacity to observe (and aspiration to be of) the adult world. Actual doing of drama, rather than being merely audience, gives a full and enriching fulfilment to the basic need, again microcosmically; and experience of doing drama to music adds depth to the experience. If, for example, a two hour play shows the full range of logical development of life and relationships, this is one level of microcosmic experience; but the same quality of experience might well be contained within the more concentrated span of a passage of music the full duration of which is only four or five minutes; the microcosmic level is changed, but the experience can still be very much the same, and what a play takes two hours logically to unfold, the passage of music will unfold, in no less logical terms, in a much shorter period; but because a play depends on words, the demands for intellectual understanding can, for young human beings, overstretch their capacities for following the fullness of the logic, and make demands mentally that outweigh the harmony of all aspects; music, and doing drama or dance to music, avoids this, retains the balance, and therefore provides experience at all levels.

The emotional experiences will include experiences of mood and atmosphere of every kind – and of life, for all humans are made up of moods and atmospheres, the majority of which have an inner source resulting from outer causes; often the outer causes cannot be changed, so that the individual has to learn to rely on inner resources to create change from within – adapting oneself to the causes in such a manner that one is able to rise above the predominant mood. The logical structure of music gives practice at the use of these inner resources, helping each individual to be less dominated by the external causes of inner emotional reaction. And further, music will, through the concentration of this inner process, give simple and momentary experiences of the spiritual nature of man, for it is this transcending experience that symbolises man's spiritual capacities; except in moments of severe crisis, this transcending experience is seldom observable; but in the microcosmic, concentrated experience of drama with music it is not only observable, but, and this is the root essence of the importance of this work in education, it is also *created* by the individual and each individual in relationship to the group. We are told that man is made in the likeness of God; the full significance of this would seem to lie in man's capacity, like God's, to be creative – and not only creative in his manipulation of external and material factors, but creative in the discovery and use of the energy of all facets of personality, the ability to master these and to learn to live in harmony with his own nature.

6

Speaking

SPEECH AND PERSONALITY

Speech has its roots in the very essence of personality, for the individual, for the family, for the community, for every regional grouping of communities, for nations. Because the roots are in personality, the basic necessity in any consideration of speech as part of drama in education must be linked to thoughts on developing the whole person. For the purpose of this book, speech is another point on the circle, a part of each human being, and, like the other parts, one that needs practice at one's own level in order to reach towards each individual's maximum fulfilment. But of all the many points on that circle, speech is the one most obviously concerned with 'communication' and therefore most readily thought of in terms of audience.

The factor of audience leads to concern from teachers that children should make certain kinds of sounds, many of them often as foreign to the children's own background as would be a foreign language, and further that these sounds should be made with strong volume in order to be heard either from the front of the class or down the length of the hall. In addition to these problems, the children are confronted also with the worst discomforts of self-consciousness, listened to by the whole class and expecting criticism of factors which, within themselves, they feel to be as natural as breathing and eating and having a roof over their heads – as natural in fact as their own home environment and their family roots and traditions.

Speech has been described by many fine teachers as 'the music of the soul'. As such, it is important not to interfere at the wrong moment in the wrong way, otherwise the effects can well extend beyond the factor of speech and undermine many other facets of personality. One of the most odious notions held by some educationists is the idea of 'catching them while they're young'. The odium is seen by all within such factors as political indoctrination, but is far more subtle where the arts are involved, including the art of living, part of which art is to be able to talk confidently and easily within ordinary human communication, putting one's own thoughts and feelings and imaginings into one's own words, and at the same time being able to listen to and to enjoy the communication of others. To believe that children will 'talk proper' if they are forced to speak in a particular way from an early age is to impose restrictive rituals which, though they may achieve results with a few children, are more likely for the majority to create fear, muddle and distaste for speaking at all, and to undermine the many root factors that could be developed if they were accepted for what they are – fundamental aspects of personality. The difficulties usually arise from teacher's trying to achieve short term results by aiming immediately at *end* results, with the imagined end product arising from the premise of an entirely different intention. We take religious instruction in school without any thought of turning all children into parsons; we introduce number without thought of all being scientists (that is still *nearly* true); we introduce various forms of sports without thinking of professional futures in sport – and yet we so often approach the arts as though we were intent on producing professional actors, and we approach speech as though we were concerned with the growth of professional orators on the one hand, or, on the other, as though the one hope of succeeding in the rat race of a competitive civilisation depended on an ability to 'talk proper', irrespective of the personal, emotional strains so often involved when attempting to sustain an artificial or partly artificial mode of speech.

Undoubtedly the factor of speech can affect future employment, though there are generally more liberal attitudes to this factor. The teacher's responsibility must include the possibility – but not by ignoring the potential harm that can arise from implied or actual attacks on human roots, no matter how well intentioned these may be. No teacher today would suggest to a child of any age group that it should leave home because the physical environment of that home is unpleasant or even because father is a drunkard and mother a loud-mouthed wastrel; nor would a teacher, even in such extreme circumstances, say, for example, 'I don't like your father and mother and I don't like the way they behave'; to do so would be to strike at the very roots of family life, leaving the child 'a fish out of water'. But the results can be precisely the same if a teacher says, in effect: 'I don't like the way your father and mother and the rest of your family talk, and you're going to have to learn to talk differently from them.' The problem of speech becomes less difficult if, once again, our premise is that of developing children rather than speech, and if we consider some of the factors of speech that develop in the pre-school child from babyhood.

Feeling for Language

It has already been suggested that children hear sound emotionally, not intellectually; during the early part of life, the speech music root is fully formed, based on the speech music of the family. This root will lead to the speech music that the child itself will naturally make, even from the very earliest months experimenting with the making of sounds and practising talking. The processes are intuitive and unconscious, and can be interfered with by being made either cerebral or conscious too often or too soon through such factors as family becoming 'audience' to early speech attempts and laughing *at* some of the delightful errors that arise, or else from too much of the correction type of remark, particularly in the middle of conversation flow. The intuitive pleasure in the music of language, together with the intuitive absorption of greater vocabulary, grow in parallel through simple and natural practice. Mass media of communication such as radio and television expose the child to further new musical sounds and more new words, many of which are unconsciously absorbed and used, irrespective of any understanding of meaning. The musical pattern of language is always more important for young children than meaning, which is why they often use made-up words or sounds to complete musical structure of sentences, whether or not the additions make any difference to actual meaning. The child's words may not be precise or accurate for a long period of time, particularly in terms of subtleties of verb changes etc., but it will be rich in its actual expression.*

This emotional feeling for and use of language is what the child brings to school from the start. Indeed, it would be little short of the truth to suggest that children learn more about language and speech in their first five years than they need to for the rest of their lives – for in those first five years they are beginning from scratch, whereas from any given point afterwards they are concerned with developments and enrichments and other forms of mastery of what *already exists*. So that with speech, as with the other points on the circle, we return to the thought that drama in education is concerned with developing and enriching factors that *already exist*, different as each factor may be for each individual. The importance of this cannot be stressed too often or considered too deeply if we are to avoid the mistake of imposing new facets in a vacuum. Furthermore, in those first five years there are none of the tensions which ultimately bar each child from the natural rhythms of life, including the rhythms of breathing and thus the rhythms of speech, the rhythms of intuitive thinking (leading ultimately to deductive thinking), the rhythms of movement, and so on.

Emotional Mastery

The function of drama where speech is concerned is quite simple. Basically, the teacher is concerned with developing personal confidence to speak at all, putting one's own thoughts and ideas and feelings into one's own words in an wholly uncritical atmosphere, until speech as such – one's own speech from one's own music

---

* Some teachers have drawn attention to the fact that very often the vocabulary of children is much richer before attendance at school, when the necessity for spelling correctly, for writing down words and for punctuation leads to a natural and wise preselection of words, throwing off the richer and more complex in order to master the new skill. The case, including the factor of grammatical accuracy, is similar where speech is concerned. Too much cerebral concern for grammar, for volume, for quality of vowels etc. leads, at its ultimate worst, to not speaking at all for fear of making mistakes and being taken to task for them – and the worst form of taking to task in speech is public exposure to the rest of the class; at least mistakes in written work can be kept more private.

background – is fully mastered in personal terms. This is emotional mastery, deeply interrelated to the factor of individual human dignity, family unity and community awareness and acceptance. Out of this deep root of confidence comes the opportunity to realise quite dispassionately and fearlessly the existence of many other ways of speaking, including 'good' speech, or 'standard English' or 'Queen's English' – but also including all the many different forms of regional speech with which the English-speaking world is so richly endowed. Out of the awareness, coupled with the constant exposure to these other forms through mass media, can be stimulated a simple interest in attempting to use them oneself, first through the opportunities provided by drama to be people other than oneself – to be the people who speak in those other ways – and ultimately through a straightforward ability to appreciate the significant appropriateness of when to use certain kinds of speech, not from artificial, insincere, snobbish or expedient evaluations of the situation of the moment, but from a simple and real sensitivity to other people. Through this approach we achieve not an unintended bilingualism but an intended, enjoyed and fully appreciated multilingualism. Unintended bilingualism arises from the attempt to impose one type of speech on a group of people whose speech root is different, without allowing for the fact that the latter has arisen from nature and cannot be uprooted; intended multilingualism arises when we build confidence in the root speech, and offer a variety of alternatives without implying that we wish to uproot that which is indigenous. Further, by acceptance of and encouragement of the basic indigenous speech, enrichment of that way of speaking is fully developed, and it will be added to other ways of speaking only if it is clear that the potential enrichment exists within the former and not only within the latter.

How is this to be achieved? There is only one way, and that is through abundant and infinitely patient opportunities to practice speaking always within an uncritical framework. Drama will provide, in many varied ways, the opportunities for practice – and most of the remainder of this chapter is concerned with suggestions as to the kind of practical work that might be attempted. Already a great deal has been suggested. If the reader will recall the suggestions for practical work in the foregoing chapters, it will be noticed that over and over again the suggestion is made that the class be allowed to talk about this, that or the other experience, either in pairs or in threes or in small groups. This simple, private opportunity to put one's own thoughts into words is all part of the factor of practising speaking; there cannot be too many such opportunities. The following practical suggestions are concerned with direct rather than incidental opportunities to speak.

Beginnings

Whatever the age group, if there has been little or no practice at speaking, it is wise to begin with the whole class all talking at the same time. In this way the factor of self-consciousness is fully eliminated because no one is exposed to audience. We must expect little absorption to start with, and little ability to sustain a flow of conversation on any topic for very long, so it is wise for the teacher to be prepared with many different topics to suggest. As confidence grows, there will often be a tendency to over-excitement, with a corresponding increase in the volume of sound made by the whole class, and to counter this it is wise to include in the suggested topics of conversation, or the circumstances, logical reasons for speaking more quietly.

One such logical reason, particularly when working in the classroom or in a hall with classrooms surrounding, is the fact of other classes working at different subjects and not wishing to be disturbed. Occasionally pointing out this kind of circumstance is all part of social training. On the other hand, we must be ready to accept a certain amount of noise in drama, particularly when absorption is strong and the class may simply not realise that they are making 'a noise'. Certainly the factor of noise should not be used as an excuse for not doing the activity or for avoiding speech aspects of drama; there is inevitable noise from many other classes in the hall, and usually an impossible din from kitchen workers, all of which has to be tolerated as part of the general work of the school. Every opportunity should be taken to explain to other members of staff the reason for the noise, in its fullest educational terms; by these means the antagonism of other members of staff is usually placated; as one teacher put it: 'I am never disturbed by sounds from another class if they are clearly intended, no matter how strong the sounds may be.'

With younger children – even right up to the first year of secondary schools, one way of beginning with everybody talking at the same time is through some general group activity such as a market-place. A quick discussion on what kinds of things might be sold in a market is followed by each person deciding for themselves what they are going to sell, and then the whole room is used as the market, with everybody calling out their own particular wares. If there is any self-consciousness about beginning, this will be overcome if gramophone music accompanies the start; the sound of the music covers the 'awkward silence' and helps people to start talking – and once they have started, the music can be slowly faded out as there is no longer any dependence on it. If voices become too loud, then the activity is stopped by the teacher (it is wise to have the tambour or cymbal on hand for immediate control, including perhaps one or two practices at stopping as soon as they hear the sound), who then suggests some logical reason for speaking more quietly – e.g. a hospital to one side of the market-place has sent a message to say they have some very sick patients who need rest and quiet. The activity is started again and this time will be quieter, with each person imposing *their own personal control* over the volume of sound they are making. As has already been mentioned, and cannot too often be emphasised, the factor of personal control is a vital part of personal development and general social and emotional training; drama provides natural opportunities for this kind of development, but teachers must not expect immediate full results and be disappointed if they do not get them: for some children, depending on such circumstances as whether they have ever been allowed to be responsible for their own actions, the development might take some while; but it will have deep roots when finally achieved through these means.

OTHER GROUP OPPORTUNITIES FOR TALKING:

Railway stations, bus stations, airports, various types of café or restaurant, supermarket and other kinds of shopping centre, various kinds of sports grounds or stadiums (with or without the actual sporting activity being brought in at some point, e.g. at a boxing stadium there might be included an imaginary contest, with the teacher supplying the sound of the beginning and end of the round), bowling alleys, fairgrounds, amusement arcades, night clubs, circuses, the seaside, parks.

Developments

Simply to use one of the above as a way of starting people talking might be the only immediate intention, the whole exercise lasting no more than two or three minutes. But one development might be to divide the class into two groups, one half being – in the case of the market-place – people who are involved with selling, the other half people who are shopping; then the experiences can be reversed and the shoppers become sellers and the sellers become shoppers.

The teacher might then decide that this was a useful moment * to build a short dramatic scene by introducing certain circumstances of conflict. Ideas will come from the class if the teacher asks for them. For example:

TEACHER (*stopping the activity*): What sort of thing might happen to stop all the buying and selling in the market-place? Anyone any suggestions to make?

VARIOUS ANSWERS: A car knocks somebody down. Somebody steals something. Someone gets murdered. A lion breaks loose. A big storm comes. Someone knocks over a fruit stall. People start quarrelling.

The teacher selects from the various ideas the one that seems easiest to deal with, if new to the work, or the one that seems to provide the best opportunity for the class, irrespective of how easy or not it may be to carry out the idea. (Again this cannot be too often reiterated; the teacher's confidence is often the most

* The teacher needs always to be on the lookout for such moments. They arise quite unexpectedly, so that although it is necessary to start each drama class with a specific intention or series of intentions, and wise also to start with very clear ideas of particular exercises to do, it is equally important to grow towards full flexibility, so that some aspects of the work can arise spontaneously from the work the class is doing.

125

important – and the most vulnerable – factor in early drama lessons, and it is always wise to keep to work with which one feels safe.) Of the alternatives above the easiest to carry out, because it affects everybody in a similar way, is the storm; so the market is started again, and the teacher, using either the tambour or the cymbal, supplies the sounds of the storm, leaving it to the class to decide on and carry out what seems right to them when the storm comes – they may pack up their stalls, they may simply run away; in either case, we have provided a new experience, including finding a simple ending for the incident. In certain circumstances – e.g. if a great deal of interest and enjoyment has been generated – it might then be wise to try out one of the other ideas from the class, discussing, in whatever detail is necessary, the happening itself before attempting it, and continuing to build the incident in so far as general absorption is ready for the extension.*

Other developments, all concerned with practice in speaking, arising from the market-place, might include:

WORKING IN PAIRS

A quarrel about the price or quality of an article
Suspicion about 'false coins', or some aspect of thieving
Searching for a very rare article
Trying to explain exactly what one wants and so on.

Still working in pairs, but beginning to be characters different from oneself

A bad-tempered man buying from a deaf stall keeper

* If it is intended to use some such experience as the market-place as a way of getting talking going, it is wise to think over any developments one might make, including a way of ending; then, if having decided on a particular ending – e.g. the storm – it might be advisable to use that particular idea, even if it is not among the suggestions that actually come from the class; it is of course possible to stimulate the suggestion by asking something like 'What about the weather? Could anything happen where the weather is concerned that might stop the buying and selling?' This will almost certainly bring the suggestion of a storm, and one proceeds from there. This is not being dishonest to the classes' ideas, if the teacher is in the early stages of the work. At the same time, it is important not to give any impression of rejecting the other ideas as being 'no good' or as being inaccurate or stupid – e.g. we may not feel the idea of 'a lion breaking loose' has much to do with a market-place; but it may well have something to do with it in the child's mind, and nothing will be gained by our making any derogatory comment on the idea.

A haughty duchess disliking a fish stall, arguing with a very proud fishmonger

A very shy person talking to an angry seller

A very shy seller talking to an angry customer

A very poor person trying to make a bargain with a skinflint.

In the next chapter the question of characterisation as such is considered in more detail; where these simple speech exercises in pairs or small groups are concerned, the attempt to be somebody different from oneself is useful because it is often one's personal self that is shy about speaking, and if one is somebody else the process may be a little easier or may contain logical justification for the inability to speak; so, to be an urgent salesman in a market-place may help speech to start flowing; to be a shy and timid customer may make one feel more comfortable about not being able to say much, and so on; many are the values of the teacher suggesting that the class be other people. However, it is important for the teacher to bear in mind that this is not theatre training, concerned with the communication of detailed characterisation; there will in fact be little such characterisation in the early stages, and what there is will quite likely be very much overdone in a kind of burlesque or parody of the character. There will be little absorption and practically no ability to sustain the character for more than a few seconds or minutes; and if audience were allowed, the character would either die away altogether, or, through exhibitionism, become even more burlesqued. If the teacher keeps constantly in mind that all that is being attempted is the provision of simple opportunity to practice speaking, and avoids all theatre considerations (including, of course, all temptations to demonstrate or otherwise show how such and such a character would behave), then all these pitfalls will be avoided and, little by little, confidence in speaking will grow. Eventually, over a period of time that will be in proportion to the amount of opportunity provided, the confidence will become really strong, bringing with it an easy flow of speech that is sincere and unhesitating.

It is wise for each teacher to make and have readily available a long list of different topics of conversation to use with the class divided into pairs. The list should be appropriate to the particular age range with which the teacher is concerned. In the following list – which is intended as a stimulus and contains therefore only a minute proportion of possible material – it will be noted that there is, for each suggestion, either a simple intended conflict or a slight difference in character, even if the difference is really only one of mood. This approach is often most valuable in the early stages because it provides a little firmer intention to the duologue. In the first topic suggested below, A and B are arguing about what programme to watch on television: the resulting conflict gives greater purposefulness to the speech and therefore helps the flow. When there is firm confidence, there would be no need for the suggested conflict and the exercise could be set simply as 'A and B are discussing what programme to watch on television'. The class is divided into pairs, calling themselves A and B. It is important to feel flexible about changing the pairs every now and then, so that each person in the class has an opportunity to work with many other people. This should not be forced, particularly in the early stages, as often the most fluent work, with the greatest degree of confidence, arises from people working in close friendship groups.

TOPICS

Two or three examples are given under each group heading.

Domestic

A and B are talking about what programme to watch on television; A wants to watch channel 9, B is determined to have channel 1.

A wants to go out for the evening; B wants to stay at home.

Discussing changing round the furniture; A wants the table by the window; B wants the couch by the window.

Discussing a meal; A wants one dish; B wants something quite different.

A is mother (or father); B is son or daughter; the parent is complaining about the state of the young person's room; or the friends they keep; or the hours they keep.

All of the above, and many of the following, could be repeated, with characters reversed.

Holidays

A and B are planning a holiday; A wants to go to the seaside; B wants to go to the country.

On holiday: A wants to go sightseeing by rail; B wants to go by coach.

A wants to join the Mods and Rockers battle; B thinks it a waste of time.

After the holiday: A thinks it the best holiday ever; B thinks they could have had a much better time.

Travel

A wants to travel overnight; B thinks its more interesting by day.

A wants to save time by going by plane; B thinks the sea trip would be more in keeping with the holiday as a whole.

A wants to eat foreign dishes; B wants to stick to English food.

A thinks everything foreign better than England; B feels the reverse.

Sport

A thinks cricket is boring; B thinks it is the best of all sports.

A thinks so-and-so will win the Cup; B thinks another team will.

A wants to play on Saturday in an amateur game; B wants to watch the professionals.

A thinks sport should be allowed on Sundays; B does not agree.

Space Travel

A thinks we shall soon have people on the moon; B does not think it is possible.

A thinks there is life on another planet somewhere; B does not.

A thinks there are such things as flying saucers; B does not.

A would like to go to the moon; B would prefer to stay on earth.

Zoos

A thinks it is wrong to put wild animals in cages; B thinks the wild animals do not mind and that zoos are interesting.

A likes to see animals 'in the flesh'; B thinks it is more interesting to see films about them.

A has never been to a zoo and does not want to go; B is persuading A.

Weather

A thinks the weather recently has been just right; B thinks it has been awful.

A likes thunderstorms; B doesn't like them and thinks them dangerous.

A thinks atom bombs cause bad weather; B thinks that is rubbish.

A believes the weather forecasts to be very accurate and helpful; B thinks they are inaccurate and never helpful.

Crime

A and B are two crooks planning a robbery of a bank; A wants to break in at night time; B thinks it would be easier by day.

A and B are two detectives planning to prevent the bank robbery; A believes they will try the robbery at night; B believes by day.

A and B have just come out of prison; A wants to 'go straight'; B wants to commit another crime.

A and B are two magistrates considering a 'sentence'; A thinks they should be lenient; B thinks they should teach a thorough lesson.

Building

A and B are planning to put up a shed in the garden; A thinks a wooden shed would be best; B believes a brick one would be wiser.

A thinks modern buildings are ugly; B thinks they are not ugly.

A would like to live in an old country cottage; B would like to live in a luxury modern flat.

A thinks it is a waste of money building new cathedrals; B doesn't.

Fuel

A likes the old-fashioned coal fire; B prefers central heating.

A thinks all coal mines should be shut and atom power be used; B thinks we shall never do without coal.

A likes steam trains; B prefers electric.

A likes to cook by gas; B prefers electricity.

A likes jet aeroplanes; B prefers piston.

At the Fairground

A and B have two shillings left; A wants to go on the dodge 'em cars; B wants to go on the roller-coaster.

A likes the games of skill (darts, rifle ranges etc.); B prefers the more mechanical factors;

A thinks the big-dipper is dangerous; B does not believe this.

The above list will give some indication of the limitless possibilities of finding different material for simple discussion or argument in pairs. It should be noted that all are concerned with A or B 'liking' or 'believing' or 'thinking' or 'wanting', providing opportunity for simple verbal expression of a *personal* emotional or intellectual view. In some instances, indication has been made of being someone else, but all of the exercises could be approached from this point of view, so that, for example, the weather might be discussed by two seamen or two farmers, fuel might be discussed by two old age pensioners or two government planners; the introduction of character will open up each topic to new and different points of view, at the same time still providing the opportunity for practising talking.

FURTHER DEVELOPMENTS

All of the above suggestions have been concerned with work in pairs; under each of the headings it is possible to develop the same kind of opportunities in groups, according to the readiness of the class. Early groups should have no more than three people per group, growing by natural stages to four, five, six or seven; generally speaking, five is quite a large enough group to work in, as beyond that number demands a very experienced sensitivity. By trial and error the teacher is able to gauge the readiness of the class for particular group sizes (see next chapter). It is always worthwhile to experiment to see if there is readiness for larger groups, returning to smaller if the evidence indicates that the development has been attempted too soon.

If we consider one further example from each of the previous headings, it is possible to see how the developments, both of character and of the larger group, can arise from what has already been attempted in pairs.

Domestic

A family (the size of family depending on the size of group the teacher is attempting to work with) is arranging the evening: father wants to do the pools; mother has ironing to do; the son wants to watch channel 9 on television; one daughter wants to watch channel 1; another daughter has homework to do and wants the television off; granny wants to rest; grandfather wants to read. They discuss the arrangements.

Holidays

A family (the size again depending on the teacher's intention and the class's readiness) is discussing or planning a summer holiday: mother wants to go to Butlin's; father would like to have a caravan; the son wants to stay in a boarding house at the seaside; the daughter wants to stay on a farm in the country; another daughter doesn't mind but wants to bring a friend of hers; granny wants to stay at home and go to different places each day; grandad wants to go abroad. They discuss.

Travel

A family (the same factors governing the size) are going to cross the channel: father wants to go by rail and sea; mother wants to take the car; the son wants to fly; the daughter doesn't want to go at all; another daughter wants to go by air ferry with the car; grandma doesn't mind as long as they travel overnight; grandad wants to travel by day.

Sport

A group of sporting fans (again the size of group depending on teacher's intention and the class's readiness) are discussing the relative merits or popularity of their particular favourite sport – cricket, football, rugger, boxing, wrestling, swimming, tennis, etc. Or the same topic discussed by a group of actual sportsmen.

Space Travel

A group of astronauts, together with their engineers, are planning a landing on the moon, including what to expect and what to take with them.

Zoos

A group of people, some of whom are experts, others of whom are zoo workers, are planning to build a new zoo, which will be pleasant for the animals as well as exciting for the customers.

Weather

The crew of a small ship are discussing whether or not to continue a voyage which will take them through a particularly severe storm, or whether to turn back; some have experienced such a storm before, others haven't.

Crime

A group of crooks are planning a robbery; or a group of police and detectives, having heard of the intended robbery, are planning its prevention.

Building

Some architects are discussing with a group of people who need a particular new building, what form the building should take.

Fuel

A varied group of people – housewives, government smoke abatement officials, atomic experts, coal mine engineers etc. are planning a new town.

Fairground

A group of people are discussing a special fair they are going to run for charity on August bank holiday.

N.B. It is always useful to keep in mind the family unit for these groups; such a unit is familiar to all members of the class, including a realisation of the many different points of view that can exist within one family.

The above development into group work is not only concerned with opportunities for practising speaking, but is also very much concerned with the development of simple improvisations within the general class drama, linking with the exercises in Imagination in Chapter 4.

Developing a Crowd Scene

Linked with the improvisation potential, briefly mentioned above, but still mainly concerned with opportunity for speech work, is the possibility of building a crowd scene, stage by stage, working upwards from pairs, through smaller and larger groups, to a scene involving the whole class. The class will not be ready for such a scene until it has had practice at simpler work in pairs – and the gauge to readiness is found both in the degree of absorption within the work as a whole and the degree of flow in speaking; once these are strongly established, it is worth attempting such a scene, even if the attempt should indicate that perhaps the moment has been chosen too soon. Below, one example is given in some detail, and then suggestions for other topics follow without any detail. The detailed suggestion is shown in its various stages of development.

STAGE 1

In pairs. Two factory workers are grumbling about conditions of work: long hours, bad canteen arrangements, low wages, dangerous machinery. (Each topic of grumbling might be suggested separately, or all the topics suggested at the same time.)

STAGE 2

Each pair joins up with another pair. In fours, the grumbling continues and now includes discussion of what should be done about the conditions, the main thought of which is that the manager of the factory should be forced to do something to improve them.

STAGE 3

The groups of four begin to join up into larger groups, arguing about the best way of forcing action from the manager. Each larger group decides they should at once go to the manager's house and demand that he listens to their complaints and does something about them.

STAGE 4

The first three stages are repeated, leading to the whole group walking to the manager's house and calling for him, perhaps reaching some kind of general chant, such as 'We want the manager, we want the manager', etc.

So far, we are concerned only with class *speech* opportunities, working upwards from pairs to the whole class working together as one unit. The teacher may decide that one of those 'special moments' has arisen when it would be both wise and possible to develop the exercise further into an actual dramatic scene. In this case, and providing there are one or two people who could bear the brunt of the responsibility,* then perhaps the following might be developed:

The different stages are incorporated as one scene: in the canteen of the factory, during the break, pairs of friends are grumbling; they join up with other pairs, and then the smaller groups join into larger, until all are working as one unit; they decide to see the manager(s) at once and go straight from the canteen to the manager's home; they call for the manager(s); he or they arrive; there is a great argument, the workers hardly letting the manager(s) get out a word in their own defence; suddenly one of the workers picks up a brick and throws it at the manager(s); the brick hits the manager; the crowd are shattered and deflated by this, as they did not intend to go so far – and they go back to work, talking in pairs or in small groups about the incident.

The additional circumstances within such an episode do not take long to build and are an enriching experience, taking a simple intention of speech exercises to the kind of exciting and stimulating

* The factor of 'one or two who can bear the brunt of responsibility' is always important. All of the drama suggested in this book is concerned with helping *every* child to develop its own resources at its own rate and in its own way; but it is important not to lose sight of those people who need moments of particular 'stretching'; in a case such as the one considered above, an opportunity can arise quite naturally, without creating the artificial circumstances of 'theatricality' etc., which can be of as much disservice as use to such people. There is never any intention in drama of holding back everyone in a class to a similar level. Each person finds his or her own level out of each opportunity that is provided, and particular opportunities are made for some people at some times – but these are often according to need rather than according to ability. No comparisons are made before the class as a whole.

moment that creates further interest in the activity. Always this factor of creating further interest is important, not just for the possibilities of drama that are thus realised, but because as interest grows so do personal responsibility and effort; there develops a conscious realisation that many personal factors – concentration, sincerity and maximum effort among them – are all basically concerned with the success of the scene; it does not matter for them that the work is being done alone, with no audience and no 'occasion' – the work is done for its own sake, and success is considered as something in its own right, quite independent of 'carrots' and other encouragements. This is one of the most important factors of developing drama – to help each person feel the rightness of effort for its own sake and not for the rewards that might accrue from it.

It is important to remember again that the kind of scene suggested above, initially as a speech exercise, is still not concerned with theatre as such, and no theatrical production factors should be incorporated for their own sake. At the same time, every encouragement is given to each member of the group to be fully and genuinely involved in the circumstances of the episode; this is really *them* working in a factory and worried about conditions; they may all be part of a crowd – but a crowd is a collection of individuals, each with his or her own point of view and feelings and thoughts and wishes. For this reason, it is important to start from the pair stage rather than go straight into the group scene, when it is too easy for the crowd to be reduced to making crowd 'bumblings' with such silly shouts as 'rhubarb-rhubarb'.*

Other examples and themes for similar crowd scene development, based on opportunity for practising speech, growing from pairs to the whole class:

People preparing to welcome someone; this basic idea can be detailed in many different ways, e.g. fairies welcoming their queen; villagers welcoming the squire etc. etc.

---

* Those responsible for building crowd scenes in plays to be performed in public are often guilty of this insincere and feebly unreal type of crowd utterance. A little patience during rehearsal, with time given for actually building the individuality of expression of members of the crowd can completely transform the scene and its resulting experience both for the participants and the audience with whom the play is ultimately shared.

Sailors demanding to turn back; (all kinds of mutiny, strike and disobedience).
Preparations for and/or the election or rejection of some kind of representative
A revolution
A lynching
Colour-bar problems in a university
A siege.
With any particular scene that is ultimately concerned with 'a crowd', the basic preparation provides the simple speech opportunity, and the moment may arise when it is useful to develop outwards to the actual scene itself, though this is not always either possible or useful.

BOLDNESS AND SENSITIVITY

With all the exercises in pairs, the teacher can encourage both bold and sensitive speech by the introduction of other quite simple circumstances. For example, to help boldness of speaking (not shouting), tell the pairs that as their conversation progresses they are to put more and more space between each other, moving as far apart as is possible, but making sure they can still hear each other quite clearly without shouting or straining. Speech then has to be very bold, as all voices become stronger – and so too does the fullness of concentration on listening to one's partner despite the many other strong voices all round. Alternatively, with the same movement away from each other, tell the class that all the speech must be done in a strong whisper, without any straining; again the whispering makes increasing demands on concentration and listening, and at the same time leads to the fuller use of speech mechanisms without these having to be made conscious.
Similar developments can be made in the group work by suggesting circumstances demanding whispering (e.g. secret meetings, planning robberies etc.) or demanding really bold speech (e.g. a shipwreck in a great storm, planning a strike in a noisy factory etc.). For the latter, the introduction of music can often help to make the right background for speaking really strongly.

ADDING DIFFERENT DIALECTS

When there is considerable confidence at speaking, arising from constant, regular opportunity to practice, all the above exercises can be attempted with the addition of different kinds of dialect; children are made familiar with dialect through television, radio and cinema – often without consciously realising that familiarity. Providing the circumstances of the class are uncritical and private – again, the whole class working at one and the same time, without teacher comment – they will attempt to use many of the dialects themselves, sometimes very successfully and at others less so, but with growing ability as they have the opportunities. It should be suggested to them that they listen very carefully to the many different kinds of dialect they hear on television and the radio.

This kind of approach in pairs can often be linked to a single theme, with perhaps change of pairs after each 'conversation'.

Example: The Weather

In pairs, being yourselves, discuss the weather during the summer (or winter).

Two *West Country* farmers discussing the effects of the weather on their crops.

Two *Cockneys* grumbling about the weather spoiling a recent sporting fixture.

Two *North Country* business men discussing absenteeism among workers because of the weather.

Two *American tourists* grumbling about how the weather spoiled their holiday.

Two '*posh*' people planning a cruise because of the awful weather.

Two *Scottish* lighthouse keepers swapping yarns about terrible weather at sea.

Two *Welsh* sailors talking about a terrible storm at sea.

Two *Irish* barmen talking about lack of trade because of the weather.

Two *Midland* cinema managers talking about the way the wet weather helps them.

Two *French* (or any other nationality) deciding to go back home because of the weather.

Two *Martians* deciding the weather on earth is so terrible that they will get back into their flying saucer and go back to Mars. (For further developments arising around this kind of attempt see the section on 'Making up our own language' on p. 140). All the above are simply isolated discussions or arguments or conversation pieces linked to the weather.

All the other suggestions in this chapter for work in different sizes of groups can equally well be explored in terms of using different dialects; it is important to emphasise again that there should be a wholly uncritical framework for such activities, with no niggling demands for the kind of accuracy that may well now and forever be beyond the compass of many of the class. But this is one way of helping young people to become more fully aware of the many different forms of speech that exist – including 'good' or 'posh' speech – and is one step in the direction of intended multilingualism; meanwhile, the majority of the work will be done in their own background speech music, developing confidence to put their own ideas and thoughts and feelings into their own words, developing fluency and clarity, developing further the ability to listen to others.

Sometimes there is great value in moving away altogether from the intellectual use of language – the meaning of words – and depending on only the emotional sound values. This can be done by a serious use of 'Mumbo-Jumbo'. Mumbo-Jumbo, known also as scribble talk or jabber talk, can make a positive contribution to practical speech work (even adult artists have found it useful). Mumbo-Jumbo can, in fact, form the basis of making up one's own language, using consonants and vowels in an entirely arbitrary manner, so that the full emotional sound values are used to express the feeling essence of what one wants to say without the limitations of vocabulary impeding that expression, and without reliance on intellectual meaning of words taking over the function of full vocal expression in such a manner that there is neither the need for nor, eventually, the awareness of the emotional sound values.

There are many exciting experiments conducted in schools regarding prose and poetry writing. Often the basic intention of these experiments is to discover ways of liberating children from intellectualism to a full flood of intuitive expression; but even so, some of the liberation is often lost in the stark mechanics of writing down the flow of words, for that flow is always faster than the flow of even the fastest pen; only immediate and spontaneous speech can really catch the flow, but it is, of course, very much more difficult to record the experience! We can hardly supply each and every member of a whole class with his own tape-recorder, let alone in conditions of sufficient privacy to avoid the microphone's tendency to pick up every sound around it! Or can we? In some foreign language classes, the physical space of the classroom is divided into many small booths, each with its own elaborate equipment – perhaps something of the kind could be made available as a creative speech room; and the cost of the many small tape-recorders would work out at only a fraction of the cost of the average science or physics laboratory.

Making up our own Language

PRACTICAL APPROACH

It must first be emphasised that in making up our own language we are not concerned with making up new sets of words; that would be a very difficult intellectual process, involving all the complex problems of memory. We are simply using the sounds of vowels and consonants in any way we choose; again, this is important, because the early tendency is to develop a kind of 'slobber' talk that is rather akin to the noises we make when trying to speak with the mouth overfilled with toffee-apple. The problem is overcome if the process is not rushed and if adequate time is given in the early stages for each person to achieve a measure of personal mastery in conditions of total – or as near total as is possible – privacy. For this reason the hall is most useful, with each member of the class being invited to find a space for themselves that is not too near anyone else. If the classroom is used, then it is wise to let people sit anywhere they like, including underneath desks, if this helps them to get away from others.

Young children need little or no preparation. Let them be Martians or other people from outer space who are talking in their own language and they will quickly master the whole process; this is, after all, only an extension of their tendency to use made-up words when stuck for an actual one, or else to use the wrong word because of unfamiliarity with its true meaning. Once, therefore, there has been some basic practice in various aspects of drama – of the points on the circle – there is little or no real difficulty in attempting this aspect up to, say, the age of twelve. After that age, particularly if little or no drama has been experienced before, the process will meet with increasing difficulties and should not be started until some work has been done on concentration, on using the imagination, on beginning to move and speak – until there is some basic foundation of confidence.

Here is an example of a teacher taking a class of teenagers for a first attempt at using 'mumbo-jumbo'.

TEACHER: Each of you find a space for yourselves, as much away from everyone else as you can. Now – each of you is a kind of inventor; not a very serious inventor, but the sort of person who likes putting a lot of old junk together in order to make something or other from it – no matter how silly or useless that something may be. Of course you can make something serious if you want to – like a flying saucer; or perhaps you make a special can opener for use in outer space. You decide for yourselves. Now, each of you is surrounded by a heap of old junk – discarded wheels and other bits of motor-cars, tin, wire, bits of wood, pieces of metal and so on; and you have screw-drivers and hammers and saws and electric drills and anything else you need. Go ahead on your own, putting all the bits together; and if you can't think of any particular thing to make, then that doesn't matter; just enjoy putting all the bits and pieces together into one whole.

After the class has proceeded with the 'putting together' activity for a while, the teacher continues:

'Now, as you go on with what you are doing, begin quietly to make all the ''effort'' sounds of the work; so, if a screw is really difficult to screw in, then let the sounds of your effort come through. And you can also make the mechanical sounds of the tools you are using – hammers, saws, electric drills and so on. Go ahead – and remember, the sounds can be as quiet as you like to start with; as you feel happy making them, then you can make them a little louder if you wish, but not so loud that they could worry anyone else.'

(*Note:* Again the attempt to preserve confidence by suggesting that very quiet and simple sounds will suffice – incidentally, quiet and simple sounds can often be the best basis of speech work in all circumstances; volume is concerned only with communication, and that is the last of all our considerations, certainly at this stage. At the same time, the social training aspect of considering other people is also put forward so that the lustily confident (or the noisy exhibitionist) has his or her potential also under consideration.)

Once a few early sounds start to come, it might be wise to say something of general encouragement, like: 'Yes, its coming well now; develop what you're doing', and then give a little longer for the activity to get firmly established. Then stop it again – as always, it will be wise to have the cymbal or tambour available for full class control – and as the activity grows it may be necessary to remind the class that you want complete silence and stillness the moment you touch the cymbal or tambour.

TEACHER (*continuing*): Now – the thing you are making and inventing is going along very well, getting very near to being finished. (*Note: we do not ask if this is so – we state it as an established fact; certainly avoid getting involved in a great intellectual discussion about it.*) Now – instead of making the effort and mechanical sounds, you are going to talk about what you are doing. But this is talking with a difference, because you are going to talk in a language that is not known on this earth at all, a language that you make up as you go along, simply by putting various sounds together – not silly and half-witted sounds like chewing toffee noises, but genuine sounds that do not have any sense to them – like foreigners often sound to us, or, if you like, as people from outer space might sound if we met them one day. So, stand by; you are still doing this quite quietly and privately – but now you are this scientist talking to himself about what he is doing, so that one day he can explain what he has made to other people. To start with, talk in a whisper. (*The whisper will again preserve the privacy of the experience – but as we sense that confidence is growing, we can suggest that they talk a little louder, even though still to themselves.*

*We might, for instance, suggest that they are going to take their invention
to a national conference and they are talking out loud the various points
they will want to mention at the conference. Again we stop the activity.*)
Now – join up with a partner, taking your invention with you.
Still talking in this language you make up, explain your inventions to each other and ask each other questions and so on, as you
wish. But remember – its all in this new language. I don't want to
hear a word of English from anyone.

(Because this is new, the sudden confrontation of a partner may
well undermine some of the class's concentration; if the teacher
expects and is ready for this then there need be no undue alarm.
It is always worth while remembering that in one sense working
with a partner involves having an audience to what one is doing,
and this can create a certain self-consciousness. If the result of this
is buffoonery, then let it go on for a while before suggesting something like: 'Right, you've had your fun hearing each other for
the first time; now get your full concentration into it; remember
you are each an inventor who is interested in seeing someone
else's invention and in showing your own. Go ahead.' Once there
is some confident flow in this, again the class is stopped.)
TEACHER (*continuing*): As you go on talking and sharing each
other's invention, something begins to go wrong. Each of you
begins to be jealous and envious of your partner's invention; so
you begin to find things wrong with it and say it isn't any good;
you both do this – and you both begin to get more and more
angry with your partner. Eventually you get so angry that you
smash to pieces each other's invention until there's nothing but
a heap of junk all round you both. And then – suddenly you
realise that after all the world would have benefited by having
both inventions, so you go off together to have a drink and discuss
a new invention. All of this is still in the language that you make
up as you go along. Go ahead.

(Now we let the improvised scene take its own time with each
pair; some will very quickly reach the point of destroying each
other's machine – but we have allowed for that by suggesting
something for them to do afterwards. If possible, we let everyone
complete the whole incident. Already, in the simplest and most

common of all emotions – that of anger – we might well see the
benefit of the liberation from using real words; so often this kind
of improvisation will dry up because people cannot find enough
real words; with their own language they are freed from this
necessity and the flow of emotional sound is therefore uninterrupted.)

TEACHER (*continuing* * *when all are through the episode*): Each pair
join up with another pair to make groups of four. Call yourselves
A, B, C and D. Now, to start with, you are four friends who have
just met in the street and you are telling each other all the
different details of a street brawl you saw yesterday evening – but
you are telling each other in this same language that you have
been making up.

There are of course many other subjects one could choose for this
first discussion in fours – this one has been chosen for its vitality
and potential freedom of action together with speech; the action
stimulates the speech, which in turn enriches the action – movement and speech are always close together, particularly when
speech is liberated from entirely intellectual meaning. Already
it will have been noted, for example, that gesture has been used
very much more freely in the previous episodes as one uses the
body to amplify and reinforce what one is trying to communicate
vocally. But here are some other suggestions for the groups of four
all working together, as distinct from what follows below, when
each of the group takes it in turn to 'lead' an activity:
Four people who have just come across some strange object on
the ground and are discussing what it might be;
Four people who have just been given a conjuring outfit and are
trying out all the various tricks;
Four people plotting some action or another;
Four people discussing a sporting event that has happened or is
to happen; and see all the suggestions in the early part of this
chapter for other ideas.

* The continuity is being maintained for the purpose of this example; in actual
fact, with some classes, this may be far enough for the first occasion, in which
case the suggestions that follow might be found useful another time. It is always
unwise, in the early stages, to try to force continuity beyond the point at which
interest is sustained; in later stages, this 'stretching' can be invaluable as
general training.

Let the activity continue for about a minute and then stop it again:

TEACHER (*continuing*): Now, person A in your group is a slick car salesman at the Earls Court Motor Show. The other three are wealthy people who have come to look at the latest, most expensive, most gadget filled, automatic car that has ever been on the market – and they all have a lot to ask and a lot to say about it to the salesman during the demonstration. All of it is still in this language that you make up.

(Again, give a minute or two for the activity, before then suggesting something for person B to be leader of, then person C and then person D. The following are suggestions that have been found useful; in each example, the leader function is stated first):

A guide in a cathedral taking round a small party of peasants who have never been inside a cathedral before.

The owner of a collection of very modern abstract painting, explaining the work to a group of visitors who start off disliking it all, but grow to liking it.

An air hostess explaining the use of the life-jacket.

From this, all kinds of 'specialists' explaining some factor to laymen.

A policeman asking three suspects what their movements were on a certain day, and, from this, all kinds of investigations into people's actions and motives.

A collector of rare ancient pottery sharing his collection with a group of experts.

(This could be a collector of anything else as well – stamps, birds eggs, old coins, rare plants, animals, antiques, furniture, old manuscripts, etc. etc. And in such examples we see again the value of a language that does not depend on meaning of words. In an improvisation that includes as its main essence experts on ancient pottery, there are immediate limitations from one's lack of knowledge of anything to do with ancient pottery; in the made up language this lack of knowledge is unimportant against the possibility of 'expressing' the many different emotions arising from one's pride in collecting, from one's interest in the objects, from one's astonishment at the beauty of this or the preservation of the other, in one's disbelief that the article is genuine, in one's joy at this possession and sadness that this one broke at some point in history – and so on. Mere facts about the articles themselves, or the knowledge of historical dates pale into comparative insignificance against the human involvement and ability to share the feelings from that involvement with other people.)

Perhaps the above will give enough guidance as to the kind of subject matter that can be useful. It is wise to vary experience from the serious to the comic, from the fast moving and excitable to the calm and tranquil, from the noisy to the secret – and of course infinite variations can be given by adding (a) specific moods, (b) specific emotions for one or more of the characters, or (c) specific types of character. Much depends on the stage the group has reached.

With the changes in mood and emotion will be seen very clearly the beginnings of the full use of vowel sounds and consonant sounds for their emotional sound value; in ordinary language sound becomes dead; hot sounds the same quality as cold, hard as soft, happy as miserable; there is full reliance on meaning to create the difference. Enrichment in the use of words comes only by using words for their emotional essence as well as their intellectual meaning. Similarly with the juxtaposition of one kind of sound with another: remove concern for meaning and a new feeling for such juxtapositions is released; similarly for the onomatopoeic uses of language. And again the freeing of gesture will be noticed, and also the sensitivity of listening fully, rather than grabbing at the shallow exterior of thought.

STORY-TELLING IN MUMBO-JUMBO

Groups of four or five are invited to find their own space on the floor and to sit in a circle, fairly close together. They are a group of friends who, at Christmas, are telling ghost stories – really frightening, mysterious, ghost stories. One person will start the story and lead up to a really exciting point – and then hand over to the next person, who will continue to another really exciting moment, and then hand over to the next and so on, all round the group, the last person of all ending the story. And the story is to be told in this same language that we make up as we go along. It is wise to emphasise that no person must go on for too long, but that on the other hand it will not matter how short some people's contribution is. In this way, we make sure that the story is not dominated by someone with an easy facility for the activity and we protect any who may not be feeling too confident. Because of the different rates at which the groups work, it is almost certain that some groups will finish before others; to protect groups who have not finished from suddenly having an audience of those who have, it might be wise to suggest that as soon as a group finishes a particular story the members go on swapping mysterious experiences, as people do at Christmas parties, still using the same language.

A second story, in the same language, and again starting with one person and passing on round the whole group, can be a comic story, with every farcical situation in it that has ever been known to happen, from falling on banana skins to being in a runaway car. This time the person starting should perhaps be different – the group itself might settle this point. When the story is finished, then swap more comic stories, but still in this same made-up language.

These two stories, if they arise at a time when there has been sufficient earlier practice, will often reveal clearly the full value of the activity. The ghost story will contain a full rich use of the vowel sounds, with exciting juxtaposition of moments of sharp consonants (like ticking clocks or footsteps etc.); the controlled but full use of the arms and fingers will also be noticeable. In the comic story, there will be much greater use of sharp and fast consonant sounds, often juxtaposed with moments of vowels used for building to surprises of one kind or another; again gesture will be used with great freedom, and it is wise to expect that in this story they will not necessarily remain seated but may well suddenly stand up in order to use the whole body – and then settle down again.

Once there is some mastery of this approach, the same language will be found most useful for many improvised plays, particularly if they happen to involve subject matters of people so beyond the range of ordinary experience that it is difficult to achieve a flow of words in our own language.

Tone of voice is an expression of the whole personality. If communication of ideas and feelings is limited to the manipulation of words according to their intellectual meaning, we do not achieve an expression of the full personality but only of that part of it which is capable of or used to using words in such a manner; thus we get a flattening out of personality because only a segment of it is involved. Hence, the most brilliant people with the most exciting ideas are often the dullest and least vivid personalities when giving a lecture or through other means trying to share their ideas – only part of them is working. We call them dry or boring or dull to listen to. Well, the mind on its own is dry and boring and dull. But mind coupled to feeling (including simple excitement and genuine warmth) transcends what we so rightly call 'grey' matter (almost the dullest colour there is) into a vivid and living entity, using all the many tones of voice that then are able to express the fullness of personality. (It is interesting to note that there are as many tones of voice as there are colours in the rainbow.) Sadly enough, this full use of all the rich tones of the voice only takes place for the majority of people when they lose control of themselves, as, for example, in moments of intense anger or acute ecstasy – the latter often only in the unselfconscious state when no one else is about. The moment there is tension the first place affected is the throat, physically tightening and restricting the whole delicate speech instrument. Tension can be created by the audience factor and self-consciousness, and from such factors as 'being stuck for words', being worried about one's 'indigenous speech music' etc. As with the early suggested exercises for developing a confident speech flow, so with this making up of one's own language, tension is released or avoided, and the fullness of tone of voice can be liberated. One error of much speech work is that of trying to train the voice instead of liberating it. It cannot be liberated in isolation, it belongs to the development of the full person; indeed it is an expression of that development, for tone of voice will reveal personality more than any other source.

The most pathetic words one can hear a young person say – and the older they are the more pathetic it is – are 'I don't know what to say', or 'I don't know how to put it'. How to say it, how to put it, are highly individual matters that stem from full confidence to be oneself, to use the whole of oneself and to be able without any kind of fear or tension to express oneself. All can be achieved by constant practice at the use of what already exists – nothing is achieved by the partial and reluctant mastery of something that is new and is imposed by other people.

Movement and Speech

In the section on movement and the use of sound, reference was made to the close links between the kinds of simple sound that can be used in drama and the actual sounds of speech. Most sound can be divided into two groups – the long and continuous sounds, such as gongs and bells, and the shorter, more staccato sounds, such as drums. The sounds of speech can similarly be divided into the longer sounds of vowels and the shorter sounds of consonants; like an orchestra, the human voice makes some sounds that sing and flow and others that tap and beat – and consonants are to speech what time-beat and rhythm are to melody.

The indivisibility of drama in education is fully realised when we consider how close movement and speech work can and should be, both of them bound by the common links of:

(a) sounds, both external (music, etc.) and internal (speech);

(b) breath, the basic essential of all life, embracing both movement and speech;

(c) liberation from tensions, arising from full personal confidence;

(d) development of imagination. A two-way process – imagination stimulates both movement and speech, and movement and speech enrich imagination;

(e) social communication; though this is largely achieved through speech, both the speech itself and the full confidence underlying that speech depend on the liberation and mastery of the physical self through the intuitive development of movement;

(f) emotional control arising from sensitivity, wholly intuitive in the first instance, but ultimately fully conscious.

There are other and more complex links that are not really the concern of a book of this nature; but even this limited list should be sufficient to indicate that no matter how much specialisation (and therefore division) may be necessary with some academic subjects, the same basic premise cannot underlie drama as a genuine part of education; drama itself is not another subject – and the apparently separate aspects of drama are not at all separate but entirely interwoven within the structure of human personality.*

In practical terms, of course, it is neither easy nor necessarily desirable to strain one's teaching resources in an effort to forge or force such links; in terms of educational philosophy, however, it is important never to lose sight of the potential links, and there are some occasions when deliberate attempts can be made.

EXAMPLES

1. With infants and young juniors, use simple, short 'sentences' of sound on the drum for movement (either of the whole body or of arms only, according to space). Follow this with making up sentences of words to exactly the same sentence of drum-beats. For instance –

DRUM SOUND: Ta-tum, ta-tum, ta-tum, ta.

SENTENCES: The donkey's in the sea, sir.

I want to go to market.

Can we go home now, please.

or

DRUM SOUND: Tum-ta ta ta tum-ta ta, ta.

SENTENCES: Isn't it a lovely day, sir.

Can we have our ice-cream now, please.

What a dirty dress you're wearing.

2. With older infants upwards, do machines of all kinds, sometimes with all the class working on their own, then in pairs, threes and other small groups, but on occasions building up to the point of the whole class being one machine. The machine might start with using only fingers and arms, and then gradually in-

* Paradoxically, in our existing education system, the one member of staff who, by the very nature of his or her work, comes closest to engendering the right condition in young people for speech work is the movement specialist; but all too often specialisation prohibits such continuity; similarly the teacher in charge of speech may not only have need for but may actually give logical birth to the need for movement—and again specialisation prohibits the continuity.

corporate the whole of the body. A single time-beat on the drum or tambour will give a basic beat from which each person develops their own rhythm of machinery; the basic time-beat might be picked up with the feet by some of the class.

Once the machines (with whatever size of group) are confidently moving, invite them to make sounds with their mouths – any sounds that belong to the particular machine or part of a machine they are being. At a later stage, let them translate these sounds into any words they wish, either finding a single phrase or sentence which they repeat over and over again, or else changing the phrase or sentence as often as they wish.

3. Choose two contrasting pieces of music, one mainly staccato and fast, the other more flowing; for instance Sandy Nelson's *Let there be drums* and Leroy Anderson's *Forgotten dreams*. Use the records alternately; if the class is new, or comparatively new to the work, then continue to stimulate movement by imaginative ideas; for instance, with the drumming record, suggest they have drums all round them, perhaps all over the hall or room, and they are playing all of the drums, using feet as well as hands; with the slower record, suggest they are painting enormous canvases, or perhaps even great murals, with a brush in each hand.

Later, add to the movement, vocal sounds which, according to the stage the class is at, could be (a) any kinds of vocal sounds they wish; (b) actual words, even repetition of a single chosen word, phrase or sentence; or (c) (for more advanced stages) intended use only of consonants.

A similar procedure for the slower record with, at (c), intended use only of vowels.

For all of these examples, and those that follow, encourage use of unforced whispered sounds or speech; volume is quite unimportant, and, in the early stages, can also involve moments of self-consciousness. Once confidence has grown, greater volume will come quite naturally and simply, but even then, moments of intended whispering are useful and help to bring sound from its correct centre; the whispering must not be forced, as it then tightens the throat and can be as harmful as shouting.

4. (Perhaps secondary only.) Speaking to music, using the mood and emotion and imaginative content as well as the actual structure and form; this process is fully intuitive and should only be attempted after a great deal of other drama work has brought full confidence.

Basically, the intention is simply that of speaking to music, all of the class doing so at one and the same time, having each found as private a place as they possibly can. But it is usually wise to precede the actual speaking with moments of active drama, all connected with the theme that is eventually used for the speech. The following four examples all include suggestions for the 'active drama build-up'.

(a) *The night-club.*

Record – any one of Sandy Nelson's. For more advanced groups, consideration can be given to different kinds of night club and the experience might be based on the rather sophisticated kind that might best be accompanied by a 'Blues' record (e.g. something by Acker Bilk).

A few moments of movement to the music, perhaps including 'playing' some of the instruments; perhaps also moments of the kind of dance seen in the nightclub (this might vary from the Twist to something more intimate).

In small groups, a few moments being the different people who are visiting the night club, including wining and dining and seeing other people they know; among the visitors might be certain celebrities from the worlds of sport or entertainment or politics etc. Some moments might also be spent on being the staff of the establishment, planning the physical arrangements (tables, floor space for dancing, cabaret items, lighting, decor etc.); this could be done in pairs or in small groups.

A few moments spent making a documentary film – perhaps for a TV advertisement – of the place and its people; each person in the class works on his or her own, using the hands as a camera view-finder, taking shots from many different angles, high and low, and from different distances – long shots, close or medium shots, even big detailed shots. In pairs or small groups, they then discuss the kind of shots they have taken.

Finally, speaking to music. Each person works on his or her own, sitting privately, and holding an imaginary microphone very close to their lips so that they can speak as quietly as they wish. Explain that when the music comes they are giving a description or commentary on the radio for listeners at home who cannot see what is going on, but can hear the music and can hear – in fact, depend on – their remarks in order really to feel as though they were present. The commentary can include descriptions of the people, what they are wearing and doing and eating; details of what the place looks like; information about and descriptions of famous personalities etc. By what he says the commentator tries to give the overall feeling of what it is like to spend an evening at the club.

(b) *The Great Fire*

Record – *Mars* from the Planets Suite by Gustav Holst. Each person is a newsreel photographer for either a television or a film company. All are working separately and start either sitting or lying down in a place private to themselves. They are at home in the evening, perhaps reading, perhaps sleeping. As the music starts, they begin to be aware of the smell of smoke; they go to the window and see outside that there is an enormous fire, perhaps a warehouse or a block of flats. Being a good photographer, and hoping for a scoop, they at once go with their camera into the very midst of the fire, taking incredibly exciting shots from all angles; included in their shots can be some of people [imaginary] getting out of the fire or being rescued from it, and of firemen [imaginary] fighting the blaze.

Then play the record through, letting each person work on their own. Then divide into small groups. Each group is a family living in a great block of flats; it is night time; some of the family are asleep, others perhaps reading etc. Again, when the music comes, one or more members of the family discover that the block of flats is on fire and raises the alarm. Working as family units, but joining up if they so wish, and using speech if they feel the need of it, all the people living in the block of flats try to escape from the fire and eventually succeed; but they have a terrible job doing so as so many of their exits are cut off by the blaze.

Allow each group a few moments to discuss, then play the record
and let the whole class develop the scene.

Then, the whole class disperses to the outer edges of the room and
either lies down or 'curls up small'; this time, starting from
fingers and then letting the movement grow through the whole
body, each person is going to be the fire, starting from a mere
wisp of smoke or a small flame and eventually becoming gigantic
powerful and uncontrolled flames which burn up everything they
touch; the 'flames' can remain isolated or join up in pairs or
small groups as the fire progresses. (For this, it is sometimes wise
to put a chair as a focal point in the centre of the hall; the chair
might even represent St Joan being burnt at the stake.)

N.B. For all of the above incidents, if absorption and energy are
strong, it will be possible to play the whole of the first section
of the record, lasting about four minutes; in which case the
crescendo at the end of the music can be used as the moment
at which the fire expends itself and dies away.

Finally, having 'filmed' fire – i.e. seen it from the outside, and
been in a fire, and then actually fire itself, the great fire is described to a background of the same music; perhaps it is wise to
suggest that this is a commentary that is attached to a documentary film about a great fire; often it will be found easiest to
speak to the music if the eyes are closed and one is seeing in the
mind's eye what is actually taking place on the screen whilst one
is commentating.

(c) The Royal Procession

Similar experiences to those in (a) and (b) – including being
various people involved in a royal procession (crowd as well as
royalty) – lead to describing a royal occasion – perhaps a straightforward procession, perhaps a royal wedding, coronation or
funeral; music according to the selected occasion.

(d) The Cathedral Ceremony

Detail of build-up and of music again as at (c).

There are of course many other subjects one might choose; the
above are simply to give some indication of the approach. With

some groups, who have had a great deal of experience and are thus fully confident and interested, it will eventually be possible simply to put on a record and say 'Speak to this as you wish'. Here, at an intuitive level, we become fully involved in the factor of improvised poetry, spoken at the moment of inspiration, in no way interfered with by the mechanics of writing. And if the kind of physical arrangements mentioned earlier can obtain, then even these spontaneous utterances can be recorded and later transcribed to paper.

7

Sensitivity and Characterisation

The foregoing chapters have been consistently concerned with one main intention – the development of the resources of each individual. From the points of view of physical, emotional, intellectual and spiritual growth, suggestions have been made for developing personal concentration, use of the senses, imagination, physical mastery (movement) and social communication (speech). The intention has been that of developing what already exists, at one's own level and rate of progress, with a constant emphasis on the necessity for intuitive discovery rather than technical mastery; in essence, the aim has been the growth of harmony in all facets of personality. Inevitably, the divisions and subdivisions, which are made for no other reasons than the fundamental nature of the book itself, tend to militate against this harmony; in practice, this is avoidable if we can accept that drama is not a subject of the straight-line progression type; the basis of division and subdivision has therefore been made from the notion of a circle rather than a straight line; all the points on the circle, any one of which can be the right place of beginning (depending on each teachers relationship to both the work itself and a particular class of youngsters), exist for the whole of each human being's life. They exist, if even only embryonically, at birth, and continue to death, and the function of drama as part of education is to develop each point to each person's complete self-realisation, with full acceptance of the infinite variability of the many potentialities in each school. Personal confidence is developed by work in an uncritical atmosphere, freed from fear of failure and from comparisons of one person with another.

One constant aim has been to overcome self-consciousness, and, in part, this is achieved by allowing the work itself to take place at a largely 'unconscious' level. The teacher, but almost invariably only the teacher, knows the precise reason for the different kinds of work done, knows what results to look for, and studies the individual progression of each person; the progression is in the people doing the drama not in the drama itself, though inevitably the challenge – that is the personal demands made on each person – grow in complexity as confidence and personal mastery grow. Even so, much of the personal challenge arises eventually from within each individual rather than as an external facet of the work itself. The 'personal challenge' aspect is eventually the most important part of the progressive factor in drama even though much of it may be intangible.

Consciousness of Self

Part of this progression is the gradual development of consciousness of self, not just at an intellectual level of perception, but emotionally and spiritually as well. This consciousness of self forms the foundation (a rock-like foundation, if the growth is slow and organic rather than swift and imposed) of living in harmony with oneself, aware of and able to use all one's resources in each aspect of life, unenvious of others whose birthright may include the endowment of particular gifts that are denied to us, perceptive of both the inner and external forces of living.

Self-consciousness is one of the scourges of humanity and is responsible for many acts which are as false and unreal for the doer as they are for the observer. Basically it often arises from simple lack of confidence – which in its turn arises from lack of opportunity to practice the use of the many facets of oneself – and from fear of failure, which arises from the expectation others have of one achieving more than one is capable of doing and then comparing the lack with the results of others. In one manner of thinking, self-consciousness is the cry of unliberated individuality against the necessity to conform to an arbitrary and largely intellectually conceived norm, the standard of which has nothing to do with preparation for living, but only for a job in life. Self-consciousness, itself negative, stems from fundamentally negative attitudes and demands both of society and of education, which is but a reflection of the essence of that society. Consciousness of self is wholly positive, and springs from an intuitive awareness of the uniqueness of individual personality; it brings a capacity to use all one's own resources, with genuine humility – and part of that humility stems from an acute sensitivity to other people.

Sensitivity, the basis of human and social awareness, is not so much another point on the circle as the progression of all the points at a higher level of existence. To start with, all the points of the circle are developed for each human being as an individual; once they are developed, their progression continues in conjunction with a growing awareness – conscious and intended – of the existence of many other human beings, of the family, of the group in class, of the class as a whole, of the school, of the community, of mankind. (See diagram on page 13).

Sensitivity and Personal Control

Sensitivity, however, like the points on the circle, cannot be achieved without practice, and that practice must be fully centred in practical emotional training aimed at helping each young person to become fully responsible for control of his own behaviour, within a framework of growing realisation of the emotional self. Sensitivity will not arise from exhortations to consider the needs of other people, particularly if adults insist on holding the onus of responsibility for behaviour; it arises from practical opportunities to practice such consideration, quite unconsciously to start with, but at a fully conscious level in the later stages.

With all the work suggested so far, a great deal of sensitivity will have already been achieved at the unconscious level through the sharing of physical space, the sharing of imaginative ideas, the exchange of words through speech exercises. Add to these the fully personal growth of a sensitive response to sound, to imaginative stimuli, and the fully personal control involved in becoming deeply absorbed in many varied activities – the accumulation of these many factors gives some indication of the extent to which unconscious sensitivity will already have been practised. Even something as simple and basic as stopping activity when the sound stops, or becoming quite still and silent the moment the teacher bangs the cymbal or tambour, are making fundamental contributions towards the growth of sensitivity.*

One important essence of this unconscious growth of sensitivity and personal control is the organic nature of its development. There is opportunity to explore all facets of the emotional self and to reach a point of selectivity – the basis of selection being the appropriateness to the immediate occasion, with the provision of legal opportunities to behave 'illegally' (i.e. the *creative* exploration of the more primitive or negative emotions) as well as the discovery of *personal* wellbeing resulting from the use of positive emotion; this feeling of personal wellbeing is neither as strong nor as positive if there is no opportunity for selection nor for the contrasting experiences of negative emotion – i.e. if adult authority is the only responsible organ of choice and excludes (usually through fear of the results) the opportunity for contrast that arises through genuine exploration of the whole emotional sphere.†

The emphasis in the early stages of such experience is on the factor of *personal wellbeing*; educationists are often quite naturally worried by this emphasis for fear that one is teaching selfishness and self-indulgence – as has already been mentioned in the

* The only forms of more fully conscious sensitivity up to now have been those involved, in the earliest stages, with the handling of individual problems of behaviour which has tended to interfere with the work of other people; it has been stressed that in such circumstances it is important to be firm on the basis of direct social training.

† Relevant to this thought is the kind of conversation adults have with teen-agers on the subject of 'morality in great ones', often as depicted in epic films; they enjoy the humanity of the 'good person' who's fundamental *adventure* in life is that of 'fighting his or her own nature'; the path of the saint is littered with many such battlefields, and the healthy view is the one that sees in this the real basis of adventure in living. By refusing to acknowledge the actuality of negative emotion in each human being, and by not making provision for the exploration of all kinds of emotion, we withhold the genuine organic opportunity for the adventure at the very time in life when it arises quite organically; much immature behaviour in later life can arise from personal inner need both for the exploration and the adventure – both society and the individual suffer because there is no longer the legal framework of drama provided for creative illegality.

chapter on movement and dance drama. The danger is negligible if drama is constantly viewed as a positive way of developing all aspects of individual personality, including that of sensitivity at a more conscious level; but experience of personal wellbeing (which includes discovery and selectivity) must come first, followed by the conscious awareness of other individuals' similar experiences and the basic interdependence of individuals on each other. The only emotional experience that is tangible is that which is personal to oneself; understanding, sympathy and compassion for the emotional experience of others is a mixture of imaginative projection and the memory of similar personal experience. As will be suggested more fully later in the book, drama is perhaps the only way of helping the full development of the imaginative aspect of this process; meanwhile the personal experience aspect is rooted in those experiences which first give rise to personal wellbeing and then to a sensitive awareness that each other individual can experience the same sense of wellbeing.

The organic nature of the pattern of work already suggested follows the pattern of actual human growth both in its intended development of the human resources that already exist and also through the fact that each aspect of the work is first attempted by the individual working on his or her own, then in pairs, in threes, in small groups, and occasionally with the whole class working as one entity, even though, particularly in the earlier stages, that entity is not homogeneous but comprised of many different sized groups all working to the same end. Human growth follows a similar pattern. The baby discovers and lives most happily in a simple form of isolation until it is about three years old; then it enjoys – though many of the early processes are more agony than enjoyment – sharing with one other person; then with two others and so into smaller groups. Integration within a larger social unit is a sophisticated and later stage of development, very much dependent on full opportunity for experiencing the other stages, particularly the entirely personal. Lack of opportunity for this experience at its right organic time may result in the person resorting to personal isolationism at what should be more mature stages of life – mature in the sense of having grown naturally and organically step by step to any particular point, rather than missing some experiences by being 'hot-housed' out of the earlier stages.

Practical Work

Once personal concentration, absorption, confidence and some liberation have been achieved, two immediate developments become possible: 1. More conscious awareness of other people; 2. The beginnings of characterisation. It should again be emphasised that this is not a question of a progressive moving away from the kind of work already being done, but rather the doing of it at a more conscious level together with the beginnings of some different exercises.

EXERCISES IN AWARENESS

(a) When using the hall for any class exercises, with each person working on his own, ask the class as follows: 'Each one of you find your own space standing (or sitting, or whatever) on the floor.' In the early stages we should expect (and be prepared to accept) a natural tendency to 'bunching' in a very small area of the hall, due to lack of confidence and uncertainty as to what is expected of them; as confidence grows, there will be fuller spreading out over the whole floor space – and any sudden return to bunching is usually indicative of some undermining of confidence, often associated with new work. When confidence is at a constant level, then the teacher can be growingly insistent that each person finds a space where they can work without in any way interfering with the work of others – perhaps even asking each person to spin round with their arms raised (if space allows for this).

(b) When groups, of whatever size, are attempting any form of exercise (or improvisation – see next chapter), and whether in hall or classroom, invite each group to find a space for itself, rather than designate spaces; only designate if one group is quite clearly so on top of another that neither can work easily – and then be careful to state that that is the reason why you are suggesting the changes of chosen space. Even at the early unconscious stage of sensitivity, there is tremendous value in this simple discovery of how to share space; this is most important for teachers who are confined to work in the classroom constantly to keep in mind. Often the adult eye and mind simply cannot believe that forty people can all work at once in so small a space; children do it quite simply and easily – as, interestingly enough, do teachers when they are involved in practical work at drama courses.

(c) *Filming*. Divide the class into pairs, labelling themselves A and B. Each person thinks of a simple activity (gardening or some domestic task) which they are going to do; the A's do their activity, whilst the B's film them doing it, working with long shots, medium shots and close-ups. A has a fine concentration exercise as he or she completely ignores the camera-man; B has a full sensitivity exercise as he moves around A, including coming very close to him, without getting in his way or otherwise interfering with his concentration. Then reverse the process, with A filming B. Follow this by allowing the pairs to discuss what they found interesting to put into the film. Class discussion on this can also be useful and enriching, providing it is entirely free from cerebral criticism – the discussion must be a simple sharing.

(d) *Mirrors*. Divide the class into pairs, calling themselves A and B, and standing facing each other about a raised arms distance apart. A is standing in front of a mirror, B is his reflection in the mirror. Whatever movement A makes, B makes at the same time, as the reflection. After a few moments, A becomes the reflection, doing whatever movement B may do. Again, after a few moments, A and B attempt to 'stay together' in their movement without either of them leading. In the early stages of 'mirrors' there will be little absorption because both A and B feel their partner to be a direct audience; this feeling quickly goes as they are trying to make the same movements at the same moment in time. Encourage entirely abstract movement, starting with the arms only and then, as confidence and sensitivity grow, using the whole body. There may well be movement of the occupational mime kind to start with (e.g. brushing the hair or shaving); allow this for a little while, until confidence begins to be established and then encourage only abstract movement. It is most important not to fuss about exact accuracy, particularly in the early stages, otherwise the exercise becomes cerebral and the intuitive freedom of sensitivity is swallowed up in over-concern for exactness of detail. There are many developments of this particular exercise, linking with concentration and imagination –

1. As experience grows, encourage the pairs to hold each other's eye, without 'strained staring', throughout the exercise.
2. With the touch of a cymbal, each pair freezes in whatever position it is in; A and B decide independently of each other who they might be in what situation if they were caught by a high-speed camera in the precise position they have 'frozen' in; they discuss their ideas.
3. As at 2 above, only the independent decision is made of themselves in relation to their partner; i.e. the high-speed camera has taken a shot of both of them at the same moment; again discuss.
4. As at 2 and 3 above, only instead of making an independent decision and then discussing, the pair discuss together straightaway.
5. Add music to the movement; this can vary from music with a pronounced beat, to slow and flowing music such as Leroy Anderson's *Forgotten Dreams* or Debussy's *Claire de Lune*.

With all of the above 'mirror' exercises, encourage constant changes of partner, so that each person in the class becomes used to working with many different people.

(e) *Delayed Mirrors*. Arrange in pairs as for 4, again each pair being A and B. A makes a short sequence of movement (using only arms to start with, but whole body later), moving in slow motion. B watches carefully. The moment A is still, B goes through the same sequence of movement until arriving in the same position as A finished in; then B continues another sequence in slow motion, with A observing; when B is still, A repeats the same sequence until arriving in the position B finished in. And so on, as long as concentration will hold without undue strain.

(f) For more advanced stages, similar to (e), but the movement is not in slow motion.

(g) For more advanced stages, similar to (e), but instead of the pair remaining in one place facing each other, they use the whole floor space; in slow motion to start with, faster motion later.

(h) '*Mirrors*' *with groups of three or more*. Naturally the exact idea of reflections cannot really hold for a group of three, but the basic sensitivity exercise works in the same way. Each group of three stands in a triangle, facing inwards; the easiest way of achieving the necessary equidistance for the exercise is for each person in the group to raise their arms to their sides and then adjust until their finger-tips are touching; incidentally this is often quite a wise position from which to start the exercise. No one in the group looks directly at any other person in the group; the best position for the eyes is on an imaginary spot, about shoulder high, at the centre of the group. Again, each person is labelled – A, B, C. To start with A leads, moving as he or she wishes, with B and C making exactly the same movements at the same moment; then B takes over leading; then C; finally the three try to keep absolutely together without any one leading.

All of the developments suggested under (d) above can be adapted to work in larger groups.

After threes, the next size of group to work in is fives; it is wise to avoid working in fours as this figure lends itself too easily to breaking into two sets of pairs; after five, any number is possible, according to concentration and absorption and the growth of sensitivity. It is ultimately possible to have any number of people working with full sensitivity to each other, keeping absolutely together with no one leading. This, of course, is a most advanced stage and will come only after considerable experience. Groups of five, six, seven or eight will provide maximum possibilities for the growth of a really full sensitivity.

(i) '*Mirrors*' *in groups with added Mood or Feeling*. The procedure is precisely the same as in both (d) and (h), but now instead of A leading in an ordinary manner he or she does so within a mood or feeling set by the teacher; many are the moods or feelings one can suggest, with a different one for each member of the group, when it comes to their turn to lead. For example, A might lead 'powerfully', B 'sadly', C 'triumphantly', D 'weakly', E 'happily', F 'determinedly', G 'saucily', H 'reluctantly', etc. (See below, under 'Adverbs' for a different development of a similar idea.)

In the above, the imaginative exercise with the high speed camera can also be incorporated at some stage or another, the decision regarding character and situation to include not only the physical position but the mood or feeling from which it arose.

(j) *Follow my Leader*. Groups of four, up to a maximum of about seven or eight. Each group stands in Indian file to start with. The person in front, on the spot, moves arms only, the others keeping with the leader, not by trying to watch the leader but by keeping absolutely aware of the person directly in front of them. Once the sensitivity is beginning to come, the leader starts moving all over the hall as he or she wishes, with still a full use of the arms; the remainder continue to follow the leader, keeping all together. On a signal from the teacher (drum-beat or some such) the leader goes to the rear and the second person takes over leading, and so on until each person in the group has had a turn at leading. Rostrum blocks in different parts of the hall can add interest and variety. The same exercise can also be done to different types of music, but it is wise not to use music that is too fast before there has been some experience and a corresponding growth of sensitivity.

One interesting growth of sensitivity within this exercise is the ability of the leaders to sense where to lead their groups so that they do not get tied up with other groups.

(k) *Blind People and Guides*. Divide the class into pairs, A and B. A closes his eyes and is guided all round the room by B; each time the teacher calls 'change over' the partner with eyes closed becomes the guide and the other closes his eyes. As confidence grows, encourage less and less physical handling by the guide, until full, sensitive control and response can be achieved by the pressure of only one finger. An increasing number of obstacles (e.g. chairs etc.) can be placed over the area, again gauged by general confidence and growth of sensitivity. Two variations of this exercise:

1. Place many obstacles over the floor area. A closes his eyes; B walks just behind or to one side of A, vocally warning him about obstacles ahead and which directions to turn in order to miss them; B does not touch A except in emergency. Change

roles, but not as frequently as in the former exercise as this demands a much greater degree of sensitivity and concentration. Encourage speaking to be absolutely calm, including some occasions when everything is said in a whisper.

2. As in 1, except the vocal guidance is given from a fixed position at one end of the hall instead of walking close to the 'blind' person. Again encourage calm speaking, and on some occasions whispering only. In the first attempts at this exercise, it is necessary for each guide constantly to use the name of the person they are guiding; later it is an interesting challenge to try and depend only on recognition of the voice without hearing one's name called.

(l) *Blind Statues.* This is an advanced development of the different components of (k), particularly of 11 (a). Divide the class into even groups, small to start with (i.e. four), but eventually growing to ten or even twelve. Subdivide each group into two equal groups: in the groups of four there will be two pairs, in groups of six there will be two groups of three and so on. One subdivision of each group is 'talked into' a statue by the other half of the same group. To make clear how this is done, let us consider one group of, for example, eight. The eight divides into two groups of four, say X and Y; within each group each person is labelled A, B, C or D, and each person will be working closely with their opposite number in the other group – so XA is working with YA, XB with YB, and so on. Group X decides, privately, on a statue that they will turn group Y into; at the same time, Group Y decides, privately, on a statue for Group X. Let us assume that group X is having first turn and has decided to turn group Y into a statue called 'War'. Group X will have decided exactly what form the statue shall take, perhaps even trying it out for themselves. Now they stand next to each other with their partners in group Y standing just in front of them. Group Y close their eyes and keep them closed, whilst group X, all speaking at the same time, guide them by words into exactly the positions they are to be in for becoming the statue. Group Y do not open their eyes until the statue is complete. Then group Y guide group X into the statue they have decided on.

This is a very advanced sensitivity exercise, demanding tremendous concentration, as all the groups in the class will be working at one and the same time. In first attempts it is wise not to have the statues formed too far away from the group giving the directions; but later, it is possible to achieve the statues from across the width of the hall, or even down the length of the hall. Again, encourage calm vocal directions, sometimes speaking only in a whisper.

(m) *Moving to Adverbs*. In (i) above, a simple sensitivity mirror exercise indicated the use of mood or feeling through giving an adverbial description to each member of the group. As part of movement (and as a speech exercise) this use of adverbs can be extended. The whole class, working individually, moves to the stimulus and accompaniment of their own repetition of adverbs. For example, with the lead always given by the teacher, a few moments might be spent as follows; the teacher says the word 'lazily'; the whole class then picks up the word, continually repeating it and moving the whole of themselves within the full feeling of the word; the teacher then calls out the word 'desperately', and again the class pick up that word and their movement changes to the full feeling of the new word, and so on. The exercise helps people to use words richly for their feeling content as well as their meaning, through the full physical experience accompanying the use of the word. It is wise to give very contrasting successions of words for early experiences, but these can become subtler at a later stage – the subtle differences between 'lightly', 'happily', 'gladly' and 'delightfully' would be too difficult for groups to achieve in the first instance, but would make an interesting and achievable challenge later. It is important for the teacher to encourage a full individual use of the adverbs, as there is little or no value in the class picking up a kind of drearily chanted repetition which has no real feeling of the words. Group sensitivity among a class will, in fact, often bring a definite choral use of the word – but this will still contain the full feeling of each word if the choral aspect is not insisted on for its own sake.

After some individual and personal experience of this nature, the class can again be divided into even groups, each group being subdivided into two equal halves, in the same manner as for (l) above; now groups X and Y each decide on a simple story for their own group; the story includes three or more changes of mood, and for each mood they select an adverb, which they then tell to group Y; group Y then uses the adverbs to accompany the action of group X, sensitively feeling the moment of the various changes of mood. For example, the story decided by group X might be as follows: They are a group of people *calmly* rowing down a river; suddenly they are caught up in a strong tide and start to row more *determinedly*; but the current gets stronger and they have to row *desperately* – and at last they begin to win their battle against the tide and row more and more *triumphantly*, until once more they are in safe waters and again row *calmly*. Having decided on this story, they do not tell it to group Y, but merely ask for the adverbs 'calmly, determinedly, desperately, triumphantly and again calmly.' The actual doing of the story may well include the lead being given on the change of mood by the group of speakers, or it may come from the doers. Sometimes, one story will contain examples of each; this does not matter in the early stages; later, the groups might decide which is to lead, and eventually there will be full sensitivity without any need for leading from one group or the other.

A variation on this exercise is for group X to tell their story to group Y and let group Y decide on the adverbs to be used.

There are many interesting variations of the above idea of using the sound accompaniment of one group to the activity of another, including not only use of the voice, but also of handclaps, etc., and for those interested in creative music, the use of home-made musical instruments, either accompanying or leading the movement of another group.

(n) *Time-beat and rhythm.* The class as a whole finds its group time-beat with a handclap; when the teacher touches any individual, that person improvises a rhythm that fits the time-beat – a single sentence of rhythm, repeated over and over; the teacher touches another person who then improvises a different rhythm; the remainder of the class continue the time-beat until the teacher touches each one in turn.

A variation of this is for the rhythms to be made by stamped footfalls.

GROUP SENSITIVITY, involving the whole class working as one homogeneous unit.

The majority of the following exercises are concerned with the building of particular dramatic moments; the dramatic essence of these moments gives common ground in emotional experience, which aids sensitivity. However, there is also value in that kind of exercise which is not rooted in any significant moment. For example:

(o) Invite the class to group itself quite freely at one end of the hall – not too bunched together, but close enough to one another to feel the group as a whole. The group remains quite still and calm and relaxed, but fully aware – and when everyone feels the moment together, they walk down the length of the hall, keeping quite simply in step and in exact physical juxtaposition to the people near to them – and, as one, all stop at the other end of the hall. Again, when they feel the moment they about turn, and repeat the walk back to the other end of the hall. It is most important that the teacher does not in any way whatsoever trigger the moment for the walking to begin – and of course the class must be encouraged not to trigger it either. There are many variations on this simple exercise:

1. As above, but by group sensitivity decision, the class finds a moment to stop before reaching the end of the hall.
2. As above, but instead of walking the group runs, again either to the other end of the hall, or, at a later stage, stopping before they reach the end.
3. As 2, but just before stopping, the group leaps into the air, all landing at one and the same moment.

(p) Arrange the class in one long line down the length of the hall; if the hall is not long enough to take the whole class in one line, then use two lines, each with its back turned to the other. Each person should be close to the persons on either side, without actually touching. Again, encourage complete calm and relaxation with full awareness. Without any triggering, everyone will raise his right arm forwards and above their heads – and then, with the moment, lower it; then the same with the left arm.

(q) Arrange the class as a group at some point in the hall, where they can all see a door. Without any triggering, they all, at the same moment, see the Queen come through the door and say, together, 'God save the Queen'.*

DRAMATIC MOMENTS

(r) Group the class very close to each other in one part of the room (this can be done as easily in a classroom as in the hall). Suggest that they are a section of the crowd at the Farnborough Air Display; they are watching for a new jet plane, which is going to swoop straight over them, turn in the distance, and return, again swooping over them. On the first occasion, supply the sound of the jet's approach and departure, return and departure, by making a climax and de-climax sound on the drum, the cymbal, or simply with the hands on the top of a desk or chair. Having done the exercise once with sound, then repeat the crowd reaction to the approaches and departures of the jet without any sound at all.

(s) The same grouping; suggest that they are all people in the Ark with Noah. One of the class, as Noah, lets the dove fly out of his hands, pointing at the path of flight of the dove until it returns again to his hands. The remainder, sensitive to where he is pointing, follow the journey of the dove.

Then repeat the same exercise; this time Noah releases the dove and lowers his hands; now, without the guiding finger, the whole group watch the flight of the imaginary dove until again it lands in Noah's hands.

(t) The same grouping; they are all members of a circus who know that their tightrope walker is unwell, but insists on going through with the highlight of his act – walking the tightrope blindfold; the group watches the imaginary walker along the whole length of the tightrope.

The same exercise can be repeated with the added suggestion

* This kind of group sensitivity experience can often be quite astonishing, particularly for those seeing it for the first time. It is, however, most important to keep the atmosphere of the class free from all tension and fear of failure. Nothing will be achieved by adopting an attitude of parade ground drilling. However, it may be necessary to remind the group of the need for maximum concentration and consideration of others.

that on, say, two or more occasions, the tightrope walker nearly falls – the group senses these moments without any form of triggering.

(u) Circumstances similar to the above, but concerning a trapeze artist instead of a tightrope walker.

(v) Circumstances similar to the above, but the group are watchers of a cliff rescue operation. Or perhaps a rescue at sea. Or timber-felling. Or someone being guillotined during the French revolution. Or a train crossing a bridge that has suddenly been found unsafe. Or commandos waiting for the signal to blow up something or other.

(w) Similar arrangements to (v), but with different emotional circumstances, e.g. miners' families waiting round the pit-head for news of a disaster at the coal-face; people waiting in a hospital for the appearance of a doctor with news for them; a crowd waiting outside the palace gates for the posting of a bulletin, etc. The majority of these examples have been predominantly concerned with sensitivity arising from the use of imagination and looking. Of course, the other senses, together with imagination, can also be used to practice sensitivity in either small or large groups. For example:

(x) *Touch.* Passing along the line a lighted match, without getting either burnt or letting it out; passing along the line a small, wounded bird or other fragile creature; passing along the line a really hot object (e.g. a hot dish of food) or a really cold object (e.g. a block of ice); passing along the line something really sticky (e.g. a large block of melting toffee) and following this by passing along feathers or confetti. All of the foregoing objects are of course entirely imaginary. Examples using the whole group in a single physical effort are: pulling on an imaginary rope; lifting an imaginary roof into position; scything in a single rhythm together; holding a firemen's sheet for an imaginary person to leap into; pulling in a fisherman's net, etc.

(y) *Listening* for distant imaginary signals; for a rare bird or insect; for the approach of secret footsteps; for tapping signals in mines or caves or at secret meetings in cellars; for all kinds of sounds – at sea, in the air or on land – in thick fog; echo soundings from inside a submarine, etc.

(z) *Smell*. The group suddenly become aware of a particular smell at one and the same moment – e.g. fire or gas or food.

The reader might find it useful, when considering group sensitivity, to refer back to the exercises in the use of the senses at the beginning of the book. At that stage we were concerned with the personal and private development of each person working on his own, deliberately excluding any awareness of other people in order to master full concentration and thus to overcome such factors as self-consciousness. Now, with full concentration achieved, we are able to reconsider similar approaches from the viewpoint of full consciousness of self and a growing awareness of and sensitivity to other people.

Characterisation

Exercises in sensitivity help both the external and inner growing awareness, first of the factual existence of other people and of a relationship of the simplest kind with them, based on being able to listen fully, really to see them and, within one's own life, to allow for them, as it were, adjusting certain factors and feelings within oneself in order to incorporate or share aspects of life with them. Characterisation provides the opportunity through which depth is added to these experiences by more detailed personal awareness, both conscious and unconscious, as a result of imaginative projection of oneself either into the circumstances governing other people's lives or else into actually 'being' other people in such circumstances. Early dramatic work includes little or no actual conscious characterisation, in the sense of 'being' other people – it is largely made up of being oneself in situations and circumstances different from those that are normal and ordinary to one's personal everyday life, commonplace as the circumstances might in fact be in other people's lives. Vicarious experience of this kind has always been educationally acceptable, and is no doubt part of the cultural and personal enrichment that is intended from programmes of reading literature, dramatic and otherwise, looking at pictures and so on.

But these experiences are seldom as full or as rich as those obtained through the use of the whole self as provided in drama.

The former experiences work through the mind, affecting the feelings only to the extent that the imagination is able to bear upon the circumstances, and this in turn will depend to what degree the imagination has been practised – without practice imagination becomes atrophied – and on the ability of the recipient consciously to exert the use of imagination, which is again dependent partly on practice, but mainly on the opportunity to develop all facets of personality including the emotional.

The basic ethic of most of the world's religions embodies the idea of consideration for other people; indifference towards others (except for moments of indignation and condemnation) is as much against the ethic as are positive antisocial acts. As has already been mentioned, the difficulty is that such an ethic can only be fulfilled as a result of developing all aspects of the individual, followed by developing a really positive awareness of other individuals; neither can be developed through intellectual knowledge of the ethic, nor through forms of punishment for disobeying the ethic, but only through the positive and regular opportunity for actual practice, firstly unconscious and largely intuitive, but eventually fully conscious.

Characterisation is part of the practice and, providing there is no tendency to worry about the necessity for communication to an audience, will develop quite naturally from the unconscious and intuitive to the fully conscious, intended and controlled.

Infants – even the preschool child – and juniors, in their own drama, often achieve astonishing degrees of characterisation, including much originality, particularly with fantasy characters; but the processes governing such achievement are almost entirely unconscious and intuitive, and the characters themselves are often the expression of aspects of the eternal symbols of man's history, and often include the full cycle of man's existence – birth, marriage, death and resurrection.

Intuitive characterisation is part of the intended development of existing individual resources; it supplies at a simple, natural and organic level, the opportunity of being the characters of one's imagination, mixed with the growing awareness of the *real* world and the discovery of 'self' and 'not-self', which is part of the orientation towards becoming part of that real world, gradually becoming more and more aware of oneself – and the uniqueness and individuality of that self – and also aware of the existence of others. The process must be allowed both privacy of growth and individuality of expression.

Gradually, in drama, the characters of the real world begin to supersede the symbolical characters of the fantasy or imaginative world, parallel with the growth of more consciousness of intended creation. Like all organic processes, this growth is a slow one, differing in its genuine rate individual by individual. It is impossible to generalise, but, roughly speaking, the process *begins* to reach towards the full changeover at the top of primary schools, completing the phase in the first two or three years of secondary schools.

The early characterisations of infant and junior children are largely of *types*, mainly because of their essence in symbolism. Individuality is lent to these types through personal individuality and imagination, but there are no detailed characteristics such as become possible with more consciously created character in the later stages of development. In the changeover state from fantasy to realism the essence of type continues, affecting both the intuitive, symbolical characters and the realistic characters, the main essence of the feeling for the real being based more in circumstance and situation than in detailed characteristics of the characters involved. This is what is meant by saying that much early drama involves children and young people 'being themselves' in different circumstances; to be a miner or a bank-manager or a school-teacher in drama is to involve oneself in particular circumstances and relationships different from those of being a child or young person who goes to school and enjoys an individual private life out of school. But it is not a full and detailed involvement in actual human characteristics; it is more to involve oneself in the factor of an 'occupational disease', whatever little detail there is arising from types of person and typical behaviour associated with the occupation, sometimes based on personal experience, sometimes on vicarious experience and sometimes on purely imaginative experience. But accuracy in portrayal of type or symbol must not be confused with detailed and conscious characterisation.

Teachers who tend to impose on children a oneness of idea about say, royalty, are the first to be indignant if they see teachers portrayed from the same basis of typical oneness; 'No,' they say, 'teachers are individuals – they might be basically kind or unkind, strong or weak, considerate or selfish, pleasant or unpleasant, and so on – each one is different.' So too are kings and queens, witches and wizards – and bank-managers and miners; but the full detail of such characteristics are an advanced stage of drama, arising as much from personal inner development and sensitivity to other people as from actual practical opportunity to be different people in a manner that accords with one's own particular and personal stage of development. This is true and genuine organic growth.

The stages of the growth of characterisation are, in general terms, as follows:

1. The intuitive and unconscious exploration of characters of the inner world of fantasy and imagination.

2. The largely unconscious exploration of characters (both of fantasy and of the real world) in *action*.

   The dominant interest in both of these is in action – i.e. in the physical emotional realms of life, with little conscious use of the intellectual.

3. The beginnings of exploration of the causes and effects of the actions of characters; there is still a particular interest in action, but a growing awareness of the cause and effect of that action in its external relationship to broad characteristics of people. Here, intellectual considerations begin to impinge on the physical-emotional realms; characterisation begins to be, as does drama as a whole, more conscious.

4. The exploration not only of the external factors of cause and effect but also of the inner factors (motivations) of the actions of characters; this is part of a fully conscious form of intended creation of characters with, quite often, no major interest in action as such; it is a realm of drama that, again in general terms, belongs only to secondary education, and possibly only from about fourteen years onwards. By this stage, with proper

growth arising from natural and organic opportunity, there is a balanced use of the physical, emotional and intellectual self.*

In the next chapter on improvisation and play-making, practical suggestions are made as to how each of these phases of development can be helped in drama as a logical part of the development of individuality, including the sensitive awareness by each individual of the existence of others; already, however, in the exercises that have been our concern up to now, there has been a growth towards this full and conscious development. By being themselves in other circumstances, by being other people in either familiar or new and different circumstances, children and young people develop, first at the intuitive and unconscious level and then at a fully conscious level, a sympathy and understanding and compassion for others which is rooted in the emotional and physical and spiritual self as well as in mere intellectual knowledge; this is the ultimate *raison d'être* of drama as training for living, and is epitomised in the first sentence of this book: 'What is a blind person?' The answer 'A blind person is a person who cannot see' brings knowledge; actually 'being' a blind person through drama brings understanding to that knowledge, and out of this experience of full understanding (emotional and physical as well as intellectual) comes sympathy and compassion. Through drama, similar experiences in depth bring understanding of all kinds of people in all kinds of circumstances and conditions, each experience broadening the horizons of awareness, thus enriching and constantly adding to the factor of sensitivity towards mankind as a whole.

But at the same time another development also takes place – that of discovering fully and truly about oneself. Every adolescent is sooner or later confronted by the inner questioning of 'Who am I?' 'Where do I fit into life?' Only part of the self is involved in the question 'What am I to do with my life?' Unfortunately, this

* It is interesting to observe that this development is paralleled by children's interest in theatre, cinema, reading, etc. To start with their interest is primarily in action for its own sake, then in action logically associated with cause and effect as governed by 'people', and then in the way people behave and the logical cause and effect of that behaviour.

being the end product of education in its present form, this is almost the only aspect of development that teachers concern themselves with – but for each young person it is only a segment of a larger whole, the fundamental essence of which is 'Who am I?' The ultimate answer to this question rests with each individual human soul, but the only possibility of a true answer being found rests in the opportunity for each person to develop the whole of the self, including the emotional self. This has constantly been reiterated, but must be said again as we consider how open each young person is to becoming the prey of every kind of temptation at the emotional level, temptation which the young are incapable of dealing with unless there has been emotional training. Emotional problems cannot be answered only by the intellect any more than spiritual or intellectual problems can be answered with the body. Through every medium of mass communication young people are daily tempted to be somebody different from their true selves; naturally the temptations are largely materialistic, but the means are always insidiously emotional, appealing either directly to the baser emotions or else to a bastardisation of finer emotion; further, the temptations are couched in such terms that the receiver is left to feel that this really could be a normal part of life *if only* such and such circumstances could obtain. Always there is the great *if*, adding complexity upon complexity to the realm of wish or dream fulfilment; wouldn't it be wonderful *if* I had a sports car; wouldn't it be wonderful *if* my hair was like so and so's; wouldn't it be wonderful *if* I were handsome or beautiful like so and so; wouldn't it be wonderful if I could do wonderful work like so and so; wouldn't it be wonderful if people respected me, feared me, liked me, etc. etc. as they do so and so; wouldn't it be wonderful if I could live, work, play, love, hate, etc. like so and so. Wouldn't it be wonderful if...if... if...discontentment, envy, greed, lack of respect for one's own self, undermining of any form of simple and genuine confidence in oneself, often even a complete unawareness of that self, are some of the inevitable results of exposure to these constant temptations, and like all temptations they are fully emotional and each person can only deal with them at the emotional level for themselves. Education cannot help by serving out intellectual platitudes and exhortations to do this, that or the other about it; the platitudes and exhortations may help a few, but even for these few some of the results of the help may be quite ephemeral; something very much more tangible is necessary if there is to be real help at the emotional level.

Drama, despite its general intangibility, affords one facet of tangible help by providing the opportunity of fulfilling for a short space of time some of the tempting 'ifs'. Through drama it is possible to *try out* what happens if...what it feels like if...what it really means if...one is someone else or has this that or the other circumstances in life. And out of this trial and error slowly emerges, at a very deep level, the simple awareness of the truth: 'No, I am not really like that...I don't really want to be like that...', and the positive corollary of 'I see – that is me; I am like that and such and such is where I fit into the scheme of things'. Out of this simple discovery comes the opportunity of living in harmony with one's own personality and with one's own destiny; parallel with it come the growing horizons of awareness of and understanding of other people. And at the root of training towards such an end must be every kind of help to develop the full uniqueness of personality so that there is a deep rock of self-respect when self-discovery is fully achieved. Ultimately self-respect depends on one's own personal acceptance of the value of one's own hundred per cent – but to start with, there must be respect from and sensitivity from those responsible for releasing and developing that potential.

Inevitably, for these reasons, young people will often choose to be characters that some teachers would prefer not to see in school, and will select circumstances and actions that are repugnant to teachers. Add other influences on choice, such as television, cinema, daily papers, comic papers and so on, and it is no wonder that large numbers of the basic situations and characters meet with official disapproval. Many teachers go so far as to suggest that the characters and situations depicted in drama are the same as are played out in the playground or after school hours, and that therefore quite enough time is devoted to them without allowing the same activities to happen in school during school hours. To adopt this attitude is to misunderstand, on the one hand, the nature of drama itself as a positive force in general training, and, on the other hand, to throw away the one opportunity we have of exerting some influence on the manner and content of that drama through the ægis of adult wisdom shared in the drama lesson. The teacher does not, in fact, simply sit back and ignore what goes on; as part of the factor of building confidence and sustaining interest there must inevitably be a certain degree of permissiveness in the early stages; and for a host of other educational reasons that have already been examined, the same permissive intention continues from wholly positive intentions. At the same time, every moment is constantly watched, seeking for the natural organic opportunity to guide and influence and enrich by making the right suggestion at the right moment. Without this influence the drama might indeed remain on a very primitive level, with the more primitive instincts and emotions constantly dominant.*

This basic influence of the teacher is at the root of so many of the suggested contrasts in the exercises throughout the book. On some occasions the teacher suggests one situation or set of characters and then allows the youngsters their own choice to follow – the intention is to stimulate personal creativity, but often brings contrast of character and situation arising from personal interest; or the reverse may happen – out of creative opportunity the youngsters select one set of circumstances and characters, and the teacher immediately follows this by suggesting a contrasting set, giving perhaps an entirely different but complementary experience; and on some occasions, the teacher might deliberately suggest both sets of circumstances and

* This very charming story, told in the pulpit of a church in the north of England some years ago, may help to clarify the point: A certain man bought a new house with a garden surrounding it; but like so many new houses, the garden looked more like a forest of weeds than a garden. Diligently the man worked in his garden, clearing the weeds, tilling the soil, planting and tending flowers and vegetables; and in nine months he had a most beautiful garden. And it came to pass that a certain clergyman was walking by one evening and stopped to admire the garden at the very time that the man was putting the finishing touches to his labour. 'Good evening,' said the clergyman. 'Good evening, vicar,' replied the man. 'What a beautiful garden,' said the vicar. 'Isn't it amazing what God and man can achieve together?' 'Indeed it is,' said the man. 'You should have seen the garden when God had it on his own.'

characters to ensure the contrast of experience. Here are two simple examples:

1. A mainly speech exercise, but with interest in characters of a simple kind. The class is divided into groups of three; each group is involved in the same simple incident, concerning a shop. The groups label themselves A, B and C. The teacher explains that A is a customer who has been shopping all day and is feeling very fed up with everybody and everything; B is a shop assistant who hates working in a shop, dislikes most customers, and particularly dislikes A on this occasion because it is nearly closing time; C is the manager of the shop, a sour, Scroogelike kind of person, who likes making money but dislikes people, especially customers who arrive after he has made up the till. The group is given a moment to discuss this and to get ready, and then, with all groups working at one and the same time, the episode is done, the length of time depending on the experience and absorption of the class as a whole. As a speech exercise, the episode gives opportunity for strong speaking; as a simple exercise in characterisations, the opportunity is based on quite clear-cut and straightforward emotional attitudes.

Immediately the episode is over – and it might last anything from one to five minutes, the teacher suggests a second episode. Again it takes place in a shop, but this time there is a considerable difference in the characters. This time, the customer is rather a shy person, who is very anxious not to worry people, but all the same wants very much to buy a particular article; the shop assistant is working in a new job, likes it very much, and is anxious to be as helpful as possible with all the customers; the manager has not found it easy to get shop assistants, likes this one and is also anxious to be helpful, both to the assistant and to every kind of customer, whether or not he has made up the day's takings and is ready to close. And again the episodes are done, with all groups working at the same time. As a speech exercise, the logical opportunity is now provided for speaking with more control and so on, and as a characterisation exercise it is, again at a very simple level, a completely contrasting experience from the last.

2. Again, developing a largely speech exercise to include early attempts at intended characterisation.

The class is divided into small groups of any number from three to five. Each group makes a 'still photograph' of some straightforward activity, for instance: 'Laying the lino.' On a handclap from the teacher, the still photograph is brought to life, with speech.

After about a minute, the activity is stopped, and each group is asked to discuss what different kinds of people the group might contain. It is necessary to emphasise that these differences do not involve only such factors as one person is father, another grandmother and so on – but what sort of person is father and each other person in the group; some general suggestions should be made as a stimulus, pointing out that one person might be 'very businesslike and efficient', another is 'short tempered and rather fussy', another 'very calm and helpful', another 'very clumsy and boisterous', and so on; the groups then discuss their characters for a minute or so (in the early stages, discussion will not be very detailed and so will not last more than about a minute), and then the still photograph of the same subject matter is again made by each group, and, when brought to life, includes the different characters decided on.

There are many possible variations and developments from this approach:

(a) the same characters may be used in many different situations;
(b) many different characters may be used in the same or different situations;
(c) the 'detail' of characters can be developed further by discussion; early development of such detail can be stimulated by suggesting that each character should include contrasting characteristics; for example 'an easy going, pleasant person but with a very quick temper', or 'a very clever person who doesn't like doing things with his hands', or 'a very energetic person who has little patience and tends to do things too quickly', and so on. Even though these are very broad and obvious characteristics, they begin to form a basis for richer and more deeply considered characterisations. Over a long period of time such an approach will lead to more subtle and complex characters and thus broaden horizons and increase the sensitive awareness of other people. This is all part of the process of using drama not only to develop

one's own resources but also the relationship of those resources to one's environment, in its broadest as well as its narrowest sense. Practically every one of the exercises already mentioned in this book can be reconsidered from this approach to characterisation, involving each member of the class in new experiences from the points of view of many different people in many different situations. Even simple exercises involving the senses can be included in the approach to characterisation: what would the sounds I can hear mean to me *if* I were not me but such and such a person; and, later, that person in such and such circumstances, etc.

But perhaps the most exciting development – and it cannot be too strongly emphasised that this cannot be forced, but will grow over a very long period of time – from this kind of work on characterisation is the growth of realisation that some 'events' and 'actions' in life are shaped by 'people'; until this realisation, the dominant factor of much drama of the kind we are about to consider – improvisation – lies in situation and story; 'people' exist in order to fulfil these situations and stories, but, in the early stages, seldom either govern events or are concerned in events that arise simply from the fact that they are the people they are. It is this development of characterisation – of awareness of and sensitivity to people of every kind – that can bring significance to the trivial, and rich experience to the most commonplace of situations. From the particular viewpoint of this book, this development is an important facet of improvisation and playmaking; but there is equal impact and effect on both the intuitive and intellectual comprehension and understanding of people of every kind as might be studied in history, geography, religious instruction, English literature, science – indeed of any subject. So that even in the specialised fields of secondary education, the development of dramatic work can be of paramount importance to specialist teachers in every subject.

8

Improvisation

In essence, improvisation is quite simply a play without a script. Because there is no need for a script, an improvised play does not depend on any form of skill or ability at reading, nor of learning and remembering lines, and is thus an activity that all children of every age group and every scale of ability are able both to enjoy and to master. Furthermore, it utilises all those points on the circle that we have already considered, depending on the full use of each person's own resources without the complex necessity of interpreting an author's intentions as well.

Unfortunately, this very factor of scriptlessness, which makes improvisation of such value as an activity for all children, is often the major reason why many teachers dislike it. The reasons for this are understandable, because at its worst improvisation is much akin to charades, and the natural corollary would appear to be that it is better to have a badly read and learned scripted play, particularly if the script itself has merit, than to waste time on 'trivial games'; add to this the fact that there are usually a few people in most classes who can read very well, often with a flair for characterisation, and also that there are many readily available play-reading books carefully graded for all age groups and all standards of ability, and it is little wonder that improvisation is so often treated with suspicion. It is hoped that the kind of considerations put forward in this book, each part of which is an element of improvisation, might indicate values in the activity that are never part of scripted work except for a very few young people. At the same time it must be emphasised again and again that there are few activities undertaken by human beings that do not contain a 'scribble' stage, when there is little mastery or skill – this is certainly true of most subjects in school, none of which is given up because of 'poor' early work. Furthermore, there are a growing number of schools that can testify to the fact that, with sufficient experience, many children and young people can reach a stage in improvisation where it is almost impossible to believe that their work is not the result of a long period of production on a scripted play, and the subject matter and characters contained within these plays *do not exist* in any published scripted material. This, indeed, is one of the great values of improvisation – both subject matter and kinds and numbers of characters can be almost tailor-made to the needs of any particular group, ranging over every field of human endeavour and experience, entirely unlimited by any of the conventions that govern most scripted plays. That many more schools do not experience improvised work of such a level is more often than not due to an impatient giving up of the activity because of its lack of any kind of quality in the early stages.

Subject Matter

The subject matter of improvised plays can be either original (from teacher or pupils) or derived from any number of different sources, some directly concerned with other subjects in school. We need to be very careful before rushing into the latter; many teachers have claimed that 'drama does not work', basing this claim on a single attempt to dramatise a history lesson with a group of children who have never had any previous experience of drama! We might as well claim that P.E. is of no use because children cannot climb Everest! We cannot use one skill to aid another interest unless we have some initial practice at the skill in its own right. Drama can be most valuable as an aid to the teaching of other subjects, helping to deepen and enrich experience; but consideration of improvisation in this chapter is largely concerned with *original* subject matter in order to emphasise the need for continuity in the process of building confidence in each individual imagination. This confidence is achieved partly from regular practice in an uncritical framework, and partly from not being confronted too soon by the possibly 'better' subject matters of derived sources.

It is very easy to undermine confidence by comparisons with the more mature and practised skill of adult material. However, when considering original subject matter, it is an important part of the adults' task so to adjust their sights that they can perceive the values of simple and primitive beginnings, and, with infinite patience, to provide the opportunities through which improvement can arise. It is true that many improvisations can be utterly trite and banal, and equally true that, without guidance from adults, this stage of the work can remain at a very low level for a considerable period. However, it is important not to allow fear of this to force too much guidance too soon, with the result that confidence and genuine effort are undermined. Allowance must be made for the personal interests and tastes of each individual, and for the fact that within such opportunities as those provided by improvisation there are bound to be many products of existing pressures on different individuals; some of these will be considered in detail later in the chapter.

The Teacher's Approach to the Class

Before considering actual practical work in improvisation, the following points are put forward regarding the teacher's approach to the class:

1. It is necessary to be ready for and to expect the 'scribble' stage, which will usually include any or all of these factors: (a) an almost complete lack of 'form'; (b) there is no proper 'beginning, middle or end', particularly the latter – improvisations either peter out or else stop suddenly; on many occasions, a member of the group will quite simply inform teacher, 'that's all'; (c) people all talk at once – *they* are seldom bothered by this, but adults often are; (d) some of this talking includes any or all of the group making suggestions to one another about the next thing to do during the actual running of the improvisation; this is perfectly natural in the early stages, as initial planning is

DEVELOPMENT THROUGH DRAMA

limited by the urge to get on with the actual 'doing', thus limiting the detail of discussion and the need to clarify various points as they arise; (e) speech is faltering and unclear to everyone except the actual participants; (f) it is usually very difficult for the observer to have any clear idea as to what is going on; however, the group usually knows exactly what it is doing, and will readily explain (often in astonishing detail) in response to questions afterwards – but these questions need to be simply and straightforwardly requests for information, without any suggestion of criticism. (This is again very parallel to the approach in art.) The important fact for the teacher to bear in mind is that, because the improvisation has been made up by and then done by the group, they do know what is happening – they are not 'communicators' or actors or playwrights, so that in the early stages they will lack clarity in communication.

2. There should be no attempt whatsoever to impose conventional theatre 'shapes'; this point is fully developed in chapter 10, so for the present all that need be pointed out is that improvisation uses the ordinary, perfectly logical behaviour and grouping of everyday life. The behaviour and groupings of life on a picture frame stage are artificial and contrived because it is concerned with communication to an audience in a single direction in front of the acting area; to impose this kind of shape in improvisation leads to self-consciousness, insincerity and 'playing at being actors acting a play'. It is best therefore not to use a stage, nor the equivalent space of a stage on the floor area of hall or classroom.

3. There should be no audience whatsoever, nor any planned intention of working towards having an audience. This factor is also developed in another chapter (see chapter 10), but sufficient has already been said to point out the necessity for working towards full concentration and absorption. Audience undermines these qualities almost more quickly than any other factor, leading to either self-consciousness or shyness for some, and insincerity from others.

4. Until there is absolute confidence, there should be no form of critical discussions or post-mortems. (See chapter 11 for further points regarding this, including the approach to 'polishing' improvisation.)

5. There should be infinite variety of size of group for improvisation, ranging from work in pairs – with all pairs working at one and the same time – to work which uses the whole class as one unit. Within the various sizes of small groups, there should be constant interchange of who works with whom, but much of the work can and should be done in natural 'social' groupings, as the friendship factor of such groups often helps both the growth of confidence and the development of early sensitivity.

6. When working in groups, all groups should do their improvisations at one and the same time, whether in hall or classroom; this often seems impossible because of (a) lack of space, (b) the possibility of each group distracting other groups nearby.

(a) Lack of space. Children and young people overcome this difficulty with great ease, particularly in the early stages of improvisation when there is a certain fear of space as such and thus a natural tendency to crowd into a small area – indeed, one sign of the growth of confidence is the clear need for more space. However, even when this need arises, there are many educational values in learning to share a little space between a number of groups; herein lies a natural opportunity for growth of sensitivity.

(b) Possible distractions. Teachers should have no fear of this, as groups concentrate entirely on what is happening within their own improvisation, except for the occasional moment when something rather startling (e.g. a scream) happens in another group; even then, the distraction is only momentary. For the most part, the worst distraction any group can have is when an adjacent group finishes an improvisation first and then becomes audience to another group – indeed, so distracting can this be, that it is often at such a moment that the teacher needs to stop all the groups and lead on to the next exercise or improvisation.

7. It is wise to be ready – and ready in terms of educational philosophy – for some specific problems that might arise, the following of which appear to be the most common.

(a) 'Requests' or 'demands' from the class to use the stage, when one exists in the hall. These usually arise from groups that have had theatre types of experience of drama, and, in terms of the fact that it is often wise to begin from where the class already is, this use of the stage can make a starting point. However, in terms of the activity being concerned with the overall development of people rather than of drama, it is wise to keep the whole class working at one and the same time in exercises based on any of the already discussed various points on the circle; these are in no way concerned with the use of stage, though if the stage is large enough it might be used as a 'classroom' for the whole class to work in at one and the same time. The demand or request might on the other hand arise simply from a general notion about theatre and drama – often arising from a single visit to a pantomime – and the feeling that this is the 'proper' way of doing it. The results from this source often include a considerable amount of showing-off and exhibitionism, which will only be overcome by weaning away from use of the stage as quickly as possible. In either case, it is important for teachers to keep in mind that the best work is done on the floor space rather than on the stage.

Above all, it is important not to allow the fact that some children 'love using the stage' to undermine our own educational intention and awareness of what in fact is going to be ultimately of most value. We do not allow children to dictate to us about other activities that they 'love' or dislike. Why so with drama?

(b) Some groups will request or demand to show their improvisations to the rest of the class. More is said about this in chapter 10 as there is in fact a point when there is a certain value to this. But for much of the time there is little or no value; the quality of the work, in the early stages particularly, deteriorates under such circumstances; furthermore it is time-consuming, leaving most of the class for long periods simply watching when there is so much they should be doing. Often the way out of the difficulty is simply to suggest to any insistent group that they do their improvisation for the others during the lunch hour or after school. However, it is interesting to bear in mind that the majority of young people seldom, in fact, do make this request once they are *deeply and confidently absorbed* in opportunities of genuine creative work.

(c) Some groups (or individuals) may request or demand to do a *proper* play, usually meaning a play with a script. This may be an indication of previous experience and total lack of confidence in their own imaginative capacities, with a corresponding need for the security of the known experience. It may have theatrical connotations, rather as in the request for using a stage. It may – and this is the most important source – be a straightforward feeling of the need for more form, as a result of early improvisation experience. Whatever the reason, it is important for the teacher to handle the situation very carefully, for to rush into full use of the script at this stage may completely undo the growing interest in the scripted form of dramatic activity. There are natural links between the two activities, but it is important not to consider them in terms of progression from one to the other. Even professional actors use improvisation as part of the study and rehearsal of scripted material.

(d) Dressing-up. The use of simple dressing-up materials is an excellent way of stimulating improvisation, helping both story content and characterisation. However, the emphasis should be on *simple dressing-up materials* – lengths of cloth of different sizes and colours, which can be used creatively in many different ways. There is little or no value in the use of whole garments, particularly of the 'mother's old bridesmaid's dress' variety. These limit imaginative possibility and also tend to clutter the wearer to such an extent that most of the concentration is involved in organising the costume rather than on the character and situation. It is also important with dressing-up materials, as with 'properties' (see below), to wean away from any kind of full dependence on them, for the materialistic factor of either clothes or props always takes away a certain amount of absorption, leaving the actual improvisation at a shallower level than it would develop to without such distractions. Here again, the wisdom of the teacher must find a balance with the personal wishes of the youngsters. It may well be true, as so many teachers constantly reiterate, that children 'love dressing-up'; but it is equally true that ultimately they will do better drama without it, and by better drama is meant the full use of their own individual resources without dependence on outside factors. Because of this, part of the teacher's task is to wean them away from a love which becomes a limitation in order to liberate them to new circumstances which, once experienced, will be 'loved' just as much, and be better for their personal development at the same time.

(e) Properties. As with dressing-up, properties can form a most useful stimulus, particularly in the early stages of improvisation; for example, in the chapter on Imagination, many suggestions are made for making up stories from some simple object which the class can either look at or touch. In the same way, the use of simple material factors, used imaginatively during an improvisation, can add a focal point of concentration, perhaps even helping a kind of composure.

But, again as with dressing-up, the very materialism of properties can bring limitations by distraction from processes of inner creation. Perhaps this is seen most clearly in any form of improvisation involving fights (see chapter 9) or moments of violence (e.g. a murderer being hanged). Clearly in these circumstances it is wise to do without weapons or ropes or any other property that might result in injury, or, as is more likely, a less sincere and absorbed playing in order not to cause injury. Although this is obvious in these extreme instances, the same principal applies throughout drama, so once again, it is wise to wean away from any form of dependence on props. And when props are allowed or encouraged, there is great value in the simple use of inexact articles vested with imagination, as, for example, a pebble for one of the crown jewels.

(f) Once improvisation has started an individual or small group may say 'We've written a play; can we please do it?' Again this is usually a symptom of a need for more form in improvisation, or it may indicate a particular personal interest, which has possibly been inspired and stimulated by improvisation. This can be very difficult to deal with because, on the one hand it is a shame to discourage either the basic interest or the immediate attempt, whilst on the other hand the result of acting such written plays is often as disappointing for the youngsters as it may well be for the teacher. The problem is quite simply rooted in the impossibility of being able to write down – from the purely mechanical point of view – the full flow of dialogue that is probably running through the mind. The greater the inspiration, the more the flow of words and the more that subsequently gets left out, particularly if there is – and there nearly always is – a strong emotional urge to complete the play in order to be able to 'do' it. Often the problem is solved for the teacher by the fact that there is only one copy, laboriously written out on one or two sheets of paper, sometimes comprising as many as ten scenes, each of which has, perhaps, only four or five lines of dialogue. In such cases, the teacher can suggest that the 'author(s)' tells the story of the play to his or her group and then the group improvise it; this usually satisfies, without the disappointment that often ensues from acting the original script.

Practical Work : Stimulating Ideas

For stimulating early improvisation ideas, the reader is referred back to all the suggestions in the previous chapters. Each idea for exercising the senses, for developing imagination, for the beginnings of movement and speech, will also be useful for starting improvisations. All the ideas will need a little more time for the groups to discuss and develop, and more time in the actual doing than would normally be given for simple exercises. And further ideas and developments will arise from use of the suggestions regarding sensitivity and characterisation. In fact, by considering all of the different points on the circle we have also been considering the basic beginnings of improvisation, and by implementing exercises for the development of these different points we have also been laying the foundations for improvisations of many different kinds, involving many different types of experience. The above point regarding the previous exercises is important, as the examples that are to follow – taking improvisation a stage farther – are unlikely to work well unless there have been both the preliminary preparation of the exercises as such and of similar material developed as improvisation in its own right, followed by continuity of both kinds of approach working in parallel. And even when these further developments are being implemented there is still need for the continuity. Once again, we are confronted with the idea that the main forms of progression are in the people doing the work and in the quality of work and not in leaving one type of activity in order to go on to another.

Conflict

Fundamentally, the nature of drama is one of conflict. This may be very broad and obvious or delicate and subtle; it may be basically psychological or physical, spiritual or mental, and whatever the source it will contain a degree of the emotional. The conflict may rest in circumstances beyond the control of man or it may arise from the character of man.

Consider the following sequence of a story:

(a) A man gets into a boat and sails out to sea.

(b) He anchors his boat and sets his line to catch fish for himself and family.

(c) A great storm comes and sinks the boat.

(d) The man battles against the raging sea and eventually reaches shore.

(e) Because everybody in his village loves the man and admires his courage, they give him another boat so that he can fish for himself and his family.

Points (a) and (b) are essential starting points of drama with all age groups; they embody simple experiences, first as oneself, then as different characters. But even in the first sentence – 'A man gets into a boat and sails out to sea' – we have only to add quite simple descriptive adjectives and we at once introduce the element of conflict. For example:

A *sad, old* man gets into a boat and sails out to sea.

An *anxious and frightened* man gets into a boat and sails out to sea.

A *starving and timid* man gets into a boat and goes out to sea.

Or, we can change our attention from the *man* to the *boat*. For example:

A man gets into an *old, rusty boat* and goes out to sea.

A man gets into a *rudderless boat* and goes out to sea.

A man gets into a *boat that is not his own* and goes out to sea.

Or we can focus our attention on the *sea*.

A man gets into a boat and goes out into a *rough and dangerous sea*.

A man gets into a boat and goes out into an *ominously calm sea*.

A man gets into a boat and goes out into *the sea which is shrouded in fog*.

Or we can, of course, add to two or even three of the circumstances, as for example:

A *sad, old man* gets into a *boat that is not his own* and goes out to
sea.

or

An *anxious and frightened man* gets into a *rudderless boat* and goes
out into the *sea which is shrouded in fog.*

Each and every one of these simple additional factors adds an
element of conflict, which changes straightforward experience to
dramatic experience. The straightforward experience is still
drama in the sense meant throughout this book, but the added
factors bring additional enrichment to that experience, extending,
above all, the use of imagination.

The element of conflict is one essential ingredient arising from
the simple addition of a few descriptive words. But the examples
also serve to show the essential *oneness* of drama, whatever the age
group. The original sentence – 'A man gets into a boat and sails
out to sea' – is material that is as suitable for infants as it is for
secondary youngsters. The additional circumstances of descriptive
adjectives can be adjusted according to the age and indigenous
experience of the class and according to their actual experience
of drama. Some teachers might consider 'a sad old man' beyond
the experience of infants – but a 'jolly man' probably would not
be considered so. So with each of the other sections of the story,
the descriptive and therefore 'conflict' elements are adjusted to
the particular requirements of the class.

It is, of course, both impossible and unwise to try to arrive at
any generalised formulæ for drama with any age group, but very
roughly it is possible to consider aspects of improvisation as
follows:

Infants

Everybody in the class works at one and the same time. In the
early stages very simple incidents or episodes can be joined together into a short story, which is controlled and enriched by

sound and told by the teacher during the actual doing. For
example: Simple experiences, unconnected – (a) being a giant;
(b) being a mouse: both accompanied by sound. Story that
follows:

'A big, strong giant goes walking across the field; suddenly the
giant sees a mouse running about; and the giant is very frightened
and runs away and hides; then he creeps slowly from his hiding
place; suddenly the giant makes a big sound from just behind the
mouse; and the mouse is frightened and runs away down his
hole; and the giant walks back home; he eats his lunch; then he
goes fast asleep.'

At each break in the story, time is left for the whole class to carry
out the action. With infants it is important to keep in mind that
they change very quickly from character to character, being
everybody in the story; so they will be the mouse as well as the
giant. At a later stage, according to experience, they will simply
see an imaginary mouse, but to start with they will do all the
different characters as they arise.

Many simple and varied stories of this kind provide rich opportunity for being different people (and things and creatures); but
the stories need to be just as short and simple as the above
example, and are always helped by the moments of pre-experience
of simply being the giant, then the mouse or whatever is involved.
Fantasy characters, animals and other kinds of creature all make
useful material for one aspect of improvisation; so, too, do inanimate objects – trees, bushes, plants and so on, for, with full
simplicity, young children will bring these to life without any
problem. For example:

EXPERIENCE: Growing from a seed into a great tree (with
sound); a great wind comes and blows down the tree.

STORY: 'One day, a tiny seed grows and grows and grows into a
great big tree (sound); the tree is very happy, just waving gently
in the breeze (sound); but one day a great wind comes and blows
and blows and blows and blows the tree down (climax of sound);
but the tree is very brave and tries very hard, and grows again,
up and up and up, until it is a great strong tree again; then the
tree decides it will move to another place where the wind will
never be so strong – so, very carefully and very slowly and very

heavily it begins to move to another place (sound again); and soon it reaches a nice sheltered place; and there it stands, enjoying the gentle breeze.'

The factor of being inanimate objects is mentioned again in another context below (see Group Experiences).

But this type of fantasy experience – always valuable because of its *symbolical* significance – needs to happen in parallel with many different experiences of ordinary life, ordinary people, ordinary occupations; (the word 'ordinary' embodies the adults' fully sophisticated loss of 'wonder'; perhaps it is the earlier and earlier loss of this capacity in human beings that leads us to speak of children becoming more sophisticated at an earlier age – but drama, by its opportunity for direct experience, helps to preserve the quality by extending the horizons of imaginative detail. This is precisely what is meant by helping people to develop themselves and their own resources in relation to their environment. Meanwhile, very young children on the whole lack this type of sophisticated outlook, and for them the very ordinary things of life are not in the least ordinary.)

So our early improvisations with infants can include all the mundane experiences of life. Consider again the lists on pp. 32–34; these were originally suggested in connection with simple participation with sounds during the telling or reading of stories. But the headings alone embrace large numbers of ordinary living experiences that are useful material for simple improvisation of either the group experience or the individual kind. The everyday domestic life of home, for example, includes cleaning and looking after the house, the garden, the path outside; includes cooking and washing-up, making beds, arranging flowers, doing the washing and ironing. So one story might be simply 'doing things in the house'. The simple experience, without any form of conflict, is always useful material for early infant work. A visit to the seaside, to a farm, to a railway station, a bus station, a fire station, a dockyard, an airport – all providing simple experience which, again because of the young child's simple ability constantly to change character can include not only being the guard or the engine driver, but also being the train, not only building sand-castles or paddling in the sea, but being the sand-castle and being the sea, and being both donkey and rider in a moment of donkey riding.

Continually there is value in the teacher telling the story whilst the class are doing it; everybody works at one and the same time, discovering for themselves how to do each thing. To start with, there is little detail in the story; as concentration and absorption grow with experience, the detail can increase by the teacher's approach and type of suggestion. For example, an early story (it is one of, shall we say, a visit to the seaside) might start:

'One morning you are fast asleep in bed. The alarm clock rings, so you get up and get washed; then you get dressed; then you have your breakfast...'

At this stage there is little or no detail within any of these suggestions. At a later stage, some detail begins to come in, and the start of the story might run:

'One morning you are fast asleep in bed; the alarm clock rings, so you push back the blankets and sheets, put on your slippers and go to the bathroom; then you wash your face and hands – and don't forget your neck and behind your ears; and then you clean your teeth...' and so on. And at a later stage still, the detail grows even more, and part of the story might now run:

'So you go to the bathroom and turn the doorknob – push the door open – go inside – close the door gently behind you so that you don't wake up anybody else in the house; now you go to the basin – put the plug in – turn on the tap – it's a very stiff tap – and as the water runs in you feel it with your fingers in case it's too hot – if it is too hot, then add some cold water – just enough to make it just right – and now you pick up the soap and rub it in your hands to make a nice lather...' and so on. Such detail in the early stages would be too full and too fussy, but as experience grows, so we enrich the experience by the type of suggestion that draws further detailed thinking and imagining from each person; perhaps another reminder should be put in here that we are not concerned with communication, so there is no worrying about accuracy in mime; accuracy in mime arises from detailed thinking and imagining, not by destroying absorption through forcing audience consideration.

So it can develop for all of the many experiences we can provide;

it is seldom difficult to 'think of ideas' if what we are thinking of is the development, through experience, of human beings by providing opportunity to use all their resources; it is only difficult when we think of developing drama itself and therefore want to dash onwards to the next experience. Circuses provide an excellent example – often one sees a top infant class dashing through a circus experience, being ponies and clowns and jugglers and performing seals, and lions and lion-tamers, perhaps even accompanied by gramophone music, and this is certainly an interesting early experience, involving different kinds of movement, sometimes of speech, of mood and atmosphere etc. 'Now what?' asks the teacher – 'I've done a circus with them already; what now?' Well, if that is the only experience of circus the class has had, then there is a great deal more that can be done and–here is the important point – much of the development can arise from discussion with the class, even during the actual running of the activity. Let us consider one aspect of the circus in these terms: the whole class have just been circus ponies; we might then proceed as follows: 'And the pony boy comes and leads the pony out of the circus ring; you all be the pony boy; how will you lead the pony out of the ring?'

ANSWERS: Just call him. – Hold his reins. – Put your hand on his neck. – Pull him by the mane, etc.

TEACHER: All right, yes, you could do any of those things. Each of you is the pony boy; you decide how you're going to do it, and lead the pony out of the ring;

The class starts doing this.

TEACHER: Where are you going to take him?

ANSWERS: Back to his stable. – Into a field at the back of the circus.

TEACHER: Yes, that's two ideas. I wonder which the pony boy really would do. If the pony has been galloping, how will he feel?

ANSWERS: Jolly hot. – Bit tired. – Hungry too.

TEACHER: Yes, he could be all those things, couldn't he? Well, what do you think pony boys do when their ponies are hot from running?

They may not know, so we tell them about 'rubbing down' a pony – and perhaps go straight into that part of the activity, without detail this time, but on another occasion we could add more detail to even this simple activity.

TEACHER: Now, you've rubbed the pony down. Now what does the pony do?

ANSWERS: Have his tea. – Have a rest.

TEACHER: Yes, he'll want both, but he's going to have tea first today. What does he have for tea?

ANSWERS: Grass. – Oats. – Hay. – Sort of meal.

TEACHER: And who gives him his tea?

ANSWER: The pony boy.

TEACHER: Where does he get it from?

ANSWERS: From the field. – From the stores.

And so on. Experience is enriched, thinking and imagination are stretched, detail is developed. Naturally, it is wise and necessary to be very sensitive as to how long this kind of discussion can last and to give constant opportunity for actually doing as well as discussing. Often it is wise to leave quite an un-interrupted sequence of activity. It is also important not to 'pick on' people – and not to give praise or blame in the discussion; the opportunity is there for all, and the teacher is interested in who is taking it and in what manner; but nothing is done that might create fear of failure.

In the section on story-building, we considered 'the Ideas Game'; what is happening above is very similar to the ideas game, only we are now considering not the imaginative ideas of making up a story, but the detail within a simple activity; the basic procedure is similar.

All such simple, straightforward experiences are important parts of improvisation in infant schools; as experience grows, the dramatic incident becomes important too, but the conflict at this age is one of circumstance rather than of character. So that in the visit to the seaside, the railway line may be blocked by a landslide and everybody sets to to dig a clear path; or in the circus, the lion breaks loose or the 'big-top' is blown down; in the domestic scene, there isn't a shilling for the gas and supper won't be ready in time, or the washing-machine breaks down, and so on. In the story happening in a boat, the boat springs a leak or a big storm comes up or there are whales and sharks swimming round; in each case, conflict is created by circumstance, and even if the circumstances are associated or caused by people, the emphasis is still on the action involved and not on the studied motives of character; so the landslide may have been caused by brigands, the leak in the boat may have been fixed by 'a bad man' or 'a crook', and these wicked people may well be caught and locked up in prison. People are now associated with the conflict, but still the main interest is in the action and the circumstances; and this is not only so for infants and young juniors – it is equally so for the early work with older age groups who have never done improvisation before; detailed interest in character comes at a later stage, and interest in the motives of character comes even later.

GROUP EXPERIENCES

The above experiences are concerned with each member of the class working at one and the same time. Parallel with such work there can also be built group experiences involving the whole class in a single story; one such example has already been suggested in chapter 5.

Early group experience needs again to be harnessed to very short and simple stories; everybody is in the same story still, but now instead of all being and doing everything that arises in the story – the kind of work in which there must always be parallel continuity – there might be the beginnings of some casting, which leads to different people having a particular experience within the overall whole of the story. However, in such work, casting should not be thought of in the way that one casts adult plays; here is no case for deciding that any one particular youngster, who happens to be blessed with particular gifts, shall have the star part; nor, as so often happens in this age of half-digested psychology, the complete opposite to this, giving the star part to the least gifted (or least attractive) youngster, because it will help to 'bring them out'.

Undoubtedly both the above examples may be of value at some moment in drama, but not too often, and certainly not in the early stages of group experience; this is one of those difficult examples where generalisation is inadequate, especially if the reader takes the advice too literally. As has already been indicated, drama, in its detailed concern for the development of each child 'at its own level and at its own rate', must be as concerned for the gifted and able child at one end of the scale and the retarded or backward or slow developer at the other end, as well as with all those who roughly fall between these extremes; drama fails in its intention if it is reduced to a kind of therapy arising from too detailed consideration for less fortunate children; it fails again if it is largely geared to the intelligent and well-gifted; again it fails if it makes no provision for these extremes. The teacher's attitude and way of thinking about the work is the most important criteria at every stage.

The question, in this case, for the teacher to decide is quite simply: 'What are the intentions underlying my attempt at group experiences' in drama? The overall intention is that of extending the horizons of experience by providing particular opportunities for each individual to *use his own resources in sensitive relationship to other people*. Within this are many detailed intentions for each individual – deeper concentration, different imaginative and thinking opportunities, and, according to the nature of the story being used as a framework for the experiences, opportunity to use one's whole body (movement) and to use language (speech); and finally, the opportunity to *sustain* being somebody or something else for a longer period of time as part of the contribution to a whole in which other people are making other and different contributions.

Perhaps an analogy with music would help to clarify this latter point. Hitherto, experience has been that of trying out all the different instruments; now experience is one of sustaining the playing of one instrument *in harmony* with other instruments; and the essence of the problem regarding casting arises from the same analogy quite naturally, for in the orchestra there is not just *one* violin, but a group of violins, not just one horn, but a group of horns and so on (we are a long way from being concerned with the virtuoso opportunities of the concerto!). Within each 'group instrument' are several individuals all contributing to the 'single wholeness' of that instrument, in relationship to the larger wholeness of the orchestra. Within the group of violinists there will be one person who is, by gift and skill, the *leader* of that group, but nevertheless his experience and gifts are given to the group of violinists; another violinist in the same group may be much less gifted and certainly unable to play a solo part in a concerto; but he contributes his particular gift and is just as much part of that group; the group lends confidence to him and helps his development, and the needs of the group draws sensitivity from the leader as well as using his qualities of leadership. So too with the group play; if the play is about a king, at this stage in our infant school work we do not cast one person as the king, but a group of people. One in the group may indeed be 'cleverer' than the others – and, as with the example of the violins, will become leader of the group king; others, less gifted, still contribute whatever they are able, using the qualities of leadership of the more gifted one among them who, in his turn, is having an opportunity to use his gifts in a sensitive manner. As teachers we avoid 'exploiting' – and possibly undermining – that gift, but provide opportunity for its use in harmonious relation to others. All potential forms of conceit and exhibitionism are thus avoided in a constructive and positive manner without in any way ignoring or belittleing the indigenous gift; and for the others, constructive and positive manners are thus found of helping to develop the confidence that arises from being able to use one's indigenous gift as a contribution to a whole instead of ignoring the smallness of the gift simply because it would be of no value in virtuoso circumstances.

Let us consider the building and doing of such a group experience with a class of top infants, pursuing the original thought of a king, starting from pre-experience.

Example:

TEACHER (*to class in hall*): You are all kings and queens. Listen to the sound I make, and all be kings and queens.

Some stately sound is made on either the tambour or the cymbal, which stimulates everybody being either kings or queens, moving about the hall.

TEACHER: And the kings and queens meet one another, and whenever they do, they bow and curtsey to one another and then go on walking until they meet another king or queen.

Sound continues as before, but with every now and then a particular climax of beat which will help some of the class with the bowing and curtsying.

TEACHER: Now – you are all people in a forest, hunting, walking very carefully as you search for whatever you are hunting. Off you go. Remember, you are in a forest, with lots of bushes and trees all round . . . .

Sound different from above – it now has an element of mood and atmosphere, accompanying the whole movement of stalking.

TEACHER: Now – let's become the forest. First of all – the trees. Curl up very small into a seed in the ground. And you are all going to grow into magnificent, great tall trees. Listen.

A growing climax of sound for the growth of the trees.

TEACHER: And when I make a loud sound, you all become seeds again.

A very quick climax on either tambour or cymbal, for everyone once more to curl up very small.

There could follow experiences of being bushes, birds etc. as suggested in chapter 5.

And the sound experience is then repeated in terms of rabbits, and after rabbits the teacher might then stop to change the experience from the fully 'directed' type to the 'stimulated' type and ask: 'What else might a hunter find in the forest apart from birds and rabbits?' Answers might well include squirrels, lions, tigers, deer and so on. If we wish to include these in our story, of which we are giving pre-experience, then each one could grow in precisely the same way, and once grown the sounds we make could vary according to the kind of movement experience we wish to stimulate and to enrich.

After these many varied experiences of being royal people, hunters, trees and bushes, then of different kinds of animal, there might then be 'small group' experiences (perhaps even simply in pairs if this seems at the moment to be the right experience to give) of people growing together as bushes or trees, being together as royal people or hunters, living and working together as different kinds of animal, in each of the latter cases there being a few moments as these people or creatures discuss among themselves what they are going to eat, where they are going to get the food from, the actual going to get it, eating it and then, perhaps, going home and sleeping.

Earlier in this chapter (see p. 194) it was mentioned that one could also provide experience of being inanimate things or objects, and there may well be such an opportunity within these circumstances. So that the teacher could now continue...

TEACHER: Now – you are all wood-cutters. Off you go into the forest. Among the trees, you find a particular one that you want to cut down and make into all sorts of different things. The wood-cutter takes his big axe and starts to cut down the tree...and he cuts and cuts until the tree falls.

A rhythmic beat on either the tambour or cymbal, eventually reaching a climax of sound for the actual falling of the tree.

Now, the woodcutter gets his great saw and starts to cut off all the biggest branches of the tree....

Again a rhythm that helps the experience of sawing.

(Perhaps this might be the right moment to introduce work in pairs by talking about long double-handed saws!)

From this there might be further experiences of 'making furniture', again either on one's own or in small groups, and then, in groups of six or seven perhaps making huts or small buildings, discussing together all the necessary things there are to do. This can be followed, again in large and small groups, by themselves *becoming* different pieces of furniture or buildings, in the latter case 'making' door frames and doors and the walls of the building. By now, everybody in the class has had simple and straightforward pre-experience of all the ingredients of the group story that is to follow. Everyone has been kings or queens, hunters, trees, bushes, birds, rabbits, other animals, and various pieces of furniture and some kind of building. Let us assume the class concerned with the experience numbers thirty-five. The teacher now continues as follows:

TEACHER: Now – we are going to do a story about a king who goes hunting in the forest. At one end of the forest – over there (*pointing to a precise spot at one end of the hall; it is always necessary at this stage to be quite precise about geographical details*) is the king's special house in the forest; that's where the king has his lunch whenever he goes hunting. Now – you people (*selecting six, seven or eight*) go over there; you are going to be the hut. In that corner over there lives a family of rabbits – you four are the rabbits; and over there lives a family of squirrels – you four are the squirrels; and the king comes hunting from that corner over there – you four are the king. You people are all trees or bushes in the forest, from all the way over there where the path starts to right over there where the king's hut is. With the sound I'm going to make, you are all seeds scattered over the ground ready to grow into bushes or trees – now!

A climax of sound sends the seeds scattering, and then with the growth of sound, each seed grows into a tree or a bush.

Now – is the king's hut made? (*If not, then allow a little more time.*) Have the rabbits and the squirrels found where they live? (*again, more time if they are not quite ready*) – and the king? Have you got what you need for hunting? What are you hunting with? (*It might be guns; it might be bows and arrows; teacher advises if necessary.*)

TEACHER: Now, while I tell the story, you do everything that happens in it.

It is early morning in the forest; the trees and the bushes are sleeping; the animals and the birds are sleeping; even the hut in the forest is asleep; and the king is asleep in his palace; everything sleeps until the sun rises – and as it rises, everything and everybody wakes up.

A quiet and sensitive growth of sound on the cymbal for the rise of the sun; the sound needs to be soft enough for the teacher to speak over easily, if there is need. There may well be an immediate response to the sound itself, with all of the different groups coming to life. If there is need for the teacher to stimulate with words over the sound, then something as follows will help:

The trees and bushes open up their leaves and branches to the sunlight and gently move in the breeze; the animals and birds wake up and find breakfast in the forest; and the hut becomes ready for the day, in case the king should need it, and the king gets ready for the hunt.

(It will be interesting to observe what happens with the hut – activity could range from simple alerting and stretching, to change of character and actual dusting and cleaning types of preparation.)

And as soon as the king is ready, he comes into the forest, down that path over there (*there may be need to add other helpful directions if the king gets lost at any point*). All the trees and bushes are delighted to see the king, and as they bow to him the king fancies he hears the breeze whispering 'Good morning, your majesty'. (*The trees and bushes might pick this up – if it is too subtle, then the suggestion might be made again, more clearly.*) But suddenly all the animals and the birds realise that the king has come hunting – so quickly they all run away and hide. The king creeps quietly down every path in turn, searching for animals and birds; sometimes he sees them – but never in time to catch them.

(*There might be a very long pause in the actual telling of the story now, leaving the king and the animals to pursue the action in their own time; if concentration begins to flag, or if there is a clear completion of interest in this part of the story, then the teacher continues from there.*)

Eventually the king gets tired of the hunt; and he's hungry too. So he goes down the path leading to his favourite hut – he opens the door – and closes it after him – and prepares to have his splendid picnic lunch. (*Details of the lunch might be inserted if it will help; or it might have been suggested to the group king earlier that they discuss what they would like to take for a picnic lunch.*) And whilst the king prepares his lunch, the animals and birds creep silently through the forest, dodging from tree to tree and bush to bush, always keeping in hiding in case the king should see or hear them. And the king eats a splendid lunch, with all of the animals and birds peering through the cracks in the walls of the hut. (*Again leave time for the action.*) And the king throws out all the crumbs from his picnic, and then becomes very sleepy – and indeed, very soon he is fast asleep, and there isn't any sound to be heard in the whole forest except the gentle breeze in the trees and bushes.

(The use of trees and bushes is always helpful with a large class, but at the same time it is necessary constantly to seek opportunities for particular things that they might do, so that they do not become just 'audience' to the activity of the others in the class.)

TEACHER (*continuing*): When the animals and birds are quite sure the king is fast asleep, they go to where he threw out all the crumbs – but very quietly so that they don't wake the king. And after their feast, they run back into the forest and hide, waiting for the king to come out of the hut and go back through the forest. But a strange thing happens – the king doesn't wake up. For ages and ages the birds and animals and the trees and the bushes wait and wait and wait, but the king is still fast, fast asleep. And soon, the sun begins to set, and the forest becomes very dark.

(*Again, the cymbal or tambour sound can help the mood and atmosphere of the idea of the sun setting.*)

And when it is quite dark, and the king still has not woken up, all the trees and the bushes, the animals and the birds, even the hut, become very worried – and they all whisper: 'Your Majesty, your majesty' over and over and over again. (*Leave them time to do this; the king may hear and wake up without story instructions; if not, the teacher continues*:) and through his sleep the king hears the whispering and slowly wakes up; and all the animals and the birds cluster round him telling him that the sun has set (*leave time for this*). And the king is very worried because he has never before been in the forest in the dark and he has no light. Then one (or more) of the animals has an idea (*N.B. the teacher might specify which animal, either by just pointing, or perhaps even by some such identification as 'father rabbit', for by now it will be clear who is likely to take a confident lead on the section following.*) He tells the king that all of the animals and the birds will make a long line, holding on to one another, with the king following the last in the line; and he tells the king that the trees and bushes will lead them out of the forest by pointing the way with their branches. (*Having given the explanation of what is going to happen, again leave time for the class to take over and organise the actual action, only putting in the occasional word of help if there seems to be any doubt or confusion; possibly the rest of the story will happen without another word, until the very end, when the king is safely out of the forest:*) And the king says his thanks and goodbyes to all the animals and the birds and the trees and the bushes, and goes safely home; and then everybody and everything in the forest goes fast, fast asleep. (*And when the full silence comes, the teacher might add an ending – though this is very much a matter of personal taste – such as:*) And the king was so grateful to all those that helped him home that he made a new law in his kingdom –

nd the law was that no one should ever hunt the animals or the birds in that forest ever again.

The story has been simple and short, has involved the whole class in a group experience, preceded by pre-experience of all the different characters and action of the story, and has included simple casting experience and the opportunity to sustain a single contribution to the whole. There are, of course, many other and different details that could have been included; for example, there might well have been a group as 'the sun'; there could have been considerable activity of one kind and another in the palace before the king sets off – but, and this is an advantage all too easily overlooked – every story immediately throws up new suggestions for different experiences, either using the same people in different circumstances or even different people in the same circumstances; each experience leads naturally to another.

At a later stage one of the possible developments is for the teacher to tell the whole story right at the very beginning, then set the 'geography', then allow the story to continue without any narration, inserting suggestions only if and when people forget what is to happen next.

This simple type of group experience can use all kinds of original story material as a framework, and of course can include all kinds of derivative story material as well, using myths and legends, adventures of geography and history, scripture stories and so on. There is clearly an overlap into work that might be considered more suitable for juniors, and the reader who is concerned with infants may well find additional material in the next section. If we can differentiate in our own minds the intentions of 'academic' work and the intentions behind this type of experience, then we discover new premises from which to judge what is suitable for each age group. The discovery often includes the fact that age group has little to do with choice of material; age and degree of experience affect the approach, the intention and the expectation. As has already been pointed out, the difference in approach is as often as not simply a matter of choice of words and characters; even the above story would work with some secondary youngsters, according to their experience, and with some basic changes, as for example, the king might become 'a man on the run' – and the whole story part of a terrifying nightmare he has in which he finds himself in a strange jungle, where the very foliage and trees seem to live and speak, and where strange nightmare creatures haunt him; the detail of character changes, some aspects of the story line change–but the overall change in material is not all that great.

Juniors and Secondary

It has been suggested that infant teachers may well find useful suggestions in a section marked juniors; so, too, will the junior teacher in the section headed infants, and for those involved with top juniors, further suggestions in the section headed Seniors. This cannot be too strongly emphasised with activity of the kind considered in this book, for the many varied intentions concerned with the growth of people, over and over again point at the unity of the child, whatever convenience there may be in some aspects of education to chop the child up into several sections, treating each section as quite different from the others.

If no work of the kind suggested throughout the book has been attempted, then it is both necessary and important to start from the beginning – not just from the beginning of improvisation as reached in this chapter, but from the beginning of all the points on the circle including concentration, use of the senses, imagination, movement, speech exercises, etc. There is no difficulty in the junior school, particularly in the lower half; self-consciousness, for the majority, will not have taken a strong hold, and confidence and skill build quickly with regular practice in an uncritical framework.

Stretching

No small part of the teacher's function in the junior school is involved in 'stretching'. Always there is the challenge to use one's resources more fully and more richly, and to stretch out towards greater awareness and perception of one's environment. (The words 'awareness' and 'perception' are used advisedly rather than 'knowledge' and 'understanding', for this factor of stretching is as deeply concerned with emotional, spiritual and physical growth as with intellectual. If concerned with all four levels rather than only one, then knowledge and understanding continue to develop as much at the intuitive as at the conscious level – there is a great deal of *thinking* involved, but not all of it conscious thinking, and there is a natural rather than a forced link with associative factors such as 'memory', 'reasoning', 'proving', etc. The intuitive foundation will aid the conscious use of these at a later stage.) It is this factor of stretching that is the immediate concern of this section of the book, presupposing that earlier work has been regularly attempted so that all of the points on the circle have already been practised and reached a stage of deep absorption and confidence.

Even at this stage a continuous programme of regular activity, using all of one's resources, must be continued; these might be tabulated as follows:

(a) Regular practice at concentration through the use of the senses.

(b) Regular practice at using the senses to stimulate the imagination.

(c) Regular use of the imagination to stimulate both the use of the body and the use of language (movement and speech).

(d) Regular use of movement to stimulate further awareness of and mastery of the physical self and that physical self within its environment (space).

(e) Regular use of speech in order to communicate one's own ideas and feelings to other people (not audience) – and to be able to listen to the ideas and feelings communicated by others (not as audience).

(f) Regular practice at becoming aware of other people in order to stimulate and develop sensitivity.

(g) Regular practice at using that sensitivity to control one's own emotions (self-discipline and social awareness).

(h) Regular practice at using one's emotional self (in harmonious relation to the other facets of oneself) in order to discover more about oneself and other people (developing horizons and broadening experience).

All these are ultimately embodied in the activity called improvisation, which is in part an outer symbol of the development of each point. Within each activity, the stretching intention is achieved through more challenging opportunities and through the stages of development of detail, as outlined in the infants section; and with improvisation, stretching is achieved in the same manner – partly by extending what already is, and partly by the introduction of new factors, which in their turn are gradually developed in more detail.

The following practical suggestions for stretching improvisation are as applicable to secondary work as to primary, again depending on the foundations that have been laid and are being continuously developed.

1. SIMPLE, DIRECT EXPERIENCE

Literally, 'the world is one's oyster'. There is no field of human activity or endeavour that is not exciting material at some stage of junior drama, quite simply and straightforwardly as activity or endeavour in its own right. Every occupation, particularly of the physical and the adventurous type – for action rather than motive continues to be the key note – constitutes interesting and worthwhile material, from the fire station to the coal-mine, from sailing a four-masted schooner to crossing the desert on foot, from exploring ancient caves to discovering the need for a lever, from inventing the wheel to curing the world of all its plagues. There is nothing too challenging. Early work may be trite in its outcome – more practice will remove part of this, the stretching we are considering here the remainder; but as far as actual material is concerned there is little or no problem; the fantastic or the supernatural can be as pertinent as the real and down-to-earth; the past can be as great an adventure as the future, or vice versa, and the present is filled with everything that avid curiosity and wonder can imagine or contemplate. There is experience of conquest and defeat, of give and take, of winning and losing, of being noble and mean, courageous and cowardly, good and wicked, important and insignificant, human and inhuman, subhuman and superhuman, of beings things, animals, creatures, insects, some entirely new and imaginary, some that existed with the birth of time; and the experiences use every facet of human personality – the physical self, the spiritual, the emotional, the intellectual – and all is guided by the intuition, for much that is achieved is entirely unconscious in the early stages, growing to full consciousness – to full awareness that this 'is me and I am *making it happen*' – gradually and eventually, and most important of all, organically, according to one's readiness from within oneself. Much of this adventure in drama is quite unparticularised in its early instances, but some of it can become direct pre-experience of information and facts at a later stage. For example: a simple situation is built up round the idea of coal-mining. Working at the singleton stage, each person experiences (perhaps from a movement viewpoint) going to a low coal-face and hacking away with a pick and then gathering the coal with shovels into trucks, and pushing the trucks through the dark tunnels to the surface. There may be many such different experiences, with the whole class working at one and the same time. Then a coal-mine scene is built up using the whole class. Some work at the coal-face, some are in charge of transport, others look after lifts and so on. Then, quite suddenly a new question is brought up. 'What is it really like in a coal-mine?' (Before, we weren't worried about this, particularly at the early stages when we simply provided a movement experience.) Now we ask and discuss: What is it really like? Many different thoughts may arise from the discussion – cramped conditions, dirt, heat, and so on, but for the purpose of this example let us follow through just one aspect – the darkness. Discussion around this will include consideration of how light is actually taken to the coal-face, including the light each miner has on his own helmet, lit by a battery. But what about before batteries were invented – what sort of light did they use then? Candles perhaps, and oil-lanterns. So we return to improvisation, everybody now working down in the darkness by oil light and candle light; at some point we warn the class that we shall be making a great sound on the cymbal or the drum, and that the sound is an explosion in the mine – perhaps some people are killed, perhaps some injured, perhaps others are not hurt and try to rescue those that are; and so a simple group improvisation happens, which now includes the episode of the explosion; how long we let the rescue operations continue will depend on the depth of absorption and concentration.

Eventually, however, the scene ends, or we bring it to a close. If it ends on its own it will most likely fade away – if we intend bringing it to a close and absorption is strong, we offer the warning: 'Begin to finish it off now if you can – just a few minutes left'; this may help the ending in a constructive manner or merely expedite its petering out; but we are to consider the whole factor of endings shortly. Meanwhile, as soon as it ends we start discussion again: 'What', we ask, 'caused that explosion?' And we discuss gas and where it comes from and how it accumulates in the mine – and we discuss what caused it to blow up, namely the naked lights. At once we get the class to divide into small groups; they are all connected with mining – inventors, managers, engineers and coal-face workers. Each group has the same problem, set them by the coal-mine owners, because this is not the first disastrous explosion that has happened: they must urgently find a way of lighting the mine that will not have the same dangers – and no one has yet heard of either electricity or the dry-cell battery. This discussion is not academic – it involves real people with a real life-and-death problem; depending on the age group, they may find the answer. If they don't, then we are standing by with the relevant information about Humphrey Davy lanterns. But we do not leave it at that – we study them in detail, and then in drama we have another scene at the mine, and the miners are issued with the lanterns and work in safety – perhaps even having a scene where the lantern indicates the presence of a pocket of gas. And so on.

This is one isolated example of simple direct experience; within it was added a single moment of conflict, embracing also experience of climax and de-climax. The introduction of conflict takes us into another stage of stretching, extending outwards from simple experience of being.

2. CONFLICT

All the situations that have been suggested under the previous heading can be developed a stage further – even into entirely different directions – by the introduction of conflict. Each activity, simple and direct to start with, becomes an adventure with the introduction of circumstances that create conflict, and the circumstances can be small or large. The coal-mine was changed by the explosion; a domestic scene is suddenly changed by granny losing her brooch or because father cannot find his lighter; a calm day at sea is changed with the coming of a wind, let alone a hurricane; a farm episode is transformed when a fence is found broken down, or some sheep are missing, or the wells are drying up; a market-place is changed by a row over the price of an article; a street scene changes with an accident; a desert exploit is changed when the map is stolen, or lost, or carried away in a sand storm; an adventure through the forest is changed when the adventurers suddenly reach a clearing not marked on their map, or when they suddenly see footsteps in a land that is reputed uninhabited; a grain of sand stops the submarine periscope from rising; a leak in the petrol tank confronts the passengers on an airplane with possible disaster; the nightwatchman falls asleep at the moment he should be fully alert; a policeman recognises a face in a crowd; a football goalie has a visit from a masked man just before the match; a mountain climb is changed by an avalanche, and so on. Any simple episode can be almost completely transformed by the introduction of a single change in circumstance, and all the above are random choices which do not even begin to touch on the whole world of fantasy and 'magic' which may still be important for juniors. The simple forest scene, discussed in the infant section, had its moment of conflict simply by the king going to sleep for too long and the sun setting; but the whole world of kings and queens, princes and princesses, witches and wizards, fairies and goblins, giants and dwarfs – not to mention animals, and all the various creatures and people of outer space and of children's own imaginings – all of them confront us with two possibilities: (1) the simple experience of being; (2) the introduction of simple conflict into the lives of these people.

The circumstances of conflict can be introduced with every size of group – twos or threes, slightly larger groups (according to readiness) or the full group experience of the whole class working together, as in the coal-mining episode. Or it can involve each person working on his own, the whole class working at the same time. This is always valuable as a pre-experience introduction to the ingredients of an improvisation. But the full richness of these experiences can be helped – part of the stretching process – by experience of (and practice at) climax and de-climax.

3. CLIMAX AND DE-CLIMAX

In earlier chapters (see pp. 44–48 and pp. 97–101) we have considered moments of simple climax, using the cymbal and tambour, usually as part of an exercise and often associated with important growth factors – growing into things or people, stimulated by the sound to a simple moment of fulfilment. If this type of experience is always continuing, then the unconscious awareness and intuitive perception of climax will grow quite naturally in improvisation.

In the early stages of improvisation and other exercises, climax is often best experienced in terms of completion, and therefore, to a certain extent, with ending. (As is pointed out later in this chapter – see p. 223, this particular approach is ultimately deeply concerned with the growth of form in improvisation.) Here again, it is important to emphasise the use of sound – of the straightforward, simple sounds that the teacher can make with cymbal or tambour or improvising on the piano or some other instrument, homemade or otherwise; the use of the gramophone is ill-advised in the early stages, though it may have many values later; some of these are touched on in this chapter.

In the coal-mining episode, a climax of sound was used for the pit explosion. In those circumstances, because we were concerned with a further and different development, a suggestion was made about the scene continuing with rescue operations; in fact, the scene could have been rounded off with the explosion, not necessarily because everybody is killed in it; some may not be, but the actual working in a coal-mine ceases because of the experience, and to this extent there is ending. So too can we develop many such episodes, associated with the idea of conflict, but bringing the former circumstances to an end – so: the storm climax *ends* the market-place or the adventure at sea or the trek across the desert; the earthquake or the landslide or the avalanche *ends* other adventures; people being turned into stone or frightened away and so on again *end* other stories. There is value in building group experiences of this nature as well as giving individual experience, with all the members of the class working on their own at one and the same time.

Even within such opportunities, there can be stretching experience through the length of the accompanying sound, which can vary from a short quick climax to a long and protracted one, extending both imagination and the ability to sustain physically and even vocally a particular moment of happening.

De-climax, again useful in earlier exercises for giving experience of going from strong large movement to quieter and more controlled movement, from strong loud activity to soft and quiet activity, is now useful as an experience of *continuity*. Perhaps this can best be illustrated with an example of an avalanche. In an improvisation, a group of mountain climbers are reaching the summit of their expedition; suddenly there is a low rumbling, which grows and grows, and they realise that an avalanche has started; quickly they protect themselves as best they may – the sound comes to a tremendous climax, and then gradually and slowly fades away as the avalanche continues down to the bottom of the mountain. Whether or not the avalanche has hit the group of mountain climbers, there is immediate stimulation to continuity; if the sound had ended with the climax then there would be stimulation more related to ending, perhaps with everybody buried or even killed; but now, because those involved in the episode hear the sound continuing after its climax, there is stimulation to 'carry on'; perhaps a few are not killed and start to rescue the others, perhaps an entirely different group of rescuers are drawn in. Returning to the coal-mining episode, a climax followed by de-climax would have been more useful for the continuity of the rescue operations. So within all of the circumstances that arise from the simple introduction of conflict, the moment is found to introduce either climax, for ending, or de-climax for continuity. The storm hits the ship but eventually dies down; or the storm hits the market-place and then dies away...and so on with all of the other examples given.

There is no need, of course, for either climax or de-climax to be directly concerned with the element of conflict that is brought into the situation, but quite often there is more clarity of situation

H

if they are one and the same. As experience grows, the circumstances of conflict can be the introduction to the potential climax or de-climax, even if these are in fact delayed for a long time. For example, if the ship's rudder is found to be broken, this will at once introduce an element of conflict; but it may be days later before the ship runs aground (climax, with de-climax) leading to the new life the people on board ship now try to live on the desert island on which they have been grounded.

One of the fullest opportunities for stretching experience exists precisely within the fact of continuity associated with, first, the fullness of climax experience, and then with de-climax. (Again, perhaps it is necessary to give the reminder that there is no question of progressing from climax to de-climax; the two experiences continue throughout all drama work, constantly becoming fuller and richer; but where the continuity factor is concerned it is part of natural development to include experience of completion before that of continuity which, by its very nature, makes further demands on concentration and the ability to sustain an improvisation.)

But both climax and de-climax, as well as conflict, are closely involved with mood and atmosphere.

4. MOOD AND ATMOSPHERE

Even the most commonplace and ordinary situation in an improvisation has a potential mood and atmosphere. In ordinary life, children are very susceptible to mood and atmosphere until their senses become deadened through lack of use, and if we aim to preserve sincerity in their improvisations they will, even at the intuitive and unconscious stages of drama, develop a strong feeling for these qualities, which we can help to become stronger and more real as their drama becomes more conscious towards the top of the primary school. One aspect of developing an awareness of creating mood and atmosphere is involved in the process of stretching and of extending experience, but it is important to let this side develop in its own way in the early stages. Full absorption, which governs the sincerity, will allow for this development even in many of the simple movement and speech exercises of earlier chapters.

The factor of conflict highlights the existence of mood and atmosphere; for example, in a domestic situation, the mood may simply be one of general high spirits – suddenly father cannot find his pipe, and the mood changes; or in the coal-mining episode, the mood may be one of hardworking intent–and the explosion suddenly changes the whole feeling, the whole atmosphere. In both cases the original mood and atmosphere are highlighted by the introduction of conflict. Climax not only helps the actual moment of fulfilment of conflict, but also concludes the preceding mood and atmosphere; de-climax provides the bridge over to the next mood and atmosphere which is created by the conflict; this is perhaps an over-simplification of a quite complex sequence of different feelings, but is stated here simply to point out how closely interwoven are all of these different experiences in drama, which are dissected only in order that we might observe the different ingredients of experience and so provide further opportunities which, though designed to help the enrichment of one particular factor are, in fact, going to help many factors. What is left as a quite unconscious experience in the early years of drama begins to become more conscious at the top of the primary school, until it is fully conscious and intended later in the secondary school. But we, as teachers, do not neglect foundation experiences simply because they cannot yet be consciously absorbed; we do not do so in the intellectual sphere and nor should we in the intuitive, physical and emotional spheres. Intuitive and later conscious experience of mood and atmosphere are a vital part of the process of becoming aware of one's environment, and sensitive to people.

Atmosphere is created by the mood of people, and in drama the moods of people are stimulated through the imagination, which in its turn is stimulated by the senses. One of the most fruitful ways of providing this form of stimulus is through the use of music, and a list of useful music for such purposes appears at the end of the book. In the section on Movement (see pp. 94–105), much is said about the use of sound and music to stimulate the full discovery of the body and the exploration of space. For movement and the control of the body, it was emphasised that time-beat and rhythm are predominantly important – but even simple time-beat will create mood. A very slow and rather quiet beat will stimulate a quite different mood in people from a fast and loud beat, so that even within the directly intended development of movement there is concern for mood and the resulting atmosphere. Music can help with three overlapping but fairly distinct kinds of activity:

Dance, in which the physical self is coordinated and responsive to timebeat and rhythm in the main, and is more or less abstract in proportion to the amount of response to mood and atmosphere.

Dance Drama, in which there is fuller use of character, mood and atmosphere and conflict, at the same time as the full physical self is used in response to beat and rhythm; and

Music Plays (improvisations with partial or full use of music), in which there is again full use of character, mood and atmosphere and conflict, but much less use of the physical self; there may also be use of speech.

The latter is what concerns us in improvisation, even though there may be intended or spontaneous use of all three activities within one sequence.

Because children hear sound emotionally and pictorially, music will help not only with the creation of mood but also with the sustaining of it and with the intuitive awareness of change of mood. This intuitive awareness will gradually become, like all the other facets of drama, more conscious as the child becomes more mature; but it is again important to allow the process to find its own rate of development and to keep constantly in mind that much of the experience arising from this particular use of music is inner experience; there may even be, at times, complete physical stillness because the experience is in the realm of feeling and, particularly in early stages, it is not always either possible or desirable to express those feelings in an outer and tangible form. It is not possible because the child is not a communicator and it is not desirable because if we attempt to force outward expression we falsify the genuine experience and the result is one of illustrating, often by conventional symbols, which have no basis in sincerity. Those teachers who are upset by the whole idea of stimulating feeling, and who, if they permit such experience at all, are anxious to translate emotion into immediate action, should consider such feelings as tranquility, simple contentment, reverence, noble aspiration, resolution, determination, hope, sympathy, and even regret and shame and change of heart. Can we really deny the educational value of stimulating such experiences? And if we do permit the stimulation, can we really believe that such inner experiences will be any the richer by forcing externalised action in order to show what one feels? Why, even in the highest forms of professional theatre communication, such feelings are often both experienced and expressed through complete and total absence of movement. How much more so then for children, who are not communicators and not being trained to communicate, is it important to allow inner experience to take place in its natural way. If we feel excited by something or furious with somebody, the feeling may at once lead to action; but there are many human feelings that not only do not lead to action but cease to exist the moment there is action.

5. EMOTION

Mood and atmosphere cannot exist without people, and atmosphere is created by the mood of people. Mood is created by feelings, which are all rooted in emotion. As has been constantly reiterated, drama is as concerned with exploring and mastering the emotional self as it is concerned with discovering and mastering the physical self. Many teachers feel that children have no experience of emotion, or at any rate experience only a few. What is usually meant by this is that children cannot express emotion. In fact the whole field of human emotion exists within them, many perhaps awaiting particular circumstances before in fact they are experienced, and many at a quite different scale from that of adults. Drama provides a natural opportunity for experience, and the opportunities can include not only an outlet for more primitive or unpleasant emotions, but also the *only* opportunities for experiencing the nobler and finer emotions, simply because the general circumstances of life for the majority of people do not call upon the need for or the use of some of these. As part of the stretching of experience through drama, simple exploration of emotions can be introduced, not as such – in a kind of abstract manner – but through a more detailed concern for characterisation. Early drama is concerned with action, with people doing things. This is extended by conflict, including the creation of mood and atmosphere; ultimately it is vitally concerned with human motive as well as behaviour, and emotion provides the bridge from simple straightforward action to the effect of action on people and the effect of people on action. So that the development (the stretching process) of the mining episode would be:

(a) Simple being and doing.
(b) The above plus conflict.
(c) The above plus consideration of the kinds of people involved, and therefore their response to the conflict.

But consideration of the kinds of people is, in the early stages, of emotional factors and not of intellectual (psychological) factors. Let us consider the development again in terms of the mining episode: the following sequence develops logically –

(a) Simply being miners – i.e. oneself as a miner.
(b) Physical consideration of the miners; some are big and strong, others are old, others are small and weak, etc.
(c) Emotional consideration of the miners, often linked with physical factors, e.g. brave (possibly linked with big and strong – though not necessarily); frightened (possibly linked with small and weak); kind (possibly linked with old), etc.

Some of the early experience in this field may well arise *after* an improvisation. In the mining episode when all is over, we may say something like: 'Now, some of you were killed or injured, Would anyone like to say why this happened to them when they were a miner in the mine?' Answers will undoubtedly include such entirely physical factors as 'Well, I was right by the explosion', or 'Well, the whole ceiling of the mine fell in on me', or 'A lot of rocks fell on my leg', etc. But some might include such factors as 'Well, I was a bit old and weak and just died'. And if we carry the discussion to those who were not killed or wounded (if any), we will again get mainly physical factors such as 'Well, I wasn't very near the explosion', or 'Well, I was standing by a strong pit-prop and it sort of kept the rocks from landing on me', but we might also get 'Well, I was a big, strong chap so it didn't really affect me', and so on. In all of these cases we are concerned with either the physical circumstances of the actual episode or with the physical condition of some of the people – i.e. stages (a) and (b) above. But either within this part of the scene, or within the extension into the rescue operations, we are confronted with the possibility of there arising (or our introducing) the next stage, the simple emotional factors, now bringing in suggestions of people being 'brave' or 'frightened' or 'determined' or whatever. All of these factors might arise *after* an improvisation; but they can also be part of the original stimulus before improvisation, arising through direct suggestion or discussion – and all closely linked with characterisation.

6. CHARACTERISATION

Much has already been said about this, but from a different angle. Now we are concerned with characterisation more fully considered from the emotional point of view. In the earlier stage we considered the *development* from making up, for example, an improvisation about

– an old man, an errand boy, a doctor, and a neighbour of the old man,

to one about:

– a *sad* old man, a *cheeky* errand boy, a *kind* doctor, and a *bad-tempered* neighbour of the old man.

The emphasis will be still on story and action, but will now include some of the emotional characteristics of people, which, in turn, will gradually begin to govern the circumstances giving rise to the story and action.

So, little by little, greater and greater emphasis is placed on people, starting from quite simple characteristics from an emotional basis, but eventually becoming more and more detailed and complex. These factors can be stretched within *all* improvisations, and considered beforehand. So that in the mining episode, the decision about what kind of person you are is made *before* the improvisation, and subsequent action is governed by that person's characteristics.

The carrying out of the action, even when so governed, is still very largely an intuitive matter, concerned with generalities rather than specific detail; but with experience and practice, and the gradual growth from unconscious drama to fully conscious realisation that 'we are making this happen', so the specific and the detailed become more important, governed now by more and more use of intellectual consideration.

7. INTELLECTUAL CONSIDERATION

Within this, the *mind* begins to govern and control, eventually in great detail, both the intention and the carrying out of that intention. It controls what one does with one's body; it controls emotion to the needs and appropriateness of the moment; it controls and preselects language that is necessary and appropriate; it is in touch with the overall intention and yet the detail of each moment; it is fully aware of, and sensitive in response to, the contribution of other people, both as themselves and as the characters they in turn are being and controlling; it controls the imagination, pinning it down to what is necessary and discarding extraneous matter that may be stimulated quite spontaneously at any given moment. This is fully conscious drama, fully intended acts of creation. It arises naturally and organically, and yet needs stimulating and encouraging (part of the idea of teachers' sharing wisdom with young people). It is a deeply valuable experience to reach, affecting all facets of personality and life, of the use of self in relation to environment – it is, in the sense of fulfilment, a kind of end-product. But the full, rich nature of the experience is dependent on the development for each person, at their own level and their own rate of progress, of all the many different points on the circle – concentration, imagination, the senses, the body, speech, sensitivity etc., etc. – in a non-audience and un-critical framework. If these have been developed, then the fulfil-ment will be really personal, genuine, sincere and of lasting value. Where drama so often goes wrong is that this goal is artificially forced, and forced moreover in relation to factors of communica-tion before there is anything to communicate or any means of communicating. Only at this stage does communication really begin to have any value in terms of full educational intent, con-cerned with the development of people and an awareness of and mastery of environment. For only now have we reached the stage where what is made or created is made or created with full

consciousness and full control, using all of the thoroughly practised facets of self that are necessary for making and creating, and
then being able to retain all of the indigenous qualities of the
work at the same time as sharing with other people. The factor
of sharing is developed further in chapter 11.

Meanwhile, it cannot be too strongly emphasised that the basis
of this intellectual aspect of development is constant *discussion*;
that kind of discussion which is informal and stimulating, devoid
of petty criticisms and comparisons and long-winded analyses of
what is wrong. Discussion on what has already happened should
always start from the viewpoint of what has gone right, so that
each youngster is helped to be aware of and sensitive to positive
values and positive considerations. To start discussing an improvisation from the viewpoint of 'What was wrong with that?'
leads to the whole process of fear of failure and to doing things
for the wrong motive, usually that of satisfying some fleeting idea
of what teacher is going to approve, and forces attitudinising and
externalising, the major enemies of sincerity and truth.

8. DEVELOPMENT OF FORM IN IMPROVISATION

In order to suggest the different stages of development in improvisation, it has been necessary to go from point to point in some
form of logical sequence; but the sequence is largely overlapping
and is paralleled by a development of form, growing outwards,
further and further away from the scribble stage, according to
the amount of practice, until, ultimately, it is possible for some
groups to improvise with the finish and polish of a scripted and
rehearsed production of a play. The early development of form
is entirely intuitive and arises literally from undisturbed and un-
criticised opportunity simply to do many improvisations. But
attention to all the different aspects suggested in this chapter aids
the discovery and mastery of form, little by little, according to
confidence and total absorption being fully maintained.

The 'still photographs' of early exercises and improvisations are
helpful because they free the mind from being fussed about how
to begin. In the same manner, climax of one kind or another can
help experience of ending, again without the mind being fussed
about *how* to end. But after confidence and absorption start

becoming stronger, the teacher begins to say during the planning of improvisations in whatever sized group: 'How is it going to begin?' and 'How is it going to end?' leaving each group with the responsibility of arranging its own beginning and ending. It is also useful to suggest actual beginnings and endings as the stimulus for making an improvised story. Examples:

Beginnings:

(a) A group of people in a room, waiting... for the telephone; for a telegram; for the arrival of someone else; for one of them to make a decision.

(b) A single sentence: 'I don't think they're coming'. 'Nothing has been heard of them'. 'They're waiting for you now'. 'Give me five minutes – then follow'.

Endings

All the above would be equally stimulating as an ending, but of course there are many other circumstances or words that could be given with the simple instruction: 'Your story begins with...' or '...ends with...'.

After many experiences of *either* beginnings or endings, we might then give both the beginning and the end, and leave the detail of what happens – of how they get from one to the other in their story – to the group. And within the overall mood and atmosphere factors we can make many different suggestions, again concerned with experience of form. For example, we might say that the improvisation starts very gaily but finishes with everyone being very sad, or vice versa; or that it starts happily and suddenly something happens to make it very tense, and it ends sadly. There are many different permutations of mood and atmosphere which we can devise for stimulating story material and helping to develop a sense of form.

SUBJECT MATTER OF ORIGINAL IMPROVISATIONS:

Naturally, subject matter also has a great deal to do with the factor of form because, particularly in the early stages, there is a simple and straightforward desire to get at once to the 'meat' of the matter, to the significant moment of action. Much has already been said about this and the manner in which development outwards from such moments can be helped.

But there are other aspects of the subject matter of original improvisations which call for some detailed consideration, because many teachers are put off by them, in particular by two types: (a) unpleasant domestic situations;* (b) violence.

It is important to bear in mind that no matter how much we stimulate imagination for original story material, children (and adults for that matter) draw on their full range of experience either consciously or unconsciously, and very often factors of particular urgency or interest will inevitably govern and colour the subject matter. The whole world of experience is used, including real life experiences, or the more vicarious experiences of television, cinema, comics, newspapers, novels, overheard adult conversations, observation of adult behaviour and so on.

Within (a), unpleasant domestic situations, we often see reflected in drama a great deal about childrens' personal backgrounds (at home we see a great deal of the school background); there will almost inevitably be elements of exaggeration in the treatment or playing of such themes, usually because of the emotional impact made at a deeply personal level. It is important for us to tolerate the use of these themes from a basis of full compassion, and by taking an intelligent interest in what is revealed. The opportunity of 'playing-out' these situations affords the same kind of simple relief to children as adults achieve by talking their troubles over with a friend. The adult often concludes such talking with the statement: 'I'm sorry to bore you with all these petty troubles, but you know it really has helped me, just to talk about them – to get them off my chest.' Of course, as adults we do not necessarily mean that the troubles are petty, but we may

* By domestic situations are meant all those situations that are to do with family life as a whole, without necessarily taking place only in domestic surroundings; for example there might be scenes in pubs. One teacher had the experience of having all her improvisation work stopped by the Head because of a scene which took place in a pub, where people were drinking beer and one of the characters was a barmaid. The Head objected to all of these as belonging to the seamy side of life, and insisted that the class returned at once to its Playreaders. They did so. The first play in the Playreader was set in 'an Inn', where the people drank 'ale' and one of the characters was 'a hostess'. No comment!

see them in a new light by verbalising them instead of churning them over and over in the mind. Children also have troubles, many of which we may consider trifling in comparison with our own great adult problems, but that is the wrong comparison; we need to consider the troubles in comparison with the experience of life of the child – then we might see them in the right perspective.

More important still for our consideration is the fact that the majority of children are unable to verbalise their worries and problems and so do not have that particular way of getting things off their chests. Very few children would be able to say to any adult, let alone a teacher, something like: 'Father and mother were quarrelling again last night, and I'm sure father hit mother several times; and none of us knows what to do about the new neighbours. They really are terrible people – and their Johnnie, who is bigger than I am, has threatened to beat me up the first chance he gets'. Early experience of adult reaction to speaking about one's own personal feelings and worries often results in never risking doing so again. If the problem is something to do with adult life, then the reaction is more often than not: 'That's none of your business', and if it is deeply personal to the realm of childhood, then it is usually met with: 'Don't be silly – it's time you grew up about these things'; 'these things' may well include considerable unhappiness, uncertainty or even fear about visits to dentists or doctors or moving to a new school or a new class. Ability to verbalise such problems provides people with a perfectly natural safety-valve; inability to do so, whether it arises from lack of confidence or experience, or fear of reaction, exacerbates the problem because there is no natural safety-valve. Drama in school (and ordinary play with pre-school children) provides an even more natural form of safety-valve during childhood. Unfortunately for many teachers, the problem from their point of view is the feeling that they have to become therapists and psychologists to deal with the matter, and the feeling is strengthened by the fact that very gradually there is beginning to be a fuller realisation of the value of such an approach in clinics, both as part of diagnosis and of treatment. But this need not affect the teacher's attitude to what is a perfectly natural factor in the lives of children, and a quite simple manifestation in drama; to 'get it off their chests' is sometimes all that is necessary, and drama provides that opportunity. Meanwhile, the teacher is given a little more information about children, and is also able to provide different and pleasanter forms of experience through drama to help counteract some of the emotional effects of whatever the other experiences are. And above all, drama provides the fullest opportunity for building a really genuine confidence in oneself and in the more positive values of life as a whole.

Violence is considered separately in chapter 9 on 'Fighting', but the approach by the teacher has similarities in that one is working from a basis of compassion for the manifestation of a natural part of human growth, and, at the same time, always being watchful for the opportunity of providing different experiences and of leading from one type of experience to another.

Other considerations regarding subject matter are dealt with in chapter 12.

Secondary Beginnings : Looking with the Eye of a Camera

The greater part of the foregoing section (pp. 208 to 227) has application to both secondary and junior work, according to stage of development, experience and amount of practice, and it is important for teachers to avoid thinking that one type of drama ends in the primary school and another starts in the secondary. Indeed, because drama is so concerned with all facets of personality training, including the emotional, it is important to try to provide first year secondary children with precisely the kind of drama they have been having in their last year at the junior school, as this is one way of anchoring part of themselves in the security of the known within circumstances that are often bewilderingly unknown.*

However, there are very particular problems for starting drama with the upper half of secondary age groups, if there has been no

* It really is both pathetic and little short of criminal how ill-informed the majority of secondary teachers are about junior school education. This is part of the price paid for teaching subjects rather than children, within a system of growing specialisation.

previous experience, and the remainder of this chapter is concerned with one approach that has been found useful – namely that of film-making. (A further approach, through 'Social Drama' is considered in detail in chapter 12; but as this deals with so many important factors other than a way of beginning – in fact is perhaps one of the most significant purposes of drama – it is necessary to keep it separate.)

Filming and a camera approach to certain sensitivity and other types of exercise have already been touched on in earlier sections – see chapters 2 and 5. But now let us consider taking the matter considerably further.

It is no concern of this book to consider processes of actual film-making, though there is undoubtedly great value in such an activity. However, it is both costly and time-consuming, and in its opportunities for each and every child to be creatively occupied with the *whole* of themselves does not pretend to equal the potential value of drama. Also, with actual film-making, there can be and often is a tendency to use a great deal of time and energy on subject matter that is so trivial that it would be looked on as no more than a very early stage of improvisation – and this factor is often made doubly difficult by the necessity to confine film locations to the environment of school and subject matter to that which allows children to be children.*

The advantage of film (which word will be used to cover both film and TV) is that all children are constantly and readily exposed to it, and furthermore *enjoy* it. Whether or not they know why they enjoy it is irrelevant, although the kind of work to be suggested will undoubtedly help them to think more consciously about that aspect of their lives. Whether or not we as teachers *approve* of their enjoyment is also irrelevant – at least with the development of visual aids we are at last conceding the point that here is a medium that both arrests and holds the attention! As teachers, we are confronted with the simple opportunity of asking: 'If we were going to make a film about...what would

* Teachers interested in all aspects of film with children, from many different forms of direct activity to help in encouraging children to become selective in both film and TV watching are advised to write to The British Film Institute, 81 Dean Street, London, W1, and The Society for Education in Film and Television, 34 Second Avenue, London, E17.

we put into it? What would really be interesting (from our own point of view as well as the point of view of those seeing the film)?' At once the imagination is stimulated because of familiarity with and interest in films. But – a film of what? The answer can be given in the most general terms – a film of anything that is of direct interest to the youngsters themselves, to start with, and eventually of as wide a range of subject matter as both teacher and pupils can possibly think of and time will allow. (In fact, time is the only ultimate obstacle.) Topics will appeal as much from the factual point of view as from the fictional, particularly if the facts are closely associated with what is of dynamic interest in the youngsters' own personal lives rather than with the academic subjects of school.

PRACTICAL APPROACH

In all the early stages, discussion is of prior importance – discussion in small or large groups, discussion in pairs, discussion between teacher and the whole class. Each member of the class should be helped to feel that any ideas they put forward will be treated seriously. It is also wise for the teacher to keep in mind – and perhaps find the moment to share the thought with the class – the famous dictum of John Grierson's on documentary film, that 'there is nothing so dull or ordinary but the creative and selective eye of the camera can make exciting and vital and alive'. This was Grierson's conception of the documentary film-makers approach to the 'creative interpretation of reality'.

From this viewpoint, our film approach can start from two ends of the scale, or from any number of points within those extremes. The two points are –

(a) The searching eye of the camera, roaming over the most commonplace activity, seeking to show both the activity and the person involved, in a wide selection of different ways, the sum of the whole of which gives a creative interpretation of that activity. Even something as simple as *sharpening a pencil* will serve as an example, with individual shots of the sharpener, the pencil and the person involved, including shots of the face, the hands, the actual operation in progress or in various stages of progress, etc.

Or, take it a stage further, into a simple but *actual* creative activity – model-making, carving, painting a picture; or into a *mimed* activity – mending a puncture, changing a wheel, shaving, grooming the hair and making up.

This basic idea has already been touched on as imaginative and concentration exercises – but here it is taken a stage further as a genuine attempt to think in terms of film.

(b) The above is concerned with the small details of a single activity. The opposite end of the scale is to think in terms of a broad, general synopsis – and then to break these down into particular scenes, and to break these down again into the detail of shots, as in (a). For example, the intended subject matter of the film might be 'Our School'. 'If we were making a documentary film about our school – say, for such a film as *Look at Life*, what would be put in it? 'Lets suppose we could really make a film about the school to show other people, for instance foreign visitors or even our own parents, what would we put into it – what sort of things would we want to show, things like the actual building as well as some of the activities that actually go on in the school?' Out of these questions will arise general discussion, enabling the teacher to suggest that the class divide into smaller groups, each of which is to discuss among themselves a particular point of view. These smaller group discussions might be suggested under two main headings: (1) A life in the day of the school; (2) Highlights of the school year.

Under (1), the following aspects might be divided among many different groups:

(a) The headmaster (or headmistress) and his (or her) general day.

(b) The location and physical geography of the school.

(c) (b) in relation to the community area as a whole.

(d) (c) in relation to the different homes and streets that different pupils travel from every day.

(e) (d) in terms of the different means of transportation to school by different people – buses, trains, bicycles, cars, walking etc.

(f) A glimpse of the different members of staff.

(g) Particular facilities of the school, subheaded under different subject matters, including indoor and outdoor activities, practical and academic subjects etc. (This would obviously be so subdivided as to occupy several different groups.)

(h) A typical beginning to the day – including arrival, assembly, registration.

(i) A typical morning in the life of different forms and age groups. (Again this could be divided into work to occupy several groups.)

(j) A typical lunch hour, including school lunches, those that bring their own lunches, those that go home for lunch, and the various ways lunch hour is occupied.

(k) Similar to (i) above, but now dealing with afternoon classes and activities, perhaps from the viewpoint of different age groups.

(l) The end of the day – school dispersal, and what people do with their leisure hours during the evening, and any direct connection the school might have with such activities.

(m)Arising out of (l), different kinds of extra-curricular activity either in the evenings or at weekends, including the various hobby and special interest activities – e.g. camera clubs, rambling, drama club, sports clubs, etc.

And under (2) – Highlights of the school year, the following aspects might be divided among many different groups:

(n) Sporting highlights.

(o) Academic highlights.

(p) Special day highlights.

(q) School visits.

(r) Visitors to school.

(s) Any special factors regarding any members of staff.

(t) Beginnings of school-life in the first year.

(u) The ending of school-life in the final year.

(v) Where do some of us go from here?

and perhaps for some groups in some circumstances there might even be a section on:

(w)How and when our school began.

(x) Different developments since those beginnings (possibly including some links with general social history, both national and parochial).

(y) Special highlights during the time the school has existed.

(z) Plans and development for the future.

There is no need, of course, to use so many topics, but nevertheless it is useful to have too many rather than too few as there may not be much depth of thinking and planning at this stage, and concentration and interest may more easily be sustained through variety. Each group now has a few points arising from one or more topics that they would like to include in the film. Many of these, particularly from section (2) cannot be attempted in practical *mock* film-making terms *without the use of drama*, i.e. without some members of the class being people actually involved in the action as well as those filming the action; an obvious example would be 'the school visit or the school journey'; another would be 'sporting highlights'. Therefore, in terms of this kind of material the teacher would need to assess whether or not the class would be able, prepared or interested to take the further practical steps, or simply go into more detailed planning for a later stage. (It is always worth having the tape-recorder to hand, because this can often stimulate the beginnings of practical activity through 'interviews', 'descriptions' and so on, even though without action.)

Meanwhile, many of the topics under section (1) will lend themselves to immediate mock film-making, perhaps starting from each small group considering their own classroom and some of the activities therein, and trying-out different kinds of shot as cameramen or directors or sound recordists, or someone involved in the class situation, or, in each group, one of each. We can even suggest that they devise and bring to school anything they like to represent the camera: an ordinary cardboard or wooden box with a hole at each end can be both effective and stimulating. By the very fact that they are *being* cameramen or film directors etc., they are beginning to be involved in practical drama, using the whole of themselves, but in circumstances where self-consciousness is less worrying; and the creative intention is at a sufficiently high level for them not to feel the activity 'stupid' and 'beneath their dignity'. In other words, they are in part by-passing the scribble stage, even though, when they eventually do get on to drama itself, there will inevitably be some return to this stage. There will not be very much absorption to start with, but this will grow very quickly because they are involved with the manipulation of and mastery of physical factors outside of themselves.

As this is not a book on film-making, there is no purpose in continuing with the details of developing the film on 'Our School'. Suffice to say that, in the same way as other work has been suggested to develop from small groups, all working at once, to the whole class working as one entity, so one can develop aspects of the film; some people remain as cameramen, directors, lighting-men, sound recordists etc.; the remainder of the class might be themselves in various class situations – and here, also is one of the rare cases when the teacher could also take part, either as himself or as other characters if the class is seriously insistent.

However, the teacher should be ready for a flood of quite detailed technical questions about making films or TV programmes, and the precise functions of the various people involved. There are many useful and not too specialised books which will help (some are mentioned in the Bibliography). There will also be – or the teacher can stimulate – interest in the nature of film as an art, much springing up around what shots to take and therefore a detailed consideration of what can be done with a camera, perhaps starting from a static camera position and then discovering the differences and enrichments the moment the camera position is flexible. Links with art are obvious, each person painting an aspect or shot that interests them, then perhaps hanging these in some kind of order based on the theme being filmed; to each picture can then be added some written sentences and consideration of what would be happening on the sound track, making as it were, a strip cartoon.

The mock film-making approach is suggested as a way of arresting attention. Gradually more and more actual drama is introduced. It is not called drama, but remains part of the film-work – even exercises in sensitivity can be introduced as a way of helping the film work. And we constantly help the development of imagination and awareness through encouragement to 'look with the eye of a camera'. And if, for subject matter, we turn again and again to the kinds of topic that are of deep interest to young people, the documentary film approach will help to give them a new view of the ordinary or the extraordinary, including their own environment and lives, a more sensitive awareness of other people, and a less apathetic view of their own community existence. (Other useful subject matter will be found in the chapter on 'Social Drama'.)

The above process of mock film-making is very closely allied to play-making, which is developed in Chapter 10.

But before considering play-making, let us look a little more closely at the one factor which more than any other disturbs teachers who attempt drama – the factor of fighting and violence.

9

Fighting and Violence

Some aspects of the problem of fighting and violence in drama have already been touched on in those sections concerned with emotional growth, self-discipline and sensitivity to other people, with particular thoughts on channelling emotional and physical energy.

Fighting and interest in violent themes starts very soon in improvisation and seems to continue interminably. For this reason, drama is often dropped altogether – or, at any rate, is rapidly changed from the informal and creative to the scripted and adult dominated. However, if we can attempt to understand some of the reasons for the behaviour, we will discover the necessary tolerance with which it is possible to find practical and constructive ways not simply of overcoming the problem but of using the manifest energy and thought as part of the whole basic premis of dramatic work, the development of each individual.

As has already been pointed out, part of the problem of growing up is that of coming to terms with sets of rules and modes of behaviour that are not necessarily a natural instinct, but are essential forms of discipline as part of the structure of all societies. These disciplines can be enforced by rule of rod or other manifestations of adult power over children, but unfortunately when they are approached through these means there can be as many negative as positive results, and the positive tend to be impermanent, not necessarily lasting with any fullness beyond school leaving age. One negative result is that children tend to lose respect for adults, and this respect *is* a fundamental instinct, the loss of which can do irreparable harm not only to the growing child, but also to its own potential parenthood and adulthood; another negative result is that the child develops control and discipline only through various forms of fear; another is that the child grows up without developing the inner equipment for making personal decisions, let alone right choices in moral decisions; another is that some children will develop a deep loathing for all forms of authority, and tend to turn all forms of freedom into licence. So if we are not patiently careful, our attempts to socialise, humanise and civilise children may result in our making them antisocial, inhuman and uncivil (if not, in fact, uncivilised to a degree greater than their own primitive beginnings.)

For each child the adjustment of instinctive life in order to embrace and accept (and by habit, eventually to adopt) the various rules etc. demanded by society, sets up an internal personal battle. The outer symbol of this inner condition is the fight (in all its various forms – verbal as well as physical) – but the actual manifestation of the fight itself is of less importance than such accompanying factors as learning to win (eventually with compassion), learning to lose (eventually without loss of faith and hope), learning integrity, discovering loyalty to oneself and others, learning strength in adversity, experiencing leadership, and learning to be led as a member of a team, a family, a nation, a member of the human race, – and, if we can see no other value, discovering the astonishing potential skill of the human body.

All these values are potential parts of the fights and other violent thinking that arise from these inner battles. Further, as will be suggested in the practical section that follows, the same or similar themes and activities can form the basis of much study that is concerned with history on the one hand, and civics on the other.

So we are, in part, confronted with the manifestation of an inner battle to overcome aspects of one's primitive nature and learn to obey and to fit in with the wise demands of society. This is only one factor. Side by side with this we see, in drama, a great deal of 'playing-out' of the rubbish of adult civilisation; possibly we should even be thankful that children have this safety valve, for we tend to be utterly careless in our full sharing of the violence of adult affairs – wars, rumours of wars, the hideous and brutal details of actual wars, murder, rape, arson, etc., are all titivated and served up either as the zenith of entertainment (TV, films, cartoons, magazine stories, etc.) or as the summit of human endeavour (all aspects of the press); even our gentler activities, such as sport, are developed into competitive wars of attrition which ultimately lead to the type of hysteria among the onlookers that causes such tragedies as the Lima football massacre. A great deal of trite lip service is given to the idea that 'we are living in a highly competitive world and children must be prepared to face it'. Undoubtedly they must – though there would not necessarily seem to be any harm in at least hoping for better things, let alone preparing for them. Meanwhile, part of our preparation can include genuine emotional training, instead of reducing emotion to 'a stiff upper lip' attitude; and we can give just and rational opportunity for the full examination of, trial of and, if need be, rejection as well as acceptance of, so called adult values, many of which are as base as others are paramount.

If we do not shrink from the problem of fights and other manifestations of violence, if we try to find constructive ways of using the energy and of guiding the emotional factors involved, then we are once again using drama in terms of its primary intention: the development of each individual, his resources, his resourcefulness, and his awareness of and sensitivity to his environment, including other people within that environment. And by these means we will be helping a *gradual* but thorough mastery and understanding of the many processes involved in the full understanding of the personal demands society must and does make on each individual, not as a crippling denial of individuality, but as an embracing opportunity which provides an equal balance of success and failure, of fulfilment and frustration, which is the give and take of harmonious living.

Practical Suggestions

Many years ago I watched an Infant school drama session, which included a fair-ground sequence, one facet of which was 'being cars in the fairground'; the children themselves chose to be bumper-cars; after a little while of very exciting bumping, the teacher suggested they should now be dodge-em cars; the suggestion was met with extreme delight and equal skill. The teacher said to me: 'Part of drama involves discovering what children want to do and being permissive – the other part is helping them to discover new things to do and being encouraging'. For any teacher worried about fights in drama, I can do no better than to extend the same advice (perhaps not only for fights, but for many other aspects of drama as well). As has already been pointed out, fighting is often what the children *want* to do and *need* to do, and often *will* do despite our best endeavour. If we are able to accept these factors, then our task is that much simpler; side by side with being permissive we are also encouraging new discoveries and experiences, even if these are closely associated with the original activity.

So we permit fighting; but we *add* to it. If the fighting is with guns, then we suggest swords or battle-axes; if there is no real story to the fight, then we suggest or stimulate stories; if there is no control then we give experience of control which may range from sudden freezing in a particular position at the moment we strike the cymbal or drum, to detailed planning of each step and stage of a fight; and if we keep in mind that any fight is made up of several component parts: *physical*, the action of the fight itself; *intellectual*, the organisation of the fight; *emotional*, the driving force and *raison d'être* of the fight – then we can, little by little, extend experience in many different directions simply through the fights themselves. So the following initial practical considerations are advised:

1. Continuity of those exercises concerned with response to sound; personal physical control; and general class control.

2. Avoidance of all audience in order to curb over-excitement and exhibitionism; hence, all members of the class work at the same time in an uncritical framework.

3. Complete avoidance of all properties (such as rulers or sticks for swords etc.). Properties divert the mind from full concentration on character, situation and action, through concern with the organisation of the property.

4. With older age groups – some top primary as well as secondary – develop exercises concerned with personal control either in the

use of fists or with imaginary weapons. For example, the teacher can explain that in TV and film fights, one way of developing realism without anyone getting hurt is involved in continuous practice at attempting to hit an object, without actually making contact. An advanced stage of this is practice at being 'loose to the point of contact', where, for instance, one's fist and arm would be quite loose during its descent or approach to an object, but would freeze into stiffness and stillness just before making full impact with that object. Practice can be given at this, by walking round the hall or classroom and aiming at particular objects, but not hitting them, either from simple control or from the latter means of freezing before contact. It is advisable to make early exercises in this field be concerned with, first, objects (e.g. desks, walls, etc.), secondly, with oneself (e.g. one's other hand, own chin, etc.) before, finally, practising on another person, in pairs. And when reaching the stage of working with another person, it is advisable to insist that each movement is completed by one person before another movement is started by the other; so that, person A will aim at person B's jaw and freeze before actually making contact – and person B will not start their blow at person A before that person has completed their own attempt. This is all part of engendering personal control – and sensitivity to others.

5. WORKING OUT A FIGHT

Again, the teacher might discuss with the class the nature of fights seen on television or film; they may look entirely realistic and spontaneous, but, in fact, are worked out very carefully to the last detail – and not only worked out, but memorised and gone over again and again and again until each person knows exactly and precisely what they are going to do either in attacking their opponent or in defending themselves from that opponent. The only accidents caused in such fights arise either from careless-ness or forgetfulness, and in a full-blooded fight these could result in a very serious accident.

Let us consider the sequence of developments of organising and developing such a fight, using the whole class.

(a) On their own, each person straps a sword belt to his waist, with a sword hanging in a scabbard (the weapons are, of course, entirely imaginary). They pull out the sword and swish it about, feeling the 'power' of it; run their fingers along the edge to feel the sharpness and the length of it; see it glinting in the sunlight; cut a hair down its middle to get the full sharpness; feel the weight of it; practise getting it quickly out of its scabbard; are suddenly confronted with an imaginary opponent whom they fight and slay (accompanying climax of sound on the cymbal will help this experience); they pull the sword out of the slain opponent and are suddenly confronted with another imaginary opponent who slays them (and again the use of sound to accompany and enrich and give climax to the experience). Each individual has now had some simple and straightforward experience of using a sword, discovering its various properties and being able to use it in the emotional circumstances of actual fights. (The use of imaginary opponents at this stage helps to give fuller personal experience because one's mind is not in any way concerned with being sensitive to another person.)

(b) In pairs: work out the first ten (or five) movements of a sword fight, in which a bang on the cymbal will denote each blow of the fight. Give time for the actual working out of these movements, and then try them through with all pairs working at once, and with the sounds of the cymbal accompanying (or leading and stimulating) the action; first time through, in very slow motion; a second time through a little quicker; a third time through at top speed. It is easy to sense between each run through the amount of discussion and settling of detail that each pair may feel is necessary in terms of their originally worked out sequence of movements – and it is wise to allow time for these discussions and checkings.

(c) Further opportunity to work out the next sequence of moves (from five to ten or ten to twenty, according to how we have begun, which in its turn depends on the sustained interest and absorption of the class as a whole); further instructions regarding the end of the fight: perhaps one person is wounded or killed and the other victorious; perhaps both are wounded and neither victorious; teacher decides.

(d) Run through this second sequence of moves (with cymbal);

again, first time through in slow motion, second time much quicker, third time at top speed – with a particularly loud cymbal beat for the climax and completion of the fight. There will probably be quick recoveries and laughter at the conclusion first time through – certainly the actual wounding will not be sustained; this does not matter because the main focus of intention and interest will still be with the fight itself. Before the third time through we might suggest that when they are wounded the action is not to cease, but that they should decide what each is going to do to help himself (or herself) regarding the wound; then we might, at the end of the third run, keep a continuous, low sound on the cymbal to help the sustaining and continuity of this new idea.

(e) After time for each pair to recap over the first sequence of the fight, run the whole fight (including both sequences) at least twice, the first time a little slower than the second. With each run, preface the action with some strong verbal stimulation for fuller concentration, intention and determination – and for even more continuity after the wounding at the conclusion of the fight.

However, if this is a very early stage in drama work, we must not expect too much concentration, intention and determination. We can and should work for it, and we can and should do everything possible to stimulate the class to work for it – but we ourselves, as teachers, will be disappointed (and possibly undermined?) if we expect too much; but we shall be using the energy (both physical and emotional) and the zest and the delight in fighting in a constructive manner; and the little addition at the end – the continuity of the action after being wounded – may last only a few seconds, but is one of the first steps we can take to extending experience beyond the fight itself into the beginnings of other possibilities.

OTHER TYPES OF FIGHT

In the same manner as above, with roughly the same sequence of development, other fights can be worked out involving the use of (a) fists, (b) wrestling, (c) a mixture of both (a) and (b), and (d) battle-axes and other ancient weapons. The latter can often arise from study of different periods in history, with interest in armour and weapons etc.

The same skill, dexterity and control in using and developing fist fights and wrestling will arise with practice. If we are worried about the possibility of people actually hurting each other with fists, then fights with imaginary weapons become a natural safeguard, because of the length of the weapons keeping a little space between opponents. As soon as we see that control is becoming really strong, then we can extend opportunity to forms of closer physical contact.

Building Improvisation Round a Fight

Once the class has worked out a fight in pairs, we can use the fight in an improvisation involving the whole class.

Let us follow this through, stage by stage, with a class that has just worked out the sword fight on the foregoing pages.

(a) Each pair divides itself into A and B.

(b) The A's go to one end of the room, the B's to the other.

(c) The A's are told that they are merchants who are travelling across desert country to market. Swift discussion takes place on a few details: What are merchants? How would they travel? What kind of goods would they be taking to market? The length of the discussion depends on absorption and interest – and it is wise to keep in mind that the majority will probably want to get ahead with the actual doing of the story.

(d) The B's are told that they are brigands or robbers who lie in wait for merchants in order to steal the goods they are taking to market. Again, swift discussion on a few details: Where would they choose to wait in desert country? When would they attack? How do they themselves travel?

(e) Then – assuming that this is an early stage of drama – the teacher takes over and *outlines the whole story* that is going to be done. This is important for full control. At a later stage, the details of the story could in part be left to the class to decide in advance, and in part left to the spontaneity of the moment; but at this stage (the directed stage) the teacher has control of all aspects, including the actual geography of the improvisation (i.e. where everybody is to start from, where they go, where they finish up, together with the actual sequence of events). The story might therefore run as follows:

TEACHER: The merchants all start in that part of the desert over there (*pointing to one corner of the hall*). Go there now, and get all your goods and things ready for market. The robbers are all hiding among rocks anywhere round this part of the desert here (*indicating the outer edges of perhaps one half of the room*). Get into hiding now.

(Leave a few moments for both groups to get into their places; listen carefully to see how much of any lively chatter that may well be going on is part of intended getting ready and how much is just 'mucking about'; if the former, we need to allow a little more time; if the latter, we are firm about it as part of social training and consideration for other people. When all are settled – at the most it should take a minute – we continue.)

TEACHER (*continuing*): Now, listen to the story – as soon as I've finished telling it, we shall do it.

'A group of merchants are crossing the desert to market; all day they have been travelling, and as evening comes they are very hot and tired. Their journey brings them across this part of the desert here (*indicating the actual area of the room*) and then along here – and round and along here – until they come to a clearing surrounded by rocks – here. When they reach the clearing, they spread out over the whole space so they all have as much air as possible – and they lie down and sleep. Meanwhile, without a movement or a sound, the robbers have watched the merchants, knowing that this is a favourite resting place. And when all the merchants have gone to sleep, the robbers very slowly and secretly come from behind the rocks, and move silently among the merchants, until each robber is by the side of the merchant you arranged your fight with. When each robber has found his opponent, he stands very still by his side; when all are still, I shall call out 'Now'; immediately the merchants jump up, and I shall make the sounds on the cymbal for you to have the fights you worked out. And remember – at the end of the fight, each one of you is badly wounded and desperately tries to reach water, where you can bathe your wounds. If you want to help one another when you are wounded, you may – but you may prefer to be

243

quite on your own. Now – stand by; robbers absolutely still and quiet. Merchants, ready with your goods. A group of merchants are crossing the desert to market. . . . '

And the story starts; there is probably no need for us to tell any more of the story during the actual running, as it is a quite simple and short story; but it is as well to keep an eye open in case at any point they need reminders of the sequence – and necessary ones can be given as 'story-teller', without interrupting the flow of action. If this is an early stage of drama, it is unlikely that anyone will have the confidence to add dialogue, but if we are worried that they might and would prefer that they didn't, then we could add the sentence at the start of the story: 'The merchants are too tired even to speak to each other. . . ' If speaking should arise, stimulated by the story, it is best not to interfere as long as it is dialogue that is concerned with the story and the people in it. (For example, someone might say something like: 'Come on, we can't lie down here. It's not safe I tell you.' Usually the others would then outweigh this opinion – but if they do not, then again as storyteller we can bring them back to the original story line. In this particular example, the teacher has taken responsibility for the call of 'Now' that starts the fight; at a later stage, in similar circumstances, the responsibility could be given to one of the class as, perhaps, leader of the brigands; but in the early stages, responsibility of this kind – simple as it may seem to us – could destroy a youngster's absorption in his own part of the action through worry about exactly when he is to call out; and if he should call out at the wrong moment, then another set of unnecessary worries are started.

The continuity of wounded action after the fight will differ in its absorption and sincerity. A few may be deeply absorbed for several minutes – some others may lose all concentration within a few seconds; the remainder will fall between the two extremes. Continuity of sound on the cymbal (or perhaps by fading in music) will help the sustaining of concentration, but we should fade this out and end the scene before there is total loss of absorption and a corresponding feeling of petering out.

The comparative calm and quiet that sometimes results from the end of such an improvisation is often a good place for *ending* a drama lesson, and if one has any flexibility of curriculum, to continue with activities such as painting or story-writing, based on the same theme and stimulated by the personal experience. However, the whole episode, including the initial working out of the fight, could equally well be useful for the beginning of a session of drama, channelling and using energy; in which case, if potential absorption is still strong, we could then go on to other drama experiences involving movement or speech or sensitivity etc., perhaps again developing these on some different aspects of the merchants and robbers the class have just experienced being.

FURTHER DEVELOPMENTS

A class of nine-year olds, who had never done drama before, did the above story as the latter part of a forty minute session of many different kinds of experience (concentration, movement, speech, etc.). When the story was over the class was asked: 'Does any part of the story you have just done make you think of any other story you have read or heard or seen?'

There were many answers, including 'Marco Polo', 'Robin Hood', 'The Good Samaritan', and other less clear references to 'explorers', 'geography' and 'poems and stories' from English lessons.

Perhaps this example will serve to show how simply and readily one kind of experience can lead to others, providing us with more material to work on as themes; but it is well to keep two factors clearly in mind – (a) this 'acceptable' development arose from an equal acceptance of the desire to fight, and a simple constructive approach to fighting; and (b) we shall not have extinguished the desire to fight through only *one* such experience; we shall need to persevere, to expect more and to be ready for other constructive developments. Perhaps it helps if we remember that one of the most beautiful stories of all is that of 'The Good Samaritan' – but that story, like so many others, started from at least an aspect of fighting.

ST GEORGE AND THE DRAGON

If there is any semblance of a fight within a known story that is going to be attempted in drama, then the class will have a strong urge to reach quickly towards that part of the story. The urge can, in fact, be so strong as to diminish or fully undermine interest in any other part of the story, particularly parts that come before the fight. The story, in whatever form we approach it, of St George and the Dragon is an excellent example. The urgent interest is in the fight between St George and the Dragon. Try to build a sequence of events that lead up to the fight, and each time we ask something like: 'And what do you think happened then?', the response will be 'they had a fight'.

One of the advantages of drama is that we can extract this kind of 'significant' moment and give full experience of it, involving several different kinds of experience, at the outset, thereby helping to satisfy a perfectly natural and instinctive interest and so help fuller concentration on other parts of the story.

With one class of juniors, this same obstacle regarding the fight between St George and the Dragon was solved in seven minutes, during which time the following sequence involved the whole class working at one and the same time, either each on his own or, for some exercises, in pairs.

(a) All were St George, galloping on his horse (accompanied and controlled by sound on the drum).

(b) St George meets an imaginary dragon, fights and slays him (again with sound).

(c) St George then meets another imaginary dragon, who this time slays St George (again at the climax of sound).

(d) Each person 'curls up small' and, with a climax growth of sound, grows into an enormous dragon – then begins to move about – then meets an imaginary St George, fights him – and is slain.

(e) The class divides into pairs, each pair being A and B; the A's are St George, the B's the dragon. Dialogue between teacher and class happened as follows:

TEACHER: How does the dragon fight?

ANSWERS: With his claws and his teeth.

TEACHER: How does St George stop the dragon using his claws and teeth?

ANSWERS: With his sword. – Galloping away. – The horse kicks the dragon.

TEACHER: So the dragon really cannot get too close to St George. Then does the dragon have any other way of fighting?

ANSWERS: He breathes fire. – He swishes him with his long tail.

TEACHER: What does St George do about all this fire and the swishing tail?

ANSWERS: He keeps out of the way. – He dodges them.

TEACHER: But then, how will he manage to kill the dragon?

EVENTUAL SOLUTION: He has a long, long sword, more like a spear.

TEACHER: I see. Then, all the St George's are going to have long spears, which the dragons are going to keep away from; and the dragons are going to breathe fire, and swish their tails, which St George is going to avoid too. There were then quick fights between St George and the dragon, with St George conquering.

(f) Still in pairs, change of roles, and another fight, with St George again winning.

The fight between St George and the dragon could have been worked out in the kind of detail suggested earlier, but in this case was not because of the time factor. However, the teacher had established by discussion, perfectly logical and agreed circumstances for keeping the pairs apart so that there was no danger of anyone being hurt by fists.

The whole sequence took seven minutes, had provided various movement experiences, response to sound, including climax, some imagination in the realm of movement, different experiences of winning and losing – and above all had satisfied the original urgent interest in 'doing' the fight. Subsequent discussion on the rest of the story now held the concentration and interest of the whole class and a play was made up between class and teacher; fight experiences again came into it over and over again, but without anything like the same urgent insistence.

Part of the intention of the above sequence is that of weaning away from interest in fighting, partly by providing some logical means of fulfilment of a particular interest and instinct in a constructive way, and partly by stimulating interest in factors arising from and associated with fighting, but not necessarily always involving actual fights.

Let us consider the sequence of events which led, in a secondary

I

school, to an even more complete 'weaning away' from fighting, though entirely dependent on fights in the first instance. There are two examples, the first of which eventually concerned the building of a play about Christopher Columbus.

1. *Christopher Columbus.* For some weeks drama had consisted of little else but sequences of improvised scenes in small groups, each scene lasting for little more than a minute or two, each being almost entirely concerned with gun fights, and each ending in a final shooting-out and the subsequent death of one or more of the combatants. The story content of these episodes was little more than a straightforward vehicle for fighting. At the start there was little or no absorption, but this began to grow with experience and practice, as did the skill in the purely physical realm of action. An initial suspicion and scepticism about the teacher's permissive approach to these activities became more cooperative as the class spotted his genuine interest and concern to help the fight to reach even greater skill and reality, including discussion on how people in films managed to fight so realistically without actually being hurt.

(N.B. the area was tough; the school was tough; the youngsters were tough; in its own way, the school had a reputation of being something of a 'blackboard jungle'. The head was progressive in so far as he was prepared to trust the experiments of members of staff to a point at which there could be definite evidence as to the potential success or failure of the experiment. Certainly he could see the point of constructively using physical energy, even if he had no more than an intuitive feeling for the value of using emotional energy at the same time.)

Over a period of several weeks, the following developments took place;

(a) The teacher suggested that interest in fights could include other means than mainly guns and fists and forms of all-in wrestling; some of the class suggested swords. This was accepted, and, with the same zest and energy and with new forms of skill, fights continued as before.

(b) The teacher asked 'Who used to use swords for fighting?' The answers led to various improvisations involving pirates. These were built into whole class improvisations, involving two

pirate ships (sections of desks on either side of the classroom) and
the development of pirate crowd-scenes.

(c) The teacher asked whether it would be possible to have a
fight involving seamen and swords on one ship instead of two;
the answers led to various forms of mutiny improvisation. (As
these improvisations developed there was a growing use of dialogue – albeit largely of an expletive kind – and very slightly
more detailed discussions and plannings of scenes. Characters
were all raw and tough.)

(d) The teacher asked if anyone in the class knew of anybody
who had had mutinies to contend with on the high seas. Some
people mentioned 'Columbus' and the class discussed the kind of
sailor who would have sailed with Columbus on his voyage across
the ocean. The teacher, though now moving a little more strongly
and deliberately away from fights, felt it wiser not to take too
many steps at once, so kept interest in the new circumstances by
continuing, logically, with the same kinds of characters as was
readily accepted in the improvisations – and Columbus's crew
must have been very similar types. The class were interested in
the information that the majority of people in Columbus's time
believed the world to be flat, and were afraid to sail west because
they would drop off the edge of the world; they were fascinated
by the fact that others who did think the world might be round
were equally afraid to risk sailing underneath the world, because
knowing nothing of gravity, they believed they would fall off.
This kind of belief, the teacher explained, led to regular sailors
refusing to sail with Columbus. There was a short discussion as to
what Columbus could do about this – suggestions included various
forms of compulsion, bribery and blackmail.

These ideas were rejected as impractical in terms of raising a
whole crew for such a journey – but the class was none the less
sceptical when the teacher explained that Columbus went to
King Ferdinand of Spain (who had already given Columbus
support in terms of cash and ships), and the King decided to
release any convicts from the prisons of Spain who were prepared
to sign on as crew. (These discussions were very much based on
the IF factor of characterisation in drama: If you were Columbus
what would you feel, what would you do? If you were a seaman

who thought the world was flat, what would you feel, what would you do? It is this basic intention of recreating for oneself the genuine circumstances of the existence of other people, with an emphasis on how it really would feel to be that person, that gives drama its particular dynamic.)

(e) Remaining then as the same tough characters, there were now improvisations involving the prisoners – and discussions of what the prisons were like in those days, compared with now, and what kind of crime could send one to prison then compared with now. Some of these discussions led to simple improvised scenes, many of which, of course, still involved both violent themes and further fights. But already a firm and positive step in the weaning away process had been taken. There were now improvisations inside the prisons at the time that messengers brought the news of the amnesty, and although the messengers themselves went through some fairly tough treatment, there were 'guards' who kept firm control with imaginary cat-o'-nine-tails; in fact there were the first improvisations which were not largely based on fights.

(f) And now followed many others – processions of convicts arriving at the ships and being signed on; the loading of the ship, and so on. Again there developed a process of play-building, which resulted in a most exciting improvised play on many aspects of Columbus's journey and discovery.

2. The second example follows a similar pattern, with a major difference in the manner in which the teacher started the weaning process. Again, there were several weeks of very little else in the way of improvisation except fighting; then, over a period of weeks, the following developments took place:

(a) The teacher pointed out that in most of their stories people were constantly being murdered. He asked – 'Does anyone know what happens to someone in this country if they commit murder?' Many knew the answer – 'They gets hung.' 'Well, couldn't your stories include what happened to the murderers as well?' *No props*. There were now slightly longer improvisations in which the murder was committed even more dexterously in order to get on with the hanging.

(b) The teacher waited until confidence was established in this extension of activity and then enquired whether what was happening was really true to life – could murderers in fact just be taken by the police and hanged? 'Oh, no, they have a trial first.' So now the trial was included; trials at this stage are very simple affairs in which the judge and the accused man exchange a kind of rhythmic slanging match: 'You killed him.' 'Oh, no, I didn't.' 'Oh, yes you did.' 'Oh, no I didn't.' 'Oh, yes you did – I saw you. Take him away and hang him.'

(c) Again, when confidence was equal to coping with yet further developments, the teacher discussed whether or not that was really the way trials went. Discussion was now lengthier and more detailed, and included recalling any trials seen on films or television. This led to slightly more detailed improvisations of murder, trial scene (with witnesses) and then the hanging. (At this stage, the accused man is unlikely to meet with any real justice, because to let him off would mean losing the hanging scene!) Already interest in other factors than fighting were beginning to arise, and little by little fights were dropped altogether – until the next occasion where situation and story demanded their use. But they ceased to be in any sense the only or even the predominant interest in drama. (This particular group, in fact, was led into a most exciting consideration of many different factors in the study of civics – court procedure; prison reform; prison conditions; the C.I.D. and crime detection – even some very simple and rather moving improvisations to do with the condemned man's parents and his home life : MOTHER : 'It's all your fault really; you were too hard on him when he was little.' FATHER : 'Wasn't my fault at all ; trouble was you were too soft with him. Spoiled him, you did.' And in the condemned cell, with the inevitable warders playing draughts : 1ST WARDER (*to condemned man*) : 'Here, have a fag.' CONDEMNED MAN : 'Ta. Think I will.' 2ND WARDER : 'Don't worry mate; it'll soon be over.' 1ST WARDER : 'Yeah. And you can have egg and bacon for your breakfast if you wants to.' The essence of these scenes was a very long way from the original fight scenes – but the one led to the other, under the sensitive guidance of a teacher who knew and accepted that there are many strong inner influences behind this apparently almost desperate need to fight; by accepting them, he knew he was helping a particular aspect of emotional growth – but he gradually channelled both the physical and the emotional energy into more constructive considerations. The final example is from work in a youth club, again with a group of youngsters who had never done drama before. There were eighty of them, some still at school, others who had left school for anything up to five years. The majority were wholly sceptical, ready for a good time, prepared to 'send up' everything – but completely responsive to being treated as human beings in intelligent and adult terms. Before the session started, there were many private wars going on, a few of them serious, the majority mere horseplay – all of them indicative of an enormous reservoir of emotional and physical energy seeking some form of outlet.

The whole group was asked at once if they would help with some still shots for a film on 'Battle scenes through the ages'. To start with, the whole group worked as one unit. They gathered to one end of the hall, and on a given signal attacked an imaginary enemy at the other end of the hall – and each time the cymbal was crashed, they froze in whatever position they were in so that various still photographs could be taken. The 'advances and attacks' included storming old castles with battle axes; pirate ship attacks with swords, right up to infantry attacks with rifles and fixed bayonets. There was experience of different kinds of mood and atmosphere, varying from the secret attacks of Red Indians with tomahawks to exploits of commandos; some were fast and very loud, others slow, very controlled and quiet. Interest was immediate, but naturally absorption was almost negligible; the use of the still photograph factor gradually helped to bring more and more personal control and concentration. Once this was fairly well established, some fights with different kinds of weapons were swiftly built up in pairs, so that people got used to working with each other – and then more scenes were built in which the defenders were now real instead of imaginary; the scenes were extended in length by the suggestion that the still photograph was only a momentary pause in the action, which could continue from where it left off on the given signal.

After an hour of really hectic activity, many voices began to demand: 'Couldn't we do something a bit quieter for a while?'

And, in smaller groups, simple improvisations were discussed and planned on subjects peripherally connected with the different periods of time which had been explored in the battle scenes.

The above sequence is different from the previous ones in that it was not a case of waiting for fights actually to arise in drama and then doing something about channelling the emotional and physical energy; it was a straightforward case of arresting attention, capturing imagination and involving everybody in the fullest possible use of themselves from the outset. The point is mentioned here simply as an indication that if we can become quite fearless about the idea of people fighting in drama, we can certainly with older groups, use an approach to fights as one excellent way of stimulating a first interest in many of the aspects of drama touched on in this book.

10

Play-making and Play-building

In one sense, play-making has been a continuous thread throughout this book, ranging from simple improvisations to the more complex and detailed plays arising in the last chapter on fighting, from the story of the king in the forest to the film story based on 'our school', from the narrative stories of infant school drama to the coal-mining disaster, from improvisations in small groups to others involving the class as a single entity. The factor of this continuous thread is important to bear in mind, because it should not be thought that play-making is an intended and final end product of dramatic work. As an activity, it exists side by side with all the other activities we have been considering, and more detailed and specific considerations have not been given to it as yet in order not to detract from other more primary objectives – the points on the circle – all of which it has been necessary to isolate in order to study them in significant detail.

But play-making also is a point on the circle, and in this sense, fully employs the mind as the controlling agency governing the use of the other facets of oneself, again in a largely intuitive manner. Each person does not necessarily *know* (in the conscious sense of knowing) what it is necessary to contribute nor how to contribute it, but nevertheless, does so with considerable accuracy. Early creative work is concerned with developing each person's confidence in themselves, irrespective of the fact that there is no consciousness awareness of how that self is in fact working. Consciousness may reveal inadequacies, particularly when comparing oneself and one's own efforts (successes and failures) with others; but if we are able to sustain the factor of confidence from the unconscious to the conscious stages of work, then each person becomes able to 'trust' himself or herself, and is therefore once more able to use intuition, even though there may now be almost parallel conscious awareness of the function of that intuition. This is one way that the person of less mental facility is able (emotionally) to come to terms with that lack, and the person of greater mental facility is able (again emotionally) to increase that factor through developing other factors beyond reasoning. One example of this is in the physical realm of life. Intuitively, many youngsters will attempt the seemingly impossible, but as mind takes over more and more consideration of what is involved, doubts creep in; the overcoming of these doubts depends on how fully confidence is developed during the intuitive period of attempt, and on other factors coming in as encouragement during the phase of intellectual assessment. Ultimately, these two factors can bring about a renewal of the fearlessness of intuitive trust and dependence.

In drama, the factor of encouragement during the phase of intellectual assessment is part of what has been termed the 'sharing of wisdom between adult and youngster'. In other words, the adult is the vital cipher in the bridge between unconscious and conscious drama particularly in terms of retaining and developing personal confidence.

With constant and regular opportunity for play-making each person becomes more skilled, not only at using all the different facets of themselves but also at using the mind to govern and organise that doing. The aim in the drama itself is still for full absorption within character and situation, but gradually a fraction of this absorption takes over the conscious organisation of the self, and is always aware of what is being made – in fact, instead of character and situation taking over 'the person', that person takes complete charge of character and situation. Again – the process can develop as organically in drama as it develops organically in the development of the individual.

So – parallel with opportunities for all manner of exercises that are developing other points on the circle, this point on the circle can be developed by the full cooperation of the teacher as a general stimulator and constructive builder of different types of experience. Let us consider further examples of this, bearing in mind that some examples of the process have already been considered, without them being predominantly concerned with play-making.

1. Developing a Story about Refugees

The following are the stages of development:

(a) A concentration exercise. The whole class attempts to walk from one end of the halls to the other without making a single sound; there is no need for 'rushing', as this is not a race. Repeat if there is any sound at all.

(b) Repeat the concentration exercise in pairs; one in each pair is wounded and depends on actual physical help (short of being picked up altogether) from the other; the one who is not wounded cannot see, so in turn depends on sensitive guidance from the wounded person. Again, the whole class attempts to go down the length of the hall without making a sound (add imaginative circumstances, such as an escape, if this will help.)

(c) Build a barrier across the width of the hall, about half way along. This can be made of chairs, turned on their sides; the barrier needs depth but not height. Repeat the concentration exercise at (a), with each person working on his or her own, again not making a sound, including getting over the barrier without touching it.

(d) Repeat concentration exercise at (b), including getting over the barrier.

(e) Outline the following circumstances to the group: they are all refugees, who, for three days have been travelling in the open, constantly pursued, without food and water or proper rest, many of them wounded – all trying to reach and cross the frontier into another country where they will be safe from the revolutionary forces that have just taken over their own country. They are exhausted and frightened from the three days they have just experienced, and now they have arrived at the no-man's land separating the two countries. Half way across the patch of no-man's land, the enemy has built a barrier, of such fiendish conception that few are able to cross it; the whole barrier is electrified and at short distances along the whole length of the barrier, hidden from sight, are sensitive microphones which can pick up the slightest sound, causing machine-guns to spray bullets right across the barrier. The refugees know about the barrier, they know they dare not make a sound; they know they dare not touch the barrier – but they know that if only they can cross it, they will have reached freedom. They are to work in pairs, one of which is wounded (the other blinded if they wish); there will be occasional bursts of machine-gun fire. (These can be made by the teacher by using the edges of two pennies against a window-pane.)

Allow a minute or two for the pairs to discuss the circumstances and to think about what they have already been through – and what they are going to do.

Then run the scene.*

It is wise not to interrupt the running of the scene; but if concentration and absorption have been rather shallow, then repeat the scene, insisting that each person concentrates as fully as possible so that they do not interfere with anyone else's work (social training again).

(f) and (g) For some groups, a further sensitivity exercise could be added at this stage by allowing the class to split into two groups, each group taking it in turn to run the scene while the members of the other group film the action. The filming can include every kind of shot from long shot to big close-up and every kind of camera angle, providing that the photographers never get in the way of anyone involved in the action; those involved ignore the camera people completely.

(h) Divide the class into six groups (which in the average class size should work out at no more than seven per group; it is wise to make sure there are not more than seven per group – the ideal number per group would be five.) Explain that the scene they have just done concerns the ending of a story – remember, it has happened at the end of three days – and that now each group is going to make a separate scene, each concerned with a different episode at a different moment in time during those three days. The following suggestions indicate the kind of circumstances that

* For a secondary group that has not done much drama before, it can arrest full attention more if the scene is spoken of as the climax of a film sequence.

might be given to each group, though naturally there are many others one could devise:

1st Group

A domestic scene on the evening the revolution starts; news is either brought to the family or is heard on the radio; the family have to decide what to do – some may wish to stay, others to go.

2nd Group

Headquarters of the Revolutionary party, shortly after the revolution starts. News comes to them that many people are leaving the country (perhaps they extract this news from a prisoner, or perhaps it is brought to them by spies or fifth-columnists among the population); they make plans to stop the people escaping, including planning the no-man's land barrier, as they have not sufficient troops to patrol the whole border. Other plans formed to stop people even reaching the border.

3rd Group

A family, a few hours after starting on their journey; they had had no reason to foresee that there would be any real problem about leaving the country; now they begin to meet the first obstacles – perhaps a road barrier; perhaps being refused tickets at the rail or bus station or at the airport; perhaps their car is stopped at a road block.

4th Group

Another family, at least a day's journey away from the town they left, but still two days away from the border; the incident in which one of them is severely wounded.

5th Group

Another family, two day's journey out; one or more of them has been wounded for some while; some members of the group are dispirited and want to turn back; others are more determined; much rests on their decision regarding the most severely wounded person in their group – and much rests on that person's own decision.

6th Group

The first family to reach the barrier; they are overjoyed to see it, but they know nothing at all of what the barrier is like; by their own actions they discover what it is like – and in making the discovery only one of them survives, to go back to others who follow and to tell them about the barrier. (It is, in fact, because of the experiences of this family that the rest of the refugees know all the hideous details of the barrier.)

Allow time for each group to discuss and plan its own scene, with particular attention to characters – the kind of people they are as well as who or what they are. When all groups are ready, let all the scenes be run at the same time; suggest that if any groups finish before the others they quietly discuss what they did (in terms of what went well first) whilst the other groups finish. When all groups have finished, let them sit round informally and tell each other the story and content of their scenes.

(i) Allow time for each group to start polishing its scene, discussing what went well, then what could be improved on; draw their attention particularly to how they are going to start the scene and how they are going to end it; suggest they think in even more detail about their characters so they are absolutely clear for themselves.

(j) Possibly allow another run through of all scenes at one and the same time, followed by further opportunity for polishing. (Omit this stage if it is taxing interest too far – much will depend on how much drama has been experienced before.)

(k) Run the scenes through one at a time, possibly in the correct order of the time sequence; 'possibly', because if the groups have had little experience of being watched, some may be more reluctant than others, in which case those that are more confident can go first. It is wise to bear in mind that reluctance may arise simply because a group is attempting something more difficult than they have ever done before and are therefore quite naturally nervous about the factor of audience. (For further points about audiences and sharing, see chapter 11.)

Up to this point, we have been considering individual group and whole class play-making based on a single common theme. Depending on the experience of the group, and the overall intention of the stage of work they have arrived at, this could now be extended into further stages of play-building. The class, in fact, could go on to make its own complete play, in which there may be many different scenes, but they are all connected into one whole, with experiences varying from the whole class working together as one unit, to many individual scenes, some perhaps with only two or three people in them.

If the full play-building process was to continue with this refugee story, then much would depend on constant discussion by small groups and by the whole class, under the general guidance and chairmanship of the teacher. Side by side with the discussion, constant attempts at trying out different improvisations as they arise: this trying-out is always important, as the actual doing of a scene will reveal much more about its possibilities and difficulties than merely talking about it, and therefore further discussion sessions are enriched and informed by actual trial and error. The following suggestions are made as indications of different ways the above story might be extended as a process of play-building:

1. Having seen the different scenes, each group decides how their scene might be linked to either the one that follows or the one that went before.

2. Could the revolutionary party headquarters be used as a link from scene to scene?

3. Could the whole story focus around a particular group of people (e.g. scientists, politicians, etc.) who must, for many important reasons, get out of the country?

4. Could more be built in of conditions leading to the revolution?

Each idea that comes up provides further opportunities for improvisations and/or drama exercises that have value in their own right, irrespective of whether or not they are finally incorporated as part of the play that is being built.

In chapter 11, A Space in which Anything can Happen, suggestions are made regarding the use of space in play-making and play-building.

2. An Episode at an Airport

This example concerns the building of a single play-making episode that uses the whole class in one place and one situation. The classroom can be as suitable as the hall for this story, in which the following stages of development might take place:

(a) Explain that an episode is going to be built-up that happens in the lounge and general waiting room of an airport; discuss what such a room would be like and what it would contain – e.g. information desks, refreshment counters, seating arrangements, etc. etc.

(b) Ask for some people (in pairs or threes) to be airport staff – people at the information desk, others who give out loud-speaker announcements about various flights, staff in charge of refreshments, perhaps of a book-stall, perhaps porters in charge of luggage, possibly immigration officials etc. (For this particular scene, the main people necessary are the first three people mentioned above.)

(c) Ask the remainder of the class to divide into small groups; for this particular scene, groups of three or four are ideal; it would not matter if some were working in pairs, but on the whole five would be too many.

When they have settled their groups, explain that they are people who are coming to an airport to meet friends or relations or business acquaintances, or whatever they themselves decide, on a particular plane at a particular time. Allow a few minutes for them to decide who they are and what kind of people they are, and who it is they are meeting, why, where they are coming from, and so on. (This being an international airport, there can be wide diversity of choice on these matters without interfering with logical niceties; nevertheless the teacher might anticipate certain kinds of characters that might make aspects of the scene difficult; for example, a group of hysterical girls meeting the Beatles from their world tour could be a positive distraction to everybody else, and if the teacher is worried about this kind of factor, it is as well to mention it at this stage; on the other hand, it is both wise and interesting to leave complete freedom of choice and to expect anything, including such things as a group of assassins who have come to kill the leader of some foreign power who is arriving for a conference.)

Whilst the small groups are discussing the above details, the airport staff can be talking about the kinds of people they are, their exact function, and perhaps start getting the room ready as the airport lounge, arranging just where the buffets are to be, the information desk, etc. and, in particular where the two in charge of loud-speaker announcements are going to be. (They need some simple 'sound' for attracting everybody's attention.)

(d) Run over the geography of the room, including the main entrance to the lounge, so that all groups know where everything is. Suggest that at the beginning of the scene, some people have already been in the lounge for some while; others, who have not yet arrived can start from outside the main entrance – they need not all arrive at once, but the plane they are all meeting is due to arrive in, say, fifteen minutes or so. Give a moment for everybody to decide where they should be and to think about who they are and what they are going to do. (As with so much of the work suggested in this book, it is wise in play-making to have one's own control factor – a cymbal or drum – to hand all the time, using it each time one stops the action in order to explain the next stage, and using it again to restart the action from complete silence and stillness.) Try out the opening of the scene, with everybody's arrival, going to information desks, refreshments etc. Give enough time for each person to try out their characters and their intentions; then stop the action, and ask each group in turn to say very briefly something about the kind of people they are and who they have come to meet.

(e) Go back to the beginning of the scene and, before starting, explain that during the running of the scene this time, on every occasion that the cymbal is struck they are all to freeze action and dialogue exactly where they are – and then each group in turn will continue for a few seconds on their own, according to who is indicated at any given moment; everybody else, except the indicated group remains in the frozen position. Carry this out, so that each group has a few moments of working entirely on their own, with the remainder of the groups being aware of what they are doing, without actually becoming audience in the full sense of the word.

(f) Add the first moment of conflict, which slightly changes the atmosphere of the scene. Up until now, the plane has been expected to arrive on schedule, although there has been no particular announcement to this effect; now the announcers attract the attention of everyone with their sound, and announce that the plane has been delayed, and further information will be given as soon as it is available. Run through this part of the scene, with each group continuing according to the effect the announcement may have on their character – some may want further information, some may be worried about delay to their programmes, some may simply be glad that at least the delay gives them time for some refreshment and so on. (Again the teacher must decide, according to circumstances and the overall intention of each aspect of experience, how the introduction of this moment of conflict should take place; it might be left as a moment of surprise, by a quiet explanation to the announcers only, nobody else knowing what is coming; or the whole moment might be explained to everybody before it is tried out.)

(g) Develop the conflict further. A second announcement informs everybody that the delay to this particular flight has been cuased by engine trouble and there is no further news regarding the arrival of the plane. As soon as further information is available, another announcement will be made. This creates further consternation for some people – perhaps individuals now, rather than groups. (So one begins to build particular moments of the scene arising from actual character.) Enquire whether there is any particular person who, as a result of this second announcement, would immediately rush to the information desk with considerable anxiety. There is sure to be some such person. As he or she arrives at the desk they happen to overhear one of the people in charge of the desk say quite casually something like 'Let's hope it doesn't crash' – the person involved can decide on the actual sentence, but the sentence must include the word 'crash'. The anxious person hears the one word and immediately runs back to his or her own group calling out that the plane has crashed. Enquire again whether there is someone else who, on hearing this information might in fact scream – again, there is probably a character who would and a person who would like to do it; with the scream everybody is absolutely silenced, and in the silence the anxious person, or another person, says: 'The plane's crashed.' So we build through a sequence of changes of atmosphere, and discuss now how everyone would behave in such circumstances; then try the sequence through.

(h) Another announcement follows, saying that the plane will be arriving within a few minutes. Once more the change of atmosphere; some perhaps are sceptical and need reassurance from the information desk; others are partially comforted; others are completely relieved. Try this part through.

(i) A final announcement states that the plane has touched down and passengers will be arriving through 'Channel no. 9' (or whatever); at once the atmosphere changes again, taking the scene to its conclusion and end.

(j) Discuss the scene as a whole, perhaps even trying out again any particular moments that need a little more attention – and then run the whole scene from start to finish without any breaks.

The above, straightforward piece of play-making could be followed up by improvisation around many different types of circumstance in the lives of the characters who have come to the airport, whether directly associated with the airport and the people they are meeting or some quite different aspects of life. There are, of course, also opportunities arising from changing round the characters and giving the class different experiences within the same scene.

Many other situations can be developed around an airport – e.g. a strike of luggage porters, or the desperate need for certain people to leave a country when there are only a few seats left on the final plane.

The basis of this example is useful for many kinds of play-making that involve the whole class as one entity, unlike the first example where, although there may be some scenes built up with the whole class, others are developed by separate smaller groups independently of each other.

A similar approach can be made to play-making around many

situations in which all of the small groups are, for instance, different families in common circumstances – e.g. A Great Trek, in which a number of families seek a new life in a new part of the world; different aspects of the journey itself, different attitudes to it, different incidents arising from the relationships of characters within each family or between one family and another; also many possible occasions of unity, when the whole group work together against common foes, be it the weather, shortage of food and water, attacks or possible attacks from tribesmen. The journey is always a useful basis for this kind of full-class play-making, and suggestions are made regarding the use of space in the next chapter.

Once we have reached the stage in drama where not only conflict as such is of interest, but also conflict that arises from the basic characteristics of people, quite simple themes become really valuable material for play-making. The examples already given were originally taken from brief stories reported in the newspapers – and every day one's eye is caught by similar material, often reported in just a few lines. Many of these involve family situations within confined circumstances – i.e. there is no journey of any kind, even though there may be several different specific localities. For example, a street of houses involved in troubles over rent and landlords; another street that is due to be pulled down, but the tenants are resisting because of dissatisfaction with alternative accommodation; another street where there are problems of undesirable tenants, perhaps linking with study of such social factors as the colour problem. (Of course, each time a 'street of houses' is mentioned, we might consider a block of flats.) With each situation, a play can be built in a similar way to that above.

Enriching Experience

It is important for youngsters of all age groups to have an opportunity of using the products of their own imaginations for the *content* of their improvisations; but it has been pointed out that little of this content will necessarily be 'new' in the sense of entirely original, for the whole of conscious as well as unconscious experience of life is used. What can be new is the 'way of looking at things', and this constantly grows as each person's individuality grows in confidence. The difficulty of using derivative sources of material – well-known stories, historical events, etc. – is that too great an emphasis can be placed too soon on the purely intellectual factor of accuracy of content, with a corresponding negation of the many other factors with which we are fundamentally concerned (including imagination). In all the early stages of drama it is therefore easier to develop the different points on the circle that are concerned with personal development if we are not at the same time involved in problems regarding the accuracy of content. Concern for this factor is often at the root of the adult's objection to the trivialities of the subject matter of improvisation; but if these improvisations are not an end in themselves – as indeed they are not, once drama ceases to be considered as a straight-line development of a subject – then they are seen as the vehicle through which full attention is given to many other factors, which can be equally well served, and in the sense suggested above better served, by the use of original material.

Inevitably, however, as an extension of the circle, the time comes when intellectual and emotional experience can be enriched by using themes and stories, ideas and thoughts, feelings and characters, etc. from almost any and every available source, exploring all the tangible and intangible aspects of man's life on earth, plumbing the perennial mysteries of existence side by side with reliving (re-enacting) events both great and small that are part of the heritage of knowledge because they are known facts. Drama provides the unique opportunity for bringing *immediacy* to any situation, making what is knowledge of the past an actual discovery in the present. (See diagram on p. 13).

Drama helps the re-creation of human endeavour, and can draw on material from the beginning of time, making immediate what is now possibly dry information. Drama transcends information and makes of it living experience, significant to the heart and spirit as well as to the mind.

This approach to sources of material is very different from the expedient use of drama merely to help the memorising of facts through dramatic illustration. Indeed we must always be cautious about the latter, because the 'facts' are not always improvised correctly, particularly if we use derivative material before other aspects of the self have been sufficiently practised to reach the stage of full control mentioned at the beginning of this chapter. For example, one primary class dramatised *The Pied Piper of Hamelin*, and so horrified were the citizens of Hamelin at the actual experience of the rats that when the Piper returned from drowning the rats they and a very grateful mayor and corporation paid him handsomely and cheered him on his way. What children *do* they will remember more clearly than what they merely read or hear about, so in a case of this kind it becomes not only necessary to correct the facts of the matter, but also to give further opportunity of actually doing the new facts as well. More experience through drama of using the whole of themselves, will eventually bring about the time when there is sufficient control at all levels – including the mind – for such errors not to occur. Meanwhile, if we use derivative sources earlier, then we must be ready for such distortions of the facts to arise.

However, the time comes when we can use – and discover that children have a voracious appetite for – all the great myths and legends (abounding in symbolism and therefore closely allied to what has been called intuition throughout this book), stories from literature, stories and people from the scriptures, from history and geography, and so on.

Even for the drama specialist in the secondary school, this can provide exciting opportunities for practical cooperation with other specialists. The history teacher (who possibly has either a secret or a very open contempt for drama) may begin to view it in a different light if approached by the drama specialist with the request: 'What are you doing in history with 3b that we could use for material in drama?' He might even be encouraged to come and see some of the results. He will undoubtedly be touched by the eventual realisation that not only has his suggestion been used as part of the enrichment of experience through drama, but also that drama has helped with the memorising of the information he is imparting. There is no flippancy in this suggestion; drama could well be discovered as one of the most valuable ways of breaking out of the stranglehold of over-specialisation in secondary education.

I I

A Space Where Anything Can Happen

Throughout this book, the consistent intention of all suggestions for practical drama work has been that of helping *the natural, organic development of each individual*, exploring, discovering and mastering his own resources, and attaining a sensitive, confident relationship with his environment. The teacher has been considered as a constant, vital factor in this process, as stimulator and with a particular responsibility for stretching in each field of activity. But it has always been emphasised that genuine and sincere endeavour by each individual is more important than artificially obtained results, such as might arise from the teacher imposing (through demonstration or explanation) particular ways of doing things; so that in the early stages the teacher may suggest 'what' but not 'how', and in the later stages the teacher constantly helps each young person to develop and enrich his actual approach and achievement through his own effort and consideration, not through any short cut based on consideration of the end product.

Precisely this same attitude and philosophy should guide our thoughts concerning *where* drama should be done, for if we want to avoid artificial work then we must avoid imposing an artificial environment which, by its very nature, can undermine the *natural development of the logical organisation and use of space*. It is for this reason that we must again consider the fundamental differences between drama as a factor in education and theatre as a sophisticated art form of communication. Drama is concerned with the logical behaviour of human beings; theatre is concerned with the rearrangement of that behaviour in order to give an illusion of logic within circumstances of communication that are very often wholly illogical. To achieve that illusion is the task of the artist, be he producer or actor, and it is a task that can be fully achieved only through the proper training and continuous practice of the art of theatre. In education we are not developing actors, we are not teaching actors, and, above, all, we are concerned with developing sincere living in a myriad ways and not concerned with developing a capacity for giving others an illusion of living.

For these reasons (among others) there is really only one entirely and totally *wrong* environment for drama in education: that is the conventional picture-frame stage, raised up at one end of a large room or hall. This particular environment involves an immediate awareness of 'out there' – a single direction of playing. If the hall is large, it makes artificial demands on the use of the voice; whether small or large, it makes artificial demands on the use of space, particularly in the physical juxtaposition of two or more people using the area, where their physical relationship to each other cannot be natural and logical. It is the mastery of these circumstances and developing the ability of giving an illusion of reality, both collectively and individually, that is the function of the trained actor; brilliant actors are so superb at creating this illusion that for those of us 'out front' it looks as if they are behaving perfectly naturally in an ordinary human manner; so the viewer tends to think that all that is involved is getting up on a platform and behaving normally – but when we try it (or make others try it), we discover that it doesn't quite work; for one thing we cannot be heard and for another what we do cannot be seen always as fully as necessary – so we decide that, although we must behave naturally, the behaviour must all be that much larger than reality – we must speak louder and we must do bigger movements and gestures, and we assume that by doing these things we will simply raise the scale of our natural behaviour, which will now look real and natural within the larger dimensions of the hall. Unfortunately it is not so – and if it works for one part of the hall (say – the back), then it will not work for another (the front); the mastery of this area is the full-time job of fully trained people. From the point of view of drama as part of the development of people, the attempt to use this kind of stage can as quickly undermine the full value of the work as any other single factor – even when the people doing drama have reached the moment of needing (as another point on the circle) to share their work with other people.

The major advantage of this viewpoint is that not only does drama in school not depend on having conventional stages (whether well or ill-equipped), but that it can in fact be attempted in even the most inadequate of circumstances of any school, large or small, old or new, cramped or spacious. This is not to suggest that the teacher who has the occasional use of a multipurpose hall for drama does not have tremendous advantages over the teacher who is confined to the classroom; so has the teacher in a classroom of light modern furniture over a teacher in a classroom of heavy old-fashioned furniture; more so has the teacher with liberal use of the hall; and the most enviable of all is perhaps the teacher with a complete 'drama block', including a studio for improvisation, another for radio plays and so on. But these are all relative conditions, and some of the finest developments of children through drama are being achieved in the oldest, cramped, inadequate buildings that man has devised for any form of teaching. Fundamentally, what is required is 'a space where anything can happen'; the space may be large or small, open or cluttered – whatever it is, it does not have to be, in the sense of a conventional stage, a particular space which can be used only in a particular manner.

Of course we must always aim for and demand the ideal. The Newsom recommendations on drama are so specific as to its educational value for *all children* (see particularly paras. 478–480), that it is incumbent on us to insist on the right conditions for dramatic work – but, at the same time, drama is so fundamental to the growth of children that we must not wait for those conditions to obtain. It is also important for us not to decide too hastily what are the right conditions, otherwise we can quickly become involved in 'types of grandeur' which create heavy budgets; these are inevitably cut down, and the shell that we are left with is very often far from the right conditions.*

Our attempts to reach the ideal must depend on our observation of the needs of children in the many different types of activity in which we are involving them as part of their growth and development as people; these needs will differ in many respects from those necessary for developing drama as a subject or as a leisure interest and activity; the latter may involve many enrichments without being fundamental; the former, through being fundamental may inevitably include many features of equal value to the latter. So let us start by considering some fundamentals.

Using the Classroom

Much of the early work in drama is best attempted in the classroom rather than the hall, particularly if the hall is very large or if it is not private; there are several reasons for this:

(a) The less space the easier it is for the teacher to have full class control, without strain and without recourse to heavy-handed methods of discipline;

(b) If the hall is not private, then it is almost impossible for the majority of the class to reach anything near full concentration; disturbed by viewers, some can become more shy, others exhibitionistic – and with older groups, all are prone to the type of derogatory comment that can come from their peers (and other members of the staff) in a school where no one is familiar with such work.

* The kind of thing that can happen is that 'the ideal hall' is envisaged to include arrangements for lighting open stage and proscenium stage presentations. Just to do the lighting part of this adequately will make certain minimum demands on height of the hall; at a later stage, the budget needs pruning, so the lighting is cut out, leaving a very large space which may well prove as inadequate as too small a space. The space *plus* the opportunities of lighting would have been ideal, but either factor on its own is very far from ideal. There are many variations on this particular theme, and perhaps one of the greatest difficulties is that so often we attempt to design a multi-purpose hall and finish up with a no-purpose hall, in constant demand for assembly, music, P.E., drama, school lunches and, last but by no means least, a central corridor for everybody to have to walk through at one or more points during each school day.

271

(c) Again, if the hall is not private, the teacher is open to the same situation regarding other classes and teachers; if things go wrong in these conditions, the teachers' confidence can quickly be undermined.*

(d) In the early stages, children (and particularly young children) are afraid of too much space. Early work in the classroom helps them to develop a depth of concentration which helps them to be less conscious of space until they are ready to discover and master more space; this can be a slow process – varying in pace with each child – and is deeply bound up with the factor of personal confidence.

Most of the activities described in this book are possible in class-room conditions, there being only some aspects of movement and dance drama, and some fuller developments of play-making that depend on the extra space. However, this possibility should not be confused with the additional advantages that obtain, eventually, in all aspects of the work if there is more space than the classroom can provide. When using the classroom it is advisable to keep the following points always in mind:

(a) Wherever and whenever possible, move the desks. This can be done as part of drama, and suggestions as to how have been tabulated in chapter 5.

(b) If for some reason the desks cannot be moved, still do every-thing possible to make sure that in the early stages all members of the class are working at the same time, even for small group work. Conditions may be cramped for some groups, but, educa-tionally, there is more value in the youngsters learning to over-come problems of cramped conditions than there is in being forced to have audiences before they are ready for them.

(c) As often as possible or naturally necessary, use the desks, both

---

* The Newsom Report makes it incumbent on Headteachers to become fully familiar with the aims, intentions and methods of procedure within drama; only in this way can they be fully helpful to the teacher attempting spheres of activity that are not only often quite new, but also are without that type of immediate result which alone will win the sympathy and interest of other members of staff. Long-term, non-academic, intangible results are usually of little interest to subject teachers, and the teacher of drama, particularly the new teacher, needs strong defending against the supercilious indifference and apathetic ridicule of colleagues who have no time for 'new-fangled and unproven methods'.

over and under them. It may well be necessary to ensure that the children either take off their shoes or wear plimsolls or other appropriate footwear, but the different levels and recesses provided by desks can be so advantageous that it is worth going to some trouble with any such arrangements.

(d) Whenever possible, keep discussions, exchanging of stories (whether 'done' or merely made up and reported on) as informal as possible, with the class grouped near the teacher as well as each other, so there is no need for 'making speeches', no problem about being heard in remote parts of the classroom—in fact, no touch of the kind of formality which can rekindle the very fears of failure that the work as a whole is aimed at removing.

(e) When the class reaches the stage of sharing their small group work, do everything possible to avoid imposing conventional theatre stage playing area.

Again, if possible, move the desks so that there is a playing area in the centre of the room. When children make their own improvisations, they behave with the full logicality of ordinary movement relationships – they do not play outwards in one direction. For this reason, if the desks cannot be moved and each group *must* use the space at the front of the classroom, do not suggest anything about 'facing front' or 'speaking up' or 'not turning backs on audience' or 'announcing title of play' (in a formal manner), nor say such things as 'Are the actors ready?' or 'Audience be quiet now' or 'Curtain going up' or 'Give the actors a hand' – everyone of these expressions belongs to the entirely different activity called theatre, and each one of them contains some potential for undermining one or another of the basic values of drama as part of the development of people. If and when groups have to – or need to – do their work one group at a time, allow conditions to remain completely informal, moving swiftly from one group to the next, with those not active at any given moment sitting quite informally in any part of the room they wish, with no intimation that the classroom has suddenly become a theatre – we do not want children 'playing at being actors acting a play'.

(f) Consider again the factor regarding noise and social training suggested in chapter 5).

(g) If and when work that has been begun in the small space of the classroom is transferred to the larger space of the hall, do not expect an immediate adjustment to be made; the effect of the larger space may be that of diminishing the work, or, if the class make an intuitive or conscious attempt to adjust to size, they may overstep the mark, with possible falsifying of some of the sincerity obtained in the smaller space. If this is so, then use only part of the hall rather than the whole of it; but certainly avoid such demands as 'Yes, that was all very well in the classroom but you'll have to get it bigger than that for the hall'. This demand will destroy sincerity and lead to artificiality (and possibly showing-off by some people) which can be as bewildering for other members of the class as for the teacher.

(h) Discourage visitors to the class until concentration and absorption have begun to be so strong that they cannot be undermined. If visitors do come (including the head), ask them to avoid behaving like an adult audience visiting a theatre.

(i) Later in this chapter suggestions are made regarding the use of 'rostrum blocks'. The desks in the classroom can often be used in a similar manner, giving experience of different levels, and of the exploration of a different dimension of space.

(j) If at all possible to arrange, it is wise for the teacher not to remain always in the same place in the classroom – e.g. where the teachers' desk is. To keep moving about, without in any way interfering with the activities of the class, has many advantages. For instance, watch to see if some individuals or groups are always trying to be close whilst others are always trying to be as far away as possible; the former may be trying to impress (one form of exhibitionism) and will benefit from teacher moving farther away; the latter may be anxious to be hidden for all kinds of reasons – lack of confidence, trying things on, laziness, and so on; the quiet, unobtrusive presence of teacher at their end can often be beneficial.

Using the Hall

All the work described in this book is intended for the floor-space of the hall and not for use on the stage. If there is a platform stage with a front curtain, then it is wisest to close the curtains so that the stage does not interest or bother anyone. With the curtain closed, provided the stage is large enough, it can make a useful room for drama as an ordinary flat spaced, four-walled room. If there is no front curtain, then it is wise to discourage the use of the stage for all early work, particularly if there is no easy access by means of front steps. Later, when there is full confidence, the stage becomes useful as one particular area for drama – for example, it might be a ship, or a palace room, or a dragon's cave – but is not used exclusively, and certainly not as a stage in the conventional sense.

(a) If the hall is very large, restrict the amount of space used in the early work, particularly for very small children; increase space as confidence increases, but it is wise to keep pace with the slower developers who will not become ready for more space quite so soon as some others.

(b) Consider again the points already mentioned concerning
— sensitivity and sharing space
— confidence and the use of space
-— space and relationship to teacher
— class (and individual) control in space

(c) As for work in the classroom, it is wise to be mobile in the hall, without getting in the way, and without appearing to be studying any individual or group too closely. If remaining in one place, do not expect or ask the class always to face you.

(d) Again, as with the classroom, keep discussions and exchanges of stories etc. in as informal conditions as possible, with the group sitting fairly close together in one section of the hall, rather than being expected to make their voices carry over the large spaces.

(e) When the class is moving around the whole hall, expect to see them moving in an anticlockwise direction, which is the perfectly normal way that 99 per cent of people move. There is no need to go into the psychological reasons why this happens, but it is wise not to resist it or to try to insist that they go the other way for a change.

(f) When many groups are doing their improvisations or short scenes at the same time, let each group find its own space for itself. Only if groups tend to be on top of each other make any suggestion regarding the use of the space, and then link the suggestion quite simply to social training by asking one group if it could let the other or others have a bit more space by moving in one direction or another.

(g) When groups reach the stage of repeating their improvisations one group at a time, with the others watching, do not let it turn into formal theatre performance by special organisation of audience considerations; let each group repeat its own scene exactly on the space where it first tried it out, with other groups sitting quite informally all round the action; and avoid also all the 'theatrical' factors mentioned in 2 (e).

(h) For older secondary groups who have never before attempted drama, the factor of self-consciousness will be combated very much more quickly and effectively if the hall is blacked out. If there are any spot-lights in the roof of the hall, one or, at the most, two of these, making a pool of light in the centre of the hall will not only make for exciting and rich experiences for those ready to use the light, but will greatly increase the shadowed parts of the room, where the most self-conscious will go and stay until their concentration and confidence grow. If there are no spotlights, then it is wise to use the ordinary lights of the hall only at one end, leaving the other end in shadow as far as possible. (This suggestion is not cranky. Self-consciousness is one of the greatest agonies that adolescents can go through, often leading to all kinds of behaviour problems that would not arise if they could be helped over that one difficulty. It is often the fault of education that they have become self-conscious at all – they would go through the stage anyway, of course, but much of the attitude of adults tends to exacerbate rather than solve the problem. One of the major functions of drama is to help each young person to reach a genuine and constructive state of consciousness of self – anything that can be done to help this is worth the slight inconvenience that might be caused for a short period of time.)

Rostrum Blocks

The most useful type of equipment for drama is the rostrum block, whatever the age of the youngsters; rostrum blocks can be of different shapes, sizes and heights; they can be adapted from quite simple boxes, such as apple or orange boxes, tea chests, etc. There are sets which can be bought on the commercial market; or, most valuable of all, particularly for secondary schools where workshop facilities are readily available, they can be made by the school to meet its own particular requirements. On p. 278 is a sequence of diagrammatic suggestions for making one particular kind of block, which is robust, fairly light in weight, cannot be damaged, will not mark polished floors, and can be made in different sizes for convenient stacking.

Rostrum blocks add a dimension to drama through providing experience of different heights. They are a stimulation to the imagination, both in terms of helping with ideas for stories and in terms of the imaginative reconstruction of the area (scene) on which the story is to take place. There will often be, particularly with secondary schools, a great deal of time spent arranging and rearranging the blocks, often with changes of only a matter of inches, followed at once, perhaps, by a complete change of everything back to what had been considered right in the first place. We should not be bothered by this – it is the basis of constructive and tidy thinking about the use of physical and material resources, having its important application even to such factors as arranging their own domestic circumstances later in life. The complete change from the original arrangement to further trial and error and then a return to that original arrangement is often an interesting example of the workings of first intuition, followed by the doubts and trials of mental application followed by a final fully judged return to the first dictates of intuition.

In the early stages of small group drama, the supplying of each group with one or two rostrum blocks is an excellent way of keeping each group in one place rather than have them all roaming about the hall. An interesting example of this concerns the very early movement exercise involving 'silly people' and a veteran car. On occasions that this has been attempted with actual chairs making the car, or else with no props at all, the journey of the car has included the majority of groups moving everywhere, even dragging chairs with them; but when the same

ROSTRUM BLOCKS

**Gussets 4in on square 3 ply,
tacked to 2in x 1in, allowing
room for insertion of sides**

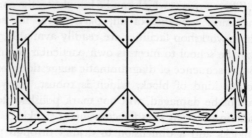

Framework—2in x 1in planed softwood

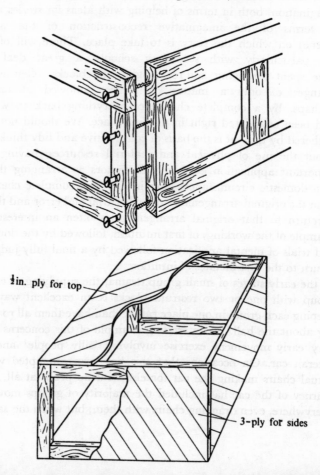

½in. ply for top

3-ply for sides

scene has been done with each group having a few rostrum blocks of different shapes and sizes, they have built their car with the blocks, and then all movement of the car has been entirely imaginary, with, very often, a fuller use of the body by each member of the group.

In dance dramas, simple rostrum blocks will help and add to all symbolical factors. In improvisations and play-making, the blocks serve for every kind of furniture or setting that anyone will need, and the very economy of such usage not only helps imaginative factors, but also aids concentration by not causing the kind of distractions that realistic settings can so often lead to.

The combination of rostrum blocks and 'a space where anything can happen' provide children with the opportunity of finding the appropriate *shape* for any kind of improvisation or play they are working on. They also indicate, together with the other general needs of the teacher and the class in drama, something of the ideal facilities necessary in school. This can best be summed up in the idea of a drama room.

A Drama Room

A simple room is all that is necessary; the ideal length for the average class would seem to be about 35 or 40 feet; the width about 25 or 30 feet; the height about 12 to 15 feet. Windows preferably only at one of the shorter sides, with each window able to be fully blacked out. Several 13 amp (or 15 amp according to local wiring and power conditions) power sockets – one for gramophone, another for tape recorder, others for use for plugging in individual or paired focus lanterns. Fundamentally that is *all* that is necessary, certainly to start with, although one would naturally add various numbers and sizes and shapes of rostrum blocks as time goes on. Nothing else is fundamentally necessary. There is no need for a platform stage, for great quantities of lighting equipment or for facilities for making scenery and costumes; of course all these things will add enrichment to some aspects of drama, but they are not fundamental to drama as part of the development of people. The overall cost of such provision is negligible when compared with the cost of such departments as the various science or physics laboratories, libraries, metal work or woodwork shops, domestic science departments and so on. (With the education officer of one L.E.A. it was worked out that these fundamental facilities could be supplied for about £2000, including room, blackout, rostra, gramophone, and two 250 watt spotlights, each with its own slider-dimmer. The same source considered that none of the other provisions mentioned above would cost less than £6000.) If this is so, and if the recommendations of the Newsom Report are to be implemented, then it is not unreasonable to advise schools continuously to apply to their authority for a drama room; and for schools with a reasonable amount of playground or field space, such a building could be erected, on a prefabricated basis, a little away from the main school building, thus solving the hoary old problem of what to do about noise.

Sharing

Another point on the circle is that of learning to share what one has made with other people, and sufficient has perhaps been said regarding this factor in relation to the work of small groups within each class. Emphasis has been made that this type of sharing should not involve a change in the approach to the activity from drama to theatre. Many teachers become worried about this issue because of the confusion between what their classes want to do and what they are ready and need to do. The latter is part of the organic growth of people – the former we may need to discourage for the sake of other developments in *all* children in the class. The following example may help to make clear one of the main issues involved. A teacher in a primary school had begun drama with his class, and before long many of the class asked if they could show their plays to one another. They were allowed to do so, enjoyed what they saw and asked time and again for the same arrangements. The teacher, feeling that if they were so keen he ought to allow opportunity for fulfilling and maintaining their enthusiasm, began to permit more and more showing of plays to each other. Inevitably, after a time, a few of the class began to emerge as being better at this activity than the others, and the less good ones were only too happy to allow these better ones to monopolise the showing, thus having less and less opportunity themselves, and, when they had the opportunity, becoming more and more discouraged about their own efforts in relation to the good actors in the class.

This is only one of many dangers inherent in our giving way too soon and too often to the desire to show each other, even within the class. Such sharing should not become a predominant activity, should be kept in the simplest and sincerest manner possible, and should have no connection with the 'good, better and best' factors outlined above; we are concerned to help each young person, and for each separate fulfilment is important in its own right, not in comparison to others.

Many of the most valuable qualities of drama are retained during the experience of sharing if the shape of the playing area is right – that is on the floor space, with the audience sitting informally around the action. In this way, grouping and physical relationships remain natural and logical and there is no vocal strain of the kind imposed by trying to be heard down the full length of the hall.

Precisely the same philosophical approach is necessary if sharing is extended beyond groups in one class, whether it be to sharing with another class, with the school as a whole, or even with parents or other adults as, for example, in the school play.

This book is not concerned with production of school plays, except in so far as the element of sharing is another point on the circle of full personal development. In these terms, it must be said that no infant school child will suffer in any way or lose one fragment of educational opportunity if it never once appears in public throughout the whole of its school life – indeed the corollary that all infant children would benefit from never appearing in public is very true. Much the same can be said for the junior school, although, if sufficient drama is being done, many children at the top of the primary school will begin to reach the kind of depth of concentration and absorption which can help them to appear in public without loss of the basic qualities of their work, providing they are playing in the right shape and are not suddenly made to perform on a picture-frame stage to a large audience. Even in the secondary school, there are major advantages to considering performances in the open stage, and for those teachers who feel that this is not proper theatre, we can only suggest that they consider the extraordinarily exciting developments in professional theatre over the last few years, many of the newest of which are open stage (e.g. Chichester Festival Theatre).

There are schools that feel, quite genuinely, that drama is a way of sharing some aspect of the life and work of a school with parents and other well-wishers; for such schools, the following brief suggestions may be of some help:

1. Consider the different diagrams on p. 284. Each one of these is a simple way of presenting a play on the open stage, relieving children and young people of many of the strains that are peculiar to working on a platform at one end of the room; it will be noted that in many of the diagrams the platform is used for seating part of the audience.

2. Consider the possibility of a drama programme that really is representative of the work of the school as a whole, showing different aspects of the actual work in drama that is attempted, even including some examples where the teacher is working with the class in front of the audience. This kind of programme is immensely valuable for primary schools who feel they must present something, but the following programme is typical of that being attempted even in some secondary schools:

(a) A short demonstration of early drama with first year classes, taken by the teacher.

(b) Movement at various stages of development.

(c) Dance dramas, and unspoken dramas with music (music plays).

(d) Processions.

(e) Crowd scenes, with simple self-contained plot or story.

(f) Various types of practice at improvised speaking.

(g) Short improvisations, from early work with the whole class working in small groups at one and the same time, to polished improvisations by individual groups.

(h) An example of play-making, where one theme is developed by many classes into a composite whole.

(i) For secondary groups, the programme could also include a polished performance of part of a scripted play.

3. With infants and young juniors (if they *must* be exposed to such experiences), explain to the audience that the children are not actors and the school is neither a theatre nor giving a training for theatre – therefore the audience must not behave like an audience at a theatre, but quietly and simply share the proceedings.

4. With older juniors and secondary, give as much preparation as possible for being looked at without any disturbance of concentration – the camera exercises described on p. 162 are very useful for this type of preparation. But as part of general training, go beyond this and make clear that in the process of sharing one gives only the finest possible. This means redoing what has been worked on, with full concentration. Incidentally, too much rehearsal rather than too little is often responsible for the breakdown in concentration.

5. Do everything possible to avoid an over-excited atmosphere of the theatrical occasion, and make sure that all involved do a few concentration exercises before the performance.

6. It is not part of the function of this book to consider the factor of using scripted plays; but it should be mentioned that if scripts are used, then the approach to production and performance should still make use of the kind of work suggested, with much opportunity for improvising on and around the words of the script, to help freshness of dialogue and getting deeply into the part and the situation. For juniors and infants, it is wiser not to use scripts.

These very few points are intended to do no more than indicate in what manner we need to approach the factor of 'the school play' if we are working from a basis of drama as part of education. The youngsters, when they are sharing with others, are the same youngsters, not a suddenly metamorphosed different race of people, and we cannot uproot educational principles simply for a few moments each year. There is no need for such up-rooting. Even with this type of activity, the basis of our thinking can and should remain precisely the same: we are concerned with developing people, not drama (and certainly not theatre); if we

OPEN STAGE SHAPES

(Stages which already exist, can be used as
a part of the playing area or for the audience)

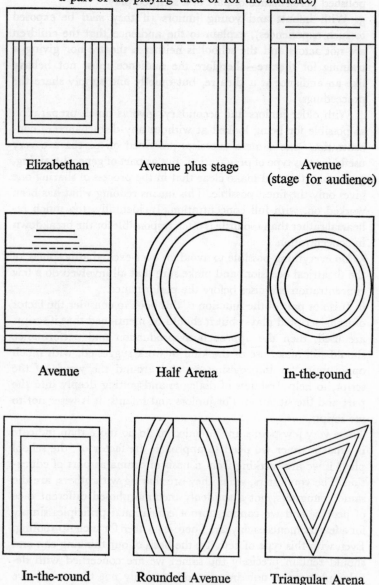

Elizabethan   Avenue plus stage   Avenue
(stage for audience)

Avenue   Half Arena   In-the-round

In-the-round   Rounded Avenue   Triangular Arena

Entrances for actors can be cut through the seating areas according to the
layout of the building.

are able to develop some of the creative and imaginative aspects of people, together with the growth of general confidence, then the drama they share will always be interesting. Audiences generally, including parents who expect the school play, are fascinated by a genuine sharing of what children can really achieve – which is always more vital, alive and exciting than watching them pretend to be actors acting plays.

12

Social Drama

Hitherto, this book has been concerned with two major streams of activity: 1. Practising the use of one's own personal resources; these are the points on the circle. 2. Practising the use of these resources in relation to one's environment and to other people within that environment; these are the same points, but developed on a different plane – the second circle in the diagram on p. 13.

All the points are further developed and enriched by the use of other material, as suggested by the outer circle in the diagram. The basic intention has been that of developing each and every child to the fulness of their own individual capacities, without reference to 'abstract standards' giving rise to comparisons or to 'failures and successes'. Each person is helped to reach towards some measure of fulfilment of what he or she *aspires* to be as a person, side by side with other aspects of education which are equally concerned with helping the fulfilment of ambition. Ambition is often most deeply concerned with the use one makes of one's life; aspiration is more often concerned with the quality of oneself as a person, which in turn affects the functional aspects; compassion – not sentimentality – will suggest to teachers that all normal human beings are fundamentally concerned with becoming the fullest and finest human being they have the capacity to be, hence the need for personal confidence against the more destructive influences of thwarted ambitions, which often have roots in external rather than inner resources.

Emphasis has been constantly placed on the necessity for continuous, straightforward practice of individual *resources*; but at various stages throughout the lives of children and young people – particularly at the closing stages of school life – it is equally necessary for education to be concerned with the development of *resourcefulness* within each person. Here again, drama has an important part to play, for it is through drama that direct experience and practice can be given at the simple and confident practical everyday use of one's resources. Drama in this sense is *social drama*, and can be considered under three main headings:

1. Manners and behaviour.
2. Aspects of general living.
3. Broader social awareness.

Manners and Behaviour

The young of all ages are blamed in each generation for their lack of manners and sensitivity, their clumsiness and seeming inability to behave appropriately in certain circumstances; in fact, most of the young people so blamed do 'know' what is expected of them, for they have been told, probably hundreds of times, and will have been through some form of schooling which rigidly imposes some of the 'rules' and constantly preaches the remainder. But 'to know' is one thing, to have the confidence to carry out that knowledge in practice is another; the bridge from one to the other is achieved through actual practice, in which real life circumstances are arranged as part of drama and the participants are provided with the opportunity of actually feeling the situation without any of the possible repercussions of failure to behave 'correctly'. Table manners form an example that ranges from school lunch to the teenager looking after his girl friend when he takes her out to dinner, from entertaining a guest to attending a civic or other special function; in any and all of these circumstances, part of the behaviour pattern is that of straightforward sensitivity to other people, part is that of understanding and having the confidence to carry out particular procedures. The mastery of the situation from either viewpoint is more readily achieved through practice than through mere verbal instruction.

287

The following situations, by no means exhaustive, may indicate some of the uses to which social drama can be put with regard to manners and behaviour. However, it is important to warn that, with youngsters who have never done any drama before, there is certain to be lack of absorption and concentration, together with a kind of burlesquing in early attempts; practice will help each person to take the episodes more seriously, and one of the teacher's aims is to make the circumstances as personal as possible for each person in the class. Most important of all is discussion; this should take place continually around each moment that is tried out – and the teacher should always take such discussion seriously, no matter how many surprises or even shocks may result.

When the work is being attempted with secondary pupils who have never done drama before, there is no need to mention the word 'drama' or the word 'theatre' or any other technicality of education; and if pupils reveal to us some of the problems that deeply concern them – particularly regarding their own personal futures – then these give us a starting place, through discussion and through the actual trial and error of real life situations. In such circumstances it is again often wise to start with all of the class working at the same time, in groups of two, three or four, according to the situation being tried out; once interest is deep and absorption begins to grow, then one group can work singly, with the rest of the class joining in discussion. However, even in these circumstances, if the atmosphere is constructive and un-critical, it is often possible to start with the single, small group of volunteers, with the rest of the class being encouraged to attempt the episodes after confidence and interest have been established through discussion.

1. Welcoming and looking after guests, at school, in the club or at home. At school, this factor is often of particular importance on special days, and can include practice at such specific duties as being in charge of car-parks, cloakrooms, handing round refreshments, guiding the way to exhibitions etc.

Practical example

Welcoming guests. Divide the class into groups of four or five; all groups are to work in their own space at one and the same time.

State the circumstances quite clearly – e.g. 'Two of you are at home and are going to meet and look after three visitors for a short while because your parents are delayed', or 'Two of you are yourselves as pupils in this class; the others in the group are members of the education committee who have come to see and hear about the school; the Head is very busy so you have been asked to look after the guests', or 'Two of you are raising funds for charity; you are welcoming the other three who are members of a pop group (or film or television personalities), who have given up some of their free time to make a personal appearance which will help your fund; you are all meeting for the first time'. The circumstances can vary from those which are typical to the youngster's own lives to broader and more imaginative themes which are of great value as general practice and in terms of helping a sympathetic understanding of what it feels like to be 'in another's shoes'.

Having stated the circumstances, allow a few moments discussion and time for arranging chairs etc. Then all groups try out the episode at the same time; this may last a very short time, be quite unabsorbed and have more the appearance of rather feeble Christmas charades than a serious attempt to master certain specific problems. It is wise to tolerate this in the early stages; we do not stop children from writing because of poor spelling!

When the episodes have ended – or we have stopped them – allow a long session of general class discussion. The teacher needs to lead this to start with, by suggesting points that can be discussed, both from the view of the immediate experience and from that of people who might actually be involved in the circumstances. These two views will differ at this stage; e.g. the 'hosts' might well be as embarrassed or as 'lost' as their guests – this could well reflect no more than the personal feelings of participants who have never before experienced this kind of opportunity.

Even the first moment of meeting will suggest numerous questions for us to ask; about such factors as shaking hands, taking coats, asking people to sit down, perhaps offering a drink, cloakroom etc., and, of course, the all important question of what to talk about.

After discussion, the episodes can be tried again, with or without changes of role; and this again can be followed by further discussion.

In social drama, each teacher finds the particular approach that will arise from his or her bond with the class; the above suggestions are general and by no means the only detailed approach. A similar pattern to that above can be followed in many of the remaining examples.

2. Introducing people to one another (including the youngsters themselves introducing their parents to the Head or to other teachers; also introducing their own friends to their parents).

3. Table manners. One interesting approach to some aspects of this factor is to ask one group to do an improvisation in which there are as many as possible examples of *bad* manners; the class then discuss the examples and the same or another group repeats the improvisation, trying to remove all the bad manners. Further discussion follows, and then the whole class divides into groups and attempts the same improvisation.

Teachers who are new to such work may well be worried by the suggestion of actually encouraging an opportunity for bad manners; the worry is without foundation, as there is no danger that we shall teach the wrong thing; indeed, by the simple opportunity for behaving illegally within a legal framework, we often find we help to remove some of the strains that exacerbate behaviour problems.

4. Manners and general behaviour on school journeys and other outings. (Some factors related to these are touched on in other examples that follow.)

5. Meeting people generally, but with particular reference to those whom one feels should have a specific mode of address, e.g. councillors, aldermen, nuns, clergymen, etc.

There are many other factors which can be considered under the general heading of manners and behaviour, but, as many might equally and justifiably be included as part of the problem of general living, they are included in the next section. However, before leaving a section concerned with manners and social behaviour, it might be helpful to point out that there is seldom, if ever, the need to despair about this aspect of living where young people are concerned, providing that as teachers we are prepared to give a great deal of practice rather than relying on other means of instruction; but much depends on the attitude inculcated in the minds of the recipients – manners for their own sake may be taboo to start with; manners as simple and straightforward sensitivity and consideration for other people are much more realistic and are the basis of a reciprocal process that is tangible. (Even the cult of masculinity – unconsciously or consciously fostered by many boys' schools – can be overcome from this basis; one does not have to be a lout to prove one's manhood!)

Aspects of General Living

The following are, again, only a few of the many possible situations that might be set as help for different age-groups, some of them concerned with life whilst still at school, some concerned with directly bridging from school to after-school life, some concerned, perhaps, only with potential problems that might arise many years ahead; the word 'problems' is used advisedly, although it is not always easy for adults to understand that what for them may constitute a perfectly straightforward aspect of ordinary everyday living may, for very many young people, constitute the very gravest of problems.

1. Using the telephone – dialling or answering, taking messages accurately, calling a number through the operator, using STD, emergency calls for police, ambulance, fire through the 999 service, etc.

It is interesting how many schools appoint telephone monitors, without giving reasonable practice at using the telephone, perhaps taking it for granted that all children have telephones at home or are familiar with their usage. These things cannot be taken for granted. On one occasion I telephoned a colleague on the staff of a secondary school, and the youngster who answered said he would go and look for the person I wished to speak to – and promptly put the receiver back on the hook. On another occasion, a similarly helpful youngster went in search of the teacher I was trying to contact – and never returned!

2. Directing people the way (e.g. to the staffroom, the Head's

room, the secretary's office, or from school to another part of the district).

3. Taking verbal messages (e.g. from class to class in school, or from school to shops, parents, etc.).

4. Helping people in the street:

(a) giving directions, or, if unable to do so, taking the trouble to find someone else who might know.

(b) Helping elderly or infirm people across a busy road or up steps or with a suitcase, etc.

(c) helping blind people across the road, through gates, doors etc.

(d) helping people who have fallen down, or someone whose hat has blown off, or whose car has run out of petrol, etc.

(e) coping with any of the above circumstances with a 'foreigner' who is barely able to make clear his requirements.

(f) obtaining information or help for oneself, including asking policemen (and when *not* to ask because of possible interference with other duties).

5. How to help at sudden emergencies, not only in terms of dialling 999, but by considering ways in which one might be helpful oneself if seeing an accident, a fire, or circumstancess that should involve the police. (The latter involves many exciting possibilities for concentration exercises, in terms of remembering detailed information as a witness.)

6. Visiting doctors or dentists or the out-patients department of a hospital, including making appointments, explaining one's needs fully and simply, etc.

7. Arising out of the above: visiting patients in hospital, including the opportunity, through drama, of experiencing the point of view of the patient.

8. Other 'difficult' kinds of visits – to elderly or infirm people, including one's own relations; or visits to various officials, e.g. taxmen, clergymen, etc.

9. Interviews for jobs. This is probably one of the most vital factors we can help with in secondary schools, and certainly constitutes one of the finest ways of starting drama with final year secondary pupils who have never had such opportunities before. The very subject matter is of prime importance to each individual, with an enormous range of problems from simple listening to

quite complex demands for expressing one's own feelings and points of view.

This particular social drama exercise is in no way arranged so that young people can 'rehearse' the right answers to questions; the object is really twofold:

(a) to help the pupil to feel the many different circumstances of the interview, thus removing fear of the unfamiliar; the details might include such factors as: knocking on the door and perhaps not hearing the reply; entering the room, not being certain where or when or whether to sit down; which chair to sit in; relaxing in it; listening clearly to questions and answering quite simply and sincerely, etc. And, perhaps most important of all, discovering the necessity for and having the opportunity of being straightforwardly and sincerely oneself – rather than putting on an act which one hopes might give the right impression, etc.

(b) to help the pupil to appreciate the employer's viewpoint of the same interview. As has already been suggested, this two-way experience can and should be at the root of much social drama, for it is by appreciating the other person's viewpoint that many deeply personal worries and concerns are seen in a new light.

10. At home: coping with strangers who come to the door when one's parents are out; or helping to make one's parents' friends welcome whilst awaiting their return.

11. Giving and receiving gifts.

12. Giving and receiving congratulations, thanks or various kinds of compliment. (The factor of receiving compliments is particularly apt for girls' schools; it is so pleasant – and so rare – when a young woman can reply to a compliment about her appearance without dissolving into a crumpled heap of embarrassment, or else looking on the compliment as one stage towards a proposal of marriage!)

13. Shops:

(a) dealing with clever and persuasive salespeople;

(b) making complaints, if necessary;

(c) returning articles that fall apart shortly after arriving home;

(d) dealing with wrong change, either for or against oneself.

14. Hairdressers: again coping with persuasive assistants in order

to have one's hair done as one wants it rather than fulfilling someone else's artistic dream!

15. Entertainment: booking seats for theatres, concerts, circuses, etc.

16. Public transport (possibly linked with school journeys):

(a) asking information about platform, times of departure and arrival, making connections, etc.

(b) booking seats (including sleepers); checking change etc.

(c) coping with the 24-hour clock – and helping others to do so;

(d) dealing with porters and luggage, tipping, etc.

(e) the use of waiting-rooms, cloakrooms, etc.

(f) in buses, or on the underground, boys offering seats to women or elderly people, including what it feels like to be rebuffed; for girls, practice at accepting such offers graciously – or turning them down, with no less graciousness. (Many boys and young men can testify to the downright rude reactions they have had to such simple offers, resulting in a simple resolve not to risk the circumstances again, however much they may be blamed for bad manners!)

(g) dealing with taxi-drivers who take apparently devious routes and so increase the fare; tipping, luggage etc.

(h) the many different problems of air transport;

(i) with many factors of all kinds of transport, much can and should be done to help girls who are travelling on their own, particularly with difficult and long waits at main line termini.

17. Restaurants: (this section includes the factor of taking a guest, particularly of the opposite sex; some of the suggestions above might be considered from a similar point of view):

(a) in some restaurants, coping with head waiters and wine waiters as well as ordinary waiters;

(b) using the menu, and asking for information about those items printed in foreign languages;

(c) looking after a guest, including a man *leading* into the restaurant (though still opening the door for the lady), finding a table, helping with coats and into chairs etc. (And the reverse of all of these for girls.)

(d) ordering wine and understanding some of the simple and

pleasant rituals attached to wine drinking (including the fact that one's palate and one's pocket remain ever the best final guides to choice); letting the wine waiter be helpful – if he knows his job, he enjoys helping those less familiar with wine; he abhors only the pseudo-wine-snob!

(e) understanding the use of different cutlery (this applies equally to special functions such as civic luncheons, from which no one can, in this epoch, consider himself exempt).

(f) complaining about bad food, dirty cutlery, dirty or broken or chipped crockery, etc. – and making the complaint without being an embarrassment either to one's guest or the rest of the establishment.

(g) guiding one's guest to the price of dishes one can afford, by making a few suggestions within or close to that price range (and experience of being the guest, responding sensitively to such suggestions).

(h) for young men taking out young women: how to accept graciously their offer to pay their own way, if it would really be helpful either to one's own pocket or to their morale; for girls, how to make such an offer without causing any embarrassment, and how to give way graciously if the man refuses.

(i) paying the bill, either at the table or at the cash desk, including the presence of a guest or guests; similarly, being a guest where one's host is paying the bill. (We can only hope that no one in our charge will ever be in the embarrassing circumstances of not having enough money to meet the bill – but it can happen to anyone, even by simply forgetting or losing one's wallet; but it makes an interesting piece of social drama, including, perhaps, what one might do if sitting at another table observing such a happening.)

(j) tipping, including the factor of ten per cent on bills, and what one does about the additional service of head-waiters, wine-waiters, etc.

18. Hotels: much of what has been said about restaurants has its application to staying at hotels, but there are additional problems of reception, luggage, garage space, keys, locking-up times, etc.

19. Parties and functions:

(a) asking for and accepting – or refusing – dances; taking or being led to the floor for a dance; leaving the floor after a dance, etc.;

(b) taking care of one's guest(s) in terms of coats, cloakrooms, refreshments;

(c) some young people are involved in particular problems such as looking after adult guests, perhaps even having to act as host for their parents during a temporary absence;

(d) saying good-bye and thank you (– and then actually *going*!)

(e) the additional problems of young people who are hosts to their own parties.

20. Weddings, funerals and christenings.

21. Having a key to the front door for the first time (and its responsibilities);

22. Earning money for the first time;

23. Having full liberty with one's own free time;

24. The many problems between children and young people at the moment of emerging fully into the independence of an adult world after many years within the security (and frustration) of the world of childhood and adolescence. Included within this is direct experience of parents and other adult points of view.

All of the above situations concern practical aspects of the direct experience of living; young people are always fascinated by discussion of such matters and usually deeply grateful for such direct opportunity of coming to grips with and mastering factors about which they may often have been preached to, either at home or at school, but still have not found the confidence fully to master.

Broader Social Awareness

The above sections have been concerned largely with *oneself* in different circumstances, and oneself in relation to *other people*, in similar or different circumstances, thereby helping one to experience and understand other peoples' points of view.

But beyond these factors, part of rich and sensitive living involves arousing one's understanding, sympathy and compassion for people whose lives are entirely different, even remote, from one's own in every conceivable facet. In a sense, this aspect of social drama has been a dominant theme throughout the whole of this book, particularly the chapters on improvisation and play-making, for it is this aspect that is often most fully concerned with providing the opportunity for deep experience of what it feels like to be other people in other situations.

One of the best sources of material is the newspaper, either national or local, using not only main headline stories but the three-line 'snippets' that so often conceal (or reveal) a wealth of human experience, ranging from the tragic to the broadly comic. The following themes have all been used by one group of teen-agers over a period of two-years:

1. The Berlin Wall. Themes have varied, according to experience, ranging from actual escapes to simple and sensitive episodes in homes on either side of the wall.

2. Various kinds of strikes, with material varying from the origins and causes of the strike to its effects on many different kinds of people, including the strikers and those who have refused to strike.

3. Thalidomide babies.

4. Housing problems, including elderly people being removed from their homes.

5. Colour bar problems of every kind, including the American University problem.

6. People going to or leaving prison; aspects of family life whilst they are in prison. Problems of rehabilitation.

7. Refugees.

8. Various types of 'fete'.

9. Assassinations (causes and effects, as well as the acts them-selves).

10. The lawn in front of the council house which was sewn with onions instead of grass seed.

11. Mining disasters; one of these was built up by two groups in a sequence of nine different scenes, four concerning the people underground, four the people above ground and the rescuers, and the final scene involving the actual rescue; at this time, the group had done so much drama, that this climax scene was not a matter of triumph and cheers but one of the meticulous problems in-volved in getting very seriously wounded and sick people to the surface.

12. 'Opening up the West' – different aspects of the lives of a community from its very beginnings.
13. Shipping disasters.
14. Airplane disasters.
15. Various types of rescue operation, often linked to the above.
16. The successful climbing of a mountain.
17. Problems of immigration.
18. Different aspects of space travel.
19. Problems besetting councillors, both in cities and in villages.
20. Many problems related to underdeveloped and under-privileged nations or communities or families or individuals.

This list is by no means all-inclusive; it includes a random selection of material that has been used, simply as an indication of the possibilities within this aspect of social drama. The procedure has already been gone into in considerable detail in previous chapters. But it is important to bear in mind that social drama, under any one of the three headings above, is often the simplest and most rewarding way of beginning drama with teenagers who have never done any before. The actual doing will inevitably be shallow in its early stages, but depth of experience will increase with practice within an uncritical atmosphere.

Whether shallow or deep, the experience is direct and personal; as was suggested at the beginning, the answer to the question 'What is a blind person?' might be 'A blind person is a person who cannot see'. But it could be: 'Close your eyes and, keeping them closed all the time, try to find your way out of this room.' The former answer gives information to the mind, the latter provides a simple means of direct emotional experience. The best way of either understanding or of teaching drama is to do it oneself. Try it for yourself – now.

Book List

ADLAND, DAVID. *Group Approach to Drama.* Longmans, 1964.

ALINGTON, A. F. *Drama and Education.* Blackwell, 1961.

BURTON, E. J. *Drama in Schools.* Jenkins, 1955.
— *Teaching English through Self-expression.* Evans, 1949.

COBBY, MAISIE. *Calling All Playmakers.* Pitman, 1956.
— and NEWTON, E. *The Playmakers.* Pitman, 1951.

PEMBERTON-BILLING, R. N. and CLEGG, J. D. *Teaching Drama.* University of London Press, 1965.

MORGAN, DIANA. *Living Speech in the Primary School.* Longmans (Education Today), 1966.

SLADE, PETER. *Child Drama.* University of London Press, 1954.
— *An Introduction to Child Drama.* University of London Press, 1958.

SOUTHERN, RICHARD. *The Open Stage.* Faber, 1953.

VIOLA, W. *Child Art.* 2nd edn. University of London Press, 1942.

WAY, BRIAN. *Three Plays for the Open Stage.* Pitman, 1958.
— and JENKINS, W. *Pinocchio.* Dobson, 1954.

WILES, JOHN, and GARRARD, ALAN. *Leap to Life.* Chatto and Windus, 1965.

WISE, ARTHUR. *Speech Education.* Longmans (Education Today), 1965.

Record List

WINIFRED ATWELL: 'More, more piano'

LEROY ANDERSON: conducts his own compositions (incl. Sleigh Ride, Syncopated Clock, Waltzing Cat, etc.).

SIBELIUS: Swan of Tuonela, Valse Triste, Tapiola

HOLST: The Planets Suite

HART AND RODGERS: Slaughter on Tenth Avenue

MOUSSORGSKY: Night on a Bare Mountain

DELIUS: On Hearing the First Cuckoo in Spring

GRIEG: Peer Gynt Suites (1 and 2)

SAINT-SAENS: Carnival of the Animals

STRAUSS: Perpetuum Mobile, Tristch Trastch Polka, Annen Polka

DUKAS: Sorcerer's Apprentice

MOZART: Ave Verum

DEBUSSY: Golliwog's Cakewalk; Claire de Lune

WAGNER: Faust Overture; Siegfried Idyll; Ride of the Valkyries

VERDI: Traviata Preludes

LECOQ: Mamzelle Angot

BLISS: Things to Come

RICHARD STRAUSS: Dance of the Seven Veils

ELGAR: Enigma Variations

BECQUART: Mammoth Fair Organ

DELIBES: Coppelia

WALTON: Facade Suite; Crown Imperial; 1st Symphony

VAUGHAN WILLIAMS: 5th, 6th, 7th Symphonies

DVORAK: New World Symphony

BERLIOZ: Symphony Fantastique

SCHUMANN: Spring Symphony

STRAVINSKY: Rites of Spring, Firebird Suite

Index

Index

Absorption, 29, 32, 38, 68–70, 72, 75, 78, 81–2, 92–5, 97, 101, 104–5, 109, 123, 126–7, 134, 154, 161–2, 186, 188, 196, 209, 211–12, 216, 223, 233, 242, 244–5, 248, 252, 255, 257, 274, 281, 288–9
see also Concentration

Adverbs, moving to, 165, 167–8

Atmosphere, 66, 86, 110, 202, 206, 216–20, 224, 263–4

Audience; in the theatre, 3, 15, 26, 115–16
in drama (usually undesirable), 14–15, 25, 43, 47, 74, 94, 143, 147, 162, 173, 186–8, 196, 209, 222, 259, 263, 272–3, 276, 281–5
and speech, 118, 120, 123, 127, 148
and fights, 238

Ball, activities with, 67–8, 71, 100

Beginnings for improvisations, 223–4

Body, discovering and using with imagination, 72–8, 81–2, 200, 209, 217, 245, 277–8
see also Movement, Physical self

Characterisation, in movement, 66, 75–8, 81–4, 88, 102, 110
in speech exercises, 126–45, 180–1, 245
in drama, 161, 218–21, 258–9
and sensitivity, 172–3
intuitive, 173–5
stages in the growth of, 175–6, 199
exercises in, 180–2, 191
from an emotional point of view, 218–22,
in play-making, 254–64

Circle of personality, 11–13, 16, 39, 64–5, 71, 118, 121, 141, 156, 158, 183, 191, 208, 222, 254–5, 266, 280, 286

Class control *see* Control of class

Classroom, use of, 270–4

Climax, 46, 48–50, 66, 81, 86, 89–91, 95–7, 98–100, 102, 104–5, 202, 204, 212, 213–17, 223, 240–1, 247
de-climax, 212, 214–16, 217

Communication; in the theatre, 2, 269
in drama, 3, 37, 47–9, 71, 94, 110, 118, 173, 196, 218–19, 222–3
in dance, 66
and speech, 118, 127, 142, 148–9, 209, 222
in improvisation, 186

Concentration, 13, 89, 186, 205, 211, 241, 244–5
importance of, 15
exercises in, 15–27, 43, 56, 68, 73–4, 78, 172, 208–9, 230, 256–7, 283
development of, 38, 96, 141, 156, 161, 196, 216, 222, 232, 271–2, 274, 276, 279, 281, 288
in speech exercises, 137, 141, 143
in sensitivity exercises, 162–3, 166–7, 170
see also Absorption

Confidence, drama builds, 41, 47–9, 56, 65, 74–7, 89, 91–3, 99–100, 101, 108, 149, 156–7, 161, 179, 208–9, 227, 254–5, 266, 272, 275–6, 285–7
in personal imagination, 42–3, 47
and use of space, 103, 106
and group work, 106
and speech, 121–3, 127–8, 138, 141–3, 148, 151–2, 155
in sensitivity exercises, 161, 165
in improvisation, 184–5, 187, 223, 250–1
teacher's, 272
see also Failure, fear of

Conflict, 111, 125, 128
the nature of drama, 192–3, 218–20
in improvisation, 198–9, 212–17
mood, atmosphere and, 217–18
in play-making, 263, 265

Continuity, in improvisation, 215–16, 241

303

Continuity (*Contd.*)
  in fights, 241
Control of classes, 16, 32, 271
  with 'arrow', 28–32, 36–7
  with sound in movement exercises, 68–9, 73–4, 79, 82–3, 88, 91, 97–9, 109, 124
  with sound in speaking exercises, 124, 126, 142
  in fighting and violence, 238–42
  in play making, 262
  see also Cymbal, Drum, Personal control
Crowd scenes, 134–7, 282
Cymbal; to control classes, 68–9, 73–5, 82–3, 109, 159, 262
  to create climax, 81, 95, 104–5
  to move to, 87–8, 90, 105
  and speech, 88, 94
  to control speaking exercises, 124, 126, 142
  to control sensitivity exercises, 162, 170
  in improvisation, 201–4, 206, 211, 214
  to control fights and violence, 238, 240–1, 243–4, 252

Dance, 46, 51, 71
  formal, 65–6
  use of sound and music for, 85, 89, 218
  dance-drama, 89, 111–12, 218, 272, 279, 282
  see also Movement
Desks; moving, 83–4, 272–3
  use of, 273–4
Development of people through Drama, 2–3, 6–7, 10, 16, 118, 160, 175–9, 181–2, 199–200, 266, 268–70, 273, 283, 286–7
  see also Circle
Discipline, 16, 38, 69–70, 271
  see also Control of classes; Social training
Discussion; and concentration exercises, 17–23
  in story sessions, 32, 49
  in movement exercises, 107–10
  in speech practice, 123–4, 126–37
  and speaking to music, 154
  in sensitivity exercises, 162–3, 166, 168
  in characterisation exercises, 181
  in improvisation, 197–8, 202, 211–12, 220, 257–60

Discussion (*Contd.*)
  in all drama, 223, 273, 275
  in 'film making', 229–30
  in fighting, 239–42, 246–51
  in play-making, 257–65
  in social drama, 288–91
Drama; its function, 1–7, 160, 176, 254–5, 268–70, 273
  in education, 1–7, 112, 150, 178–82
  a definition of, 3, 6, 219–20
  everyone finds his own level in 135–6
  conflict the nature of, 192–3
  as a safety valve, 225–7, 236–7
  sources of material for, 266–7
  space for, 268–79
  drama room, 279–80
  public performances, 281–5
  see also, Circle; Development, Theatre
Dressing-up, 189–90
Drum; to control movement classes, 68–9, 73–5, 82–3, 159
  to create climax, 81, 90, 95–7, 105
  to move to, 87–8, 91–2, 94–7, 105
  and speech, 88, 94, 149
  using imaginary, 101–2, 151
  to control speaking exercises, 124, 126, 142
  in speech with movement, 150–1
  to control sensitivity exercises, 165, 170
  in improvising, 201–3, 206, 211, 214, 262
  to control fights and violence, 238, 246

Education; academic, 1, 3–4, 7, 10–11, 113, 150, 182, 207
  drama in, 1–7, 112, 150, 178–82, 267–70
  philosophy of, 1–6, 150, 187–90
  must develop imagination, 42–3
  personal confidence the fundamental basis of, 91–2
  music and, 112–13
  fear of emotion in, 112–14
  specialisation in, 150
Emotion, 13, 101
  discovery and control of, 14, 93, 114–15, 149, 158–60, 177–8, 209, 219–22, 235, 255
  emotional harmony, 65, 79
  emotional causes of tension, 79
  emotional hearing of sound and music, 85–8, 120–1, 218

Emotion (*Contd.*)
  stimulated by music, 112-15, 218-19
  in education 112-13, 159-60
  positive and negative, 114-15, 159-60, 178
  and the use of language, 120-2, 146
  and creative illegality, 159
  and characterisation, 218-22
Endings of improvisations, 212, 223-4, 244-5
Environment, awareness of, 13, 20, 209, 217, 286

Failure, fear of, 16, 25, 38, 41, 43, 74, 75-7, 79, 89, 91, 110, 170*n*., 198, 223
  see also Confidence
Fighting in drama, 71-2, 102*n*., 110-11, 190, 227, 234-54
  reasons for, 235-7
  constructive use of, 237-40
  control of, 238-41
  organising and developing, 239-53
  weaning away from, 247-52
  in a youth club, 252
  see also Violence
Film (imaginary) in drama, 46-7, 49, 67, 76-8, 84, 152-4, 162, 227-34, 252, 257
Gong; to move to, 87-8
  and speech, 88, 149
Group work; in concentration exercises, 15, 19-23
  in story sessions, 41, 51-3
  in imagination exercises, 44, 52
  in movement, 67-8, 78, 106-12, 200
  when to start, 106-10
  early work, 106-12
  size of groups, 107
  in speech work, 122-39, 143-7, 152-4, 180-1, 200
  in mumbo-jumbo talk, 143-7
  in speaking to music, 152-4
  in sensitivity exercises, 160-72, 200
  in characterisation exercises, 180-2
  in improvisation, 186-7, 193-4, 199-212, 254, 257-9, 275-6
  compared to music, 200-1
  leaders in, 200-1
  in infant schools, 201-7
  in junior schools, 207
  in secondary schools, 207-8, 276
  in film making, 230-5
  in fighting, 239-52
  in play-making and building, 257-65

Hall, use of, 269-72, 274-6
Hearing *see* Listening

Ideas game, 40-1, 48, 198
Imagination, 13-14
  vital to develop, 42-3
  development of, 43, 55, 64, 149, 156, 158, 191, 208, 222, 233
  exercises to stimulate, 43-64, 133, 141, 191, 209, 230
  exercises in the use of, for teenagers, 57-63, 247
  exercises in using body with, 74-8, 81-2, 209
  and the use of space, 106, 209
  music stimulates, 112, 217-18
  development of sensitivity through the sharing of ideas, 158, 163
  in sensitivity exercises, 170-1
  in characterisation, 173-5
  in improvisation, 184, 190, 193
  and properties, 190
  controlled, 222
Improvisation, 133-5, 142-6, 161, 176, 182-234, 254
  subject matter, 184, 191-8, 207, 210-11, 224-6
  teacher's approach to class, 185-7
  group work in, 186-7, 193-4, 199-212, 254, 257-9, 275-6
  space in, 187
  dressing-up, 189-90
  properties, 189-90
  stimulating ideas for, 191
  aspects of, 193-4
  in infant schools, 193-207, 210
  in junior schools, 207-8, 210-14, 227
  in secondary schools, 207-8, 210
  stretching in, 208-12, 216, 219-20
  conflict and, 198-9, 212-17
  endings, 212, 223-4, 244-5
  climax and de-climax in, 212-16
  continuity in, 215-16, 241
  development of form in, 223-4
  beginnings, 223-4
  domestic situations in, 225-6
  playing out troubles in, 225-6
  fighting and violence in, 225, 227, 235, 242-53
  play-making and building, 257-66
  rostrum blocks for, 165, 274, 276-9
  public performances of, 282
  in social drama, 289-90
Individuality encouraged by drama, 3-4, 72

Infant schools, drama in, 12, 217
  audience not desirable, 14–15, 281–2
  concentration exercises in, 16
  story sessions to begin drama in, 28–56
  movement leading to stories in, 71
  movement in, 93
  movement with speech in, 150–1
  characterisation in, 173–4, 194
  improvisation exercises in, 193–9, 201–4, 210
  group work in, 201–7
  stretching in, 208–10
  public performances by, 281–3
Intellect, 13–14, 64, 175, 255
Intuition, 66, 267, 277
  development of, 4–6, 72, 115, 156, 209, 211
  intuitive experience, 101, 217–18, 255
  intuitive characterisation, 173–5
  see also Development

Junior schools, drama in, 216
  concentration exercises in, 16
  story session to begin drama in, 28–39, 56
  stretching in, 208–11
  improvisation in, 207–8, 210–14, 227
  public performances by, 281–3

Leaders in drama, 200–1
Listening, 14
  concentration exercises in, 15–20, 22–4, 68
  used to stimulate imagination, 43–51, 58–9
  used in sensitivity group exercises, 171
  see also Senses
Looking, 14–15
  exercises in, 15–16, 20–4
  used to stimulate imagination, 51, 53–4, 59–60
  sources of material for, 54
  see also Senses

Manners, 287–91
Mirror exercises, 162–5
Mood, 86, 88, 110, 164–5, 202, 206, 216–20, 224
  see also Emotion

Movement, 8, 46, 51, 71, 156, 197
  improvised, and the use of sound and music, 65, 85–117, 217
  within drama, 65, 247
  beginning, 66–71, 191
  activities with a ball, 67–8, 71, 100
  in slow motion, 71
  stories leading from, 71
  exercises in discovering the body and using it with imagination, 72–8, 81–2, 200, 209, 217, 245, 277–8
  characterisation in, 66, 75–8, 81–4, 88, 102, 110
  relaxation exercises, 78–82
  'growing from nothing' exercises, 80–2, 104–6
  teenagers and, 93, 101–2
  early group work in, 106–12
  its closeness to speech work, 149–51
  with speech work, 150–4
  rostrum blocks and, 276–9
  public performances of, 282
Mumbo-jumbo, scribble talk, 139–47
Music, 50–1, 85–6
  recorded, 51, 83, 88–9, 100–2, 110, 112, 151–5, 214, 300
  its use in movement, 84–117, 217
  emotional hearing of, 85–8
  intellectual appreciation, of 85–6, 88
  discovery and control of emotion through, 112–15, 218–19
  and logic, 112–17
  musical pattern of speech, 120–1, 149
  as a background for speech, 137, 150, 152–5
  group work compared to, 200–1
  in improvisation, 214
  to stimulate imagination, 112, 217–18
  list of, 300
Music plays, 218, 282

Newsom Report, 270, 272n., 280

Personal control, 31, 69–70, 88, 93, 108, 124, 158, 209, 235, 238–9, 252
  see also Emotion
Personality, development of, 4–6, 10–12, 286
  see also Circle; Development
Personal release and mastery of resources, 13, 286
  see also Development

Physical self, the mastery and control of, 13–14, 65, 71, 78–9, 102, 109, 149, 156, 209, 219, 222
see also Body; Movement; Speech
Play-making, 176, 182, 234, 250–1, 254–67
  play-building, 260
  space for, 272
  rostrum blocks for, 279
  public performances of, 282
  see also Inprovisation; Stories
Plays with scripts, 188–91, 283
Poetry, improvised, 155
Pre-experience, 201–3, 207, 211, 213
Properties, 189–90, 232, 238

Rostrum blocks, 165, 274, 276–9
Relaxation exercises, 78–82
Rhythm, 50, 85–91, 95, 97–102, 106, 108, 112, 121, 168, 203, 217–18
  see also Music; Sound

Secondary schools, 'film making' in 46–7, 49, 67, 76–8, 84, 152–4, 162, 227–34, 252, 257
  concentration exercises in, 17
  story sessions as the beginnings of drama in, 28–56
  drama in, 63, 217, 267
  movement leading to stories in, 71
  movement in, 93, 100–2
  speaking to music in, 152–5
  characterisation in, 175–6
  improvisation in, 207–10
  fighting in drama in, 247–51
  public performances in, 282–3
  social drama in, 286–98
  see also Self-consciousness; Teenagers
Seeing *see* Looking
Self-consciousness, 157–8
  concentration overcomes, 15, 172
  in secondary schools, 15, 101, 108, 208, 232, 276
  in drama, 16, 20, 79, 101, 110, 157, 186, 208
  and use of space, 103
  and group work, 106, 108
  in speech, 118, 123–4, 143, 148, 151
  consciousness of self, 157–8, 172, 176–8, 276
  see also Confidence
Self-discipline *see* Personal control
Senses, 13
  development and full use of, 14, 57, 64, 156, 222
  exercises in the use of, 15–27, 56–9, 64, 68, 172, 182, 191, 208–9

Senses (*Contd.*)
  used to stimulate the imagination, 43–64, 209
  exercises for teenagers in the use of, 58–63
  used in group sensitivity exercises, 171–2
  see also Listening; Looking; Smelling; Tasting; Touching
Sensitivity, 13
  development of, 21, 26, 64–6, 107, 149, 158–77, 187, 191, 209, 217, 222, 233–5, 238, 257, 275, 287, 291
  group sensitivity, 169–72
Sharing, 26, 47, 69–70, 107, 162, 223, 280–1, 283
Smelling, 15–16
  exercises in, 15–16, 24
  used to stimulate imagination, 54–5, 61–2
  in group sensitivity exercises, 172
  see also Senses
Social drama, 228, 234, 286–98
  manners and behaviour, 287–91
  aspects of general living, 287, 291–5
  broader social awareness, 287, 296–8
Social training, 16, 69–70, 83, 123–4, 159, 209, 243, 257, 273, 276
  see also Control of classes
Sound;
  use of sound and music in movement, 84–117
  basic ingredients of, 86–7
  to stimulate ideas, 88, 92
  for mood and atmosphere, 88
  for control, 88, 97–8, 238
  and speech, 88, 94, 120, 149
  response to, 247
  see also Control of classes, Cymbal; Drum; Listening; Music
Space in drama, 1, 66
  use of, 66, 101–3, 161–2, 209, 269–79
  needed for movement, 66–7, 83, 272
  exercises to help discovery of, 103–6, 209, 272
  sensitivity developed through sharing, 158, 161–3, 187, 275
  music to stimulate exploration of, 217
  in play-making, 260
Speech, 8, 13–14, 156
  use of sound and, 88, 94, 120, 149
  added to movement, 109, 149–51

Speech (*Contd.*)
  and personality, 118–22
  in education, 118–20
  communication and, 118, 127, 142, 148–9, 209, 222
  a part of drama, 118–55
  confidence and, 121–3, 127–8, 138, 141–3, 148–9, 151–2, 155
  different forms of, 122, 138–9
  multilingualism, 139
  practice in, 122–43, 191, 200, 208–9, 216
  characterisation in speech exercises, 126–45, 180–1, 245
  exercises in boldness and sensitivity, 137–8, 158
  dialects, 138–9
  mumbo-jumbo, 139–47
  tones of voice, 148
  its closeness to movement, 149–51
  speaking to music, 137, 150, 152–3
  in music plays, 218
  intellectually controlled, 222
  public performances, 282
Stage, use of in drama, 187–9, 269–70, 274–5, 247
  Open, 282, 284
Stories; as beginnings of drama, 28–46
  ideas for, 32–5
  sound participation in, 29–37, 39
  participation with action in, 35–9
  made up by class and teacher together, 39–41
  creating, 43–56, 198
  develop from movement, 71, 107–8
  sound in, 88–9
  infants improvise to, 196, 201–6
  improvised, 223–4
  using violence, 242–51
  see also Improvisation; Movement; Play-making

Tambour *see* drum
Tape recorder, 140, 232, 279
Tasting, 14–15;
  exercises in, 15–16, 24

Tasting (*Contd.*)
  used to stimulate imagination, 55, 63
  see also Senses
Teacher; importance of, 8, 268
  where to start, 8–9
  function of, 12, 26–7, 255–6, 268
  bond of control with class, 69–70, 97–8
  whether to participate, 72
  approach of, 89–91, 93–4, 185–7
  confidence of, 125–6
  influence of, 179–80
  see also Control of class, Discipline
Teenagers, 57–8
  exercises in using the senses and imagination for, 57–63, 247
  and movement, 93, 101–2
  and mumbo-jumbo talk, 141–7
  social drama and, 288–98
  see also Fighting; Secondary schools; Self-consciousness
Tension, 79–80, 121, 148–9, 170n.
Theatre; must not be confused with drama, 2–3, 6–8, 10, 15, 135–6, 186–9, 268–9, 273, 276, 280, 283
  concentration exercises in, 25–6
Time-beat, 50, 66, 85–92, 95–102, 106, 108, 151, 168, 216–17
Touching, 14–15
  exercises in 15–16, 23–4
  used to stimulate imagination, 51–4, 61
  used in sensitivity exercises, 171
  see also Senses

Violence in drama, 190, 234–53
  reasons for, 235–7
  constructive use of, 237–40
  control of, 238–41
  organising and development of, 239–53
  weaning away from, 247–52
  see also Fighting
Visitors to drama classes, 274